LINES IN THE ICE

FOR MADELEINE AND JOSHUA

PHILIP J. HATFIELD

LINES IN THE ICE

EXPLORING THE ROOF OF THE WORLD

MCGILL-QUEEN'S UNIVERSITY PRESS

MONTREAL & KINGSTON · LONDON · CHICAGO

CONTENTS

HUMAN MARKS IN THE ICE

INTRODUCTION
HUMAN MARKS IN THE ICE

Ships fighting against a freezing sea. Masts and ropes caked in ice. Crews of men hauling sledges over crumpled and broken landscapes. These are the mental images conjured when many think of the Arctic and the history of its exploration by Europeans, Russians and Americans. However, this is not the only human history of the Arctic – a polar region slippery to define but broadly consisting of the Arctic Ocean and parts of Alaska, Canada, Finland, Greenland, Iceland, Norway, Russia, and Sweden. Indigenous communities – the Inuit, Eskimo, Sami, Nenets and many others – have a long history of living in and around the Arctic, using its bounty to sustain themselves and drawing their culture and folklore from its landscape and seasonal rhythms. Elsewhere, in the present day, the idea of the Arctic has also become more multifaceted. Although exploration to find trade routes and resources is still important, ideas formed around borders, civil infrastructure, scientific research and biome conservation, among other concerns, now shape our imagination of the Arctic.

Crucially, both the distant past and the contemporary world as sketched out above are connected by the history of exploration. The work of explorers – not to mention the traders, hunters and trappers who, historically, followed them – is a bridge between these two eras. The major period of exploration by Europeans, Russians and Americans, stretching from the fifteenth century to the early twentieth century, had a huge impact on indigenous societies across the Arctic. The arrival of Western explorers broadened the horizons of these cultures, but also introduced new tools, mechanisms of economic exchange and diseases – factors that would reshape populations and create conflict between communities for generations to come. These dynamics have reshaped the Arctic world of the indigenous peoples as we see it today.

Moreover, the territories explored and endeavours undertaken by explorers have had a lasting impact on our contemporary understanding of, not just the Arctic, but the world around it. The border claims of modern nations are underpinned by the maps, lost ships, cairns and claims of Victorian explorers; strands of scientific analysis, including those relating to climate change, have been opened up and evidenced by the findings of historic expeditions; and Arctic wildlife still bears the scars of those who made the most of adventurers' finds.

H. M. S. "EREBUS" AND "TERROR."

ABOVE

The departure of the *Erebus* and
Terror depicted in the *Illustrated
London News* 24 May 1845.

P.P.7611

OVERLEAF

Front page of a facsimile
of the *Illustrated
Arctic News*.

P.P.5280

1875.c.19.

FACSIMILE
OF THE
Illustrated Arctic News,
PUBLISHED ON BOARD
H.M.S. RESOLUTE: CAPTN HORATIO T. AUSTIN, C.B.
IN SEARCH OF THE EXPEDITION
UNDER
Sir John Franklin.

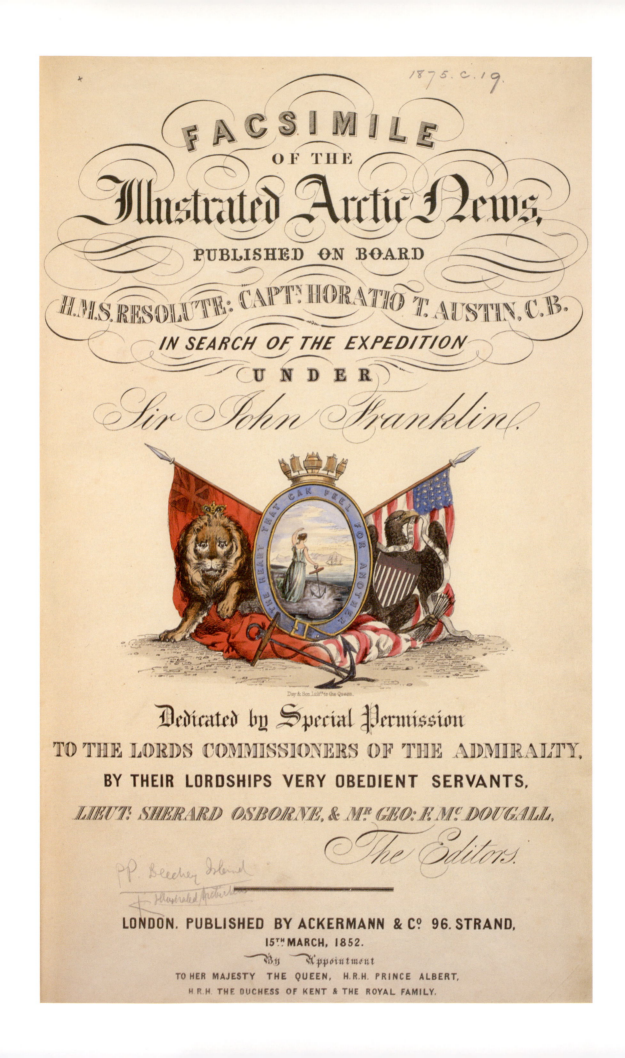

Day & Son, Lithrs to the Queen.

Dedicated by Special Permission
TO THE LORDS COMMISSIONERS OF THE ADMIRALTY,
BY THEIR LORDSHIPS VERY OBEDIENT SERVANTS,
LIEUT: SHERARD OSBORNE, & MR GEO: F. MCDOUGALL,
The Editors.

LONDON. PUBLISHED BY ACKERMANN & CO. 96. STRAND,
15TH MARCH, 1852.
By Appointment
TO HER MAJESTY THE QUEEN, H.R.H. PRINCE ALBERT,
H.R.H. THE DUCHESS OF KENT & THE ROYAL FAMILY.

On top of this, some of the names we associate with the Arctic, even those most famous, such as HMS *Erebus* and *Terror*, were also part of a growing understanding of the polar world to the south of the globe. Our understanding of the Antarctic would not be what it is today without the lessons learnt in the Arctic, the crews who gained experience there and the technologies developed on those expeditions. Even the idea of writing to endure the dark winter months of the poles, which historically produced fantastic artefacts such as the *South Polar Times*, owes its foundation to the exploration of the Arctic during the nineteenth century (see pp. 16–19).

In the contemporary era, the basic motivation of European and American explorers – the pursuit of resources and trade routes in order to gain financial and political advantage – is fundamentally unchanged. However, the search has shifted from a hunt for gold to a race for 'black gold' (oil). The Arctic continues to be reconfigured by this desire for wealth, which is also, simultaneously, inspiring creativity, cultural growth and even the development of spiritual attachments to the land, as it has done for thousands of years.

Lines in the Ice: Exploring the Roof of the World is an attempt to illustrate this rich, interconnected history through its human legacies. The collections of the British Library, as well as those of a large number of other world heritage institutions, provide windows through which we can reflect on the ways human cultures have engaged with the polar regions, especially the Arctic, over a long period of time. This book attempts to take a rounded view of the Arctic world, drawing particular attention to the importance and significance of indigenous cultures and their history to the Arctic. However, as the main focus is on how non-Arctic societies, such as Britain, relate to this polar region, it lingers particularly on the work of explorers and their agency in shaping the Arctic region we know today, not to mention how this underpins our deeper understandings of the world at large.

Taking an object-focused approach and drawing predominantly from the collections of the British Library, *Lines in the Ice* revolves around three main sections. Chapter one, 'Blank Spaces?

The Draw of the Arctic', looks at what drew the interest of non-Arctic peoples north, as well as providing insights into the history of indigenous life in the Arctic. 'One Warm Line: Seeking an Arctic Passage' focuses on the main period of European and American interest in the Arctic, especially the search for the Northwest Passage and the nineteenth-century British quest to conquer Arctic waters, which, in the case of Sir John Franklin and his ill-fated 1845 expedition, turned to tragedy and a desperate search for answers. Finally, the third chapter, 'The Arctic and the Modern World', looks at the enduring legacy of this history.

This story will be told using books, maps, photographs, prints, music and many other materials created by indigenous and Western peoples over the last five hundred years. These objects are the tip of the iceberg that is a rich material heritage depicting human engagement with, exploitation of and, perhaps most importantly, inspiration stemming from the polar regions. Through these historic records (some only a few years old), we see the variety of ways humans have engaged with this frigid space on the roof of the world and, at a time of great change and peril for the Arctic (as well as the Antarctic), I would argue that, in these objects, we should see hope for the future.

The history of human engagement with the Arctic, especially where Europeans and Americans are concerned, may not seem to be an overtly positive one, especially as we face a period in which trade and resource extraction are competing with the race to understand our changing climate. However, while we can see a long history of greed and conflict in the material laid out in this book, inspiration, diligent enquiry, a strong desire to protect and conserve, a spiritual appreciation of the land and its bounty, not to mention a will to preserve these lands for generations to come, are all also discernible. *Lines in the Ice* will show how, through an appreciation of the present's connection to the past, we can hope to see more clearly a healthy and sustainable structure for future human engagement with the Arctic.

ONE

BLANK SPACES?

THE DRAW OF THE ARCTIC

Uvilorsiortoᴋ ᴋavdlunâtsiaᴋ Kalâtdlip nuerᴋâ!
(Aᴋᴜᴘ ᴋᴀɴɢᴇʀᴍɪᴜᴘ, Nᴏᴜᴘ ᴇʀᴋᴀɴᴇ̂ᴛᴜᴘ ᴀsɪʟɪᴠᴅʟᴜɢᴜʟᴏ sᴀɴᴀ).

Today, inhabitants of much of the world still think of the Arctic as a blank space – an unspoilt, unpeopled space of spectacular ice formations and dramatic seascapes. This is far from the reality of the modern Arctic, which is peopled, holds many unique cultures and is also a site of intense political and commercial interest for the wider world. Moreover, the Arctic has long been this way. During the time of the Roman Empire the silk roads, which acted as trade routes connecting the Far East with the Mediterranean, carried amber and furs from the Arctic across the world. The high north was already part, albeit on the extreme borders, of a continent-spanning trade network.

In the fifteenth century, the exploration of the Americas by Christopher Columbus changed the operation of the world's trade networks; northern European countries, afraid of being sidelined and perhaps even threatened by the increasingly affluent Spain and Portugal, looked north for solutions. Looking to gain a trade advantage, not to mention precious resources and other trade opportunities, England and other northern European countries started to look for Arctic trade routes, and the search for the Northwest Passage began. The Northwest Passage was a sea route over the landmass of North America that, it was hoped, would be simple, ice-free and shorter than the Atlantic routes currently monopolised by the Spanish and the Portuguese. Others looked to a Northeast Passage – running via seas over the Eurasian landmass, or via the North Pole – but all of those searching for these routes hoped to find the same thing: an advantage over their competitors.

Explorers including Martin Frobisher, William Barents and James Cook began to journey north in the sixteenth and seventeenth centuries and come into increasing contact with the indigenous communities of the Arctic. This was the beginning of an intensification of the wider world's interest in the Arctic, an interest that would change the north and how it was viewed by people to the south. This section shows why Europeans went north, what they encountered and how a journey of exploration, still continuing today, began.

POPULATED PLACES
WITH RICH CULTURES

Across the Arctic there live indigenous peoples with rich, distinct and historically deep-rooted cultures, who have lived there since long before Europeans took an interest in the north. Their cultures and traditions have been handed down over hundreds of years through oral testimony and material culture, an example of such a culture being the Inuit carvings now so popular with art collectors all over the world. Inuit print culture is also extremely popular today, having seen explosive growth as an art industry in the twentieth century. Before this, Europeans had attempted to record Inuit culture in forms they regarded as more tangible, such as the printed word and artistic illustration, and some of these objects still survive today.

Kalâdlit Okalluktualliait (Greenland Legends, 4 vols., 1859–63,) is one such object, compiled and edited by Hinrich Johannes Rink, a Danish geologist, scholar and administrator, working in Greenland in the mid-nineteenth century. The book's focus is on Inuit history, culture and tradition and the four volumes tell various stories through text, in Kalaallisut (Western Greenlandic) and Danish, and prints, by Aron Kangek, a young hunter who went on to become an important oral historian for the region. The scale of the work and the variety of its content display the richness of Greenland's Inuit culture, as well as the depth of its historical memory.

Of particular note are the accounts of Inuit interaction with the Norse settlement that existed in Greenland between the tenth and fifteenth centuries. Originally founded under the leadership of Erik the Red, this settlement existed alongside Inuit communities before eventually disappearing, possibly due to climatic change that caused crops to fail and the landscape to become inhospitable to settlement. *Kalâdlit Okalluktualliait* recounts stories of, at different times, both cooperation and conflict with this settlement. Such cultural artefacts and histories are not unique to the Inuit of Greenland, nor to the Inuit as a whole. The culture of pan-Arctic indigenous peoples is repeatedly shown to be diverse and robust, not to mention constantly marked by the encroachment of European peoples. Indeed some peoples, such as the Sami, have had an impact in the opposite direction.

Kalâdlit Okalluktualliait highlights the fact that the Arctic explored by Europeans from the fifteenth century onwards was far from an empty land. Rather, it housed rich and diverse cultures that had seen Europeans come – and go – before.

OPPOSITE
Kalâdlit Okalluktualliait
[Greenland Legends]
(1859 and 1860 volumes).
RB.23.a.35373

Kâgsup ernera sakiatsiaisa paugât.
(ARUP KANGERMIUP, NOUP ERKANÊTUP, ASILIVDLUGULO SANA).

Akigssiardlo ikerssuarmiordlo arpaliútut.

Ungilagtakimut likerârtok.

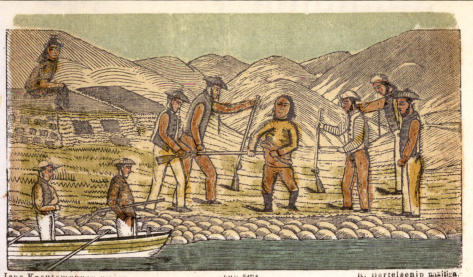

Jens Kreutsmannip assilua.   Arup sana.   R: Bertelsenip nakitiga.
(Kup: 30). Kavdlunât isigingisagssât. (Side: 31).

Aꞅigssiardlo Ikersuarmiordlo paꞣagssungmigsut.

Iluligssane Aꞅigssiap sujulê arssautut.

A FEEL FOR THE LANDSCAPE

Finding one's way in a landscape is fundamental to survival and cultural development for peoples all over the globe In the Arctic, where changes in weather are not only dangerous but can alter the features of the land, being able to navigate is particularly important. Indigenous Arctic cultures have used various navigational methods – in particular, reading the clues and marks left by weather, which provide points of orientation – but maps are still an important part of their wayfinding methodology.

Indigenous mapping of the Arctic has taken a variety of forms, including spoken description and ephemeral maps carved in ice and with stones – both practices that are important to indigenous cultures across North America. Within this tradition, the process of mapmaking is more important than the map object: it is a way of communicating knowledge, forming bonds between people and reaffirming the human relationship with land and sea.

Maps have also been carved in wood, as evidenced by surviving nineteenth-century maps of parts of the East Greenland coast. These maps are designed to be rotated and felt by hand, each notch and curve represents not only a 'bird's eye view' of the coast, but also gives a sense of it in three dimensions. While a European tradition of mapping would recognise the function of these objects, the way in which they are used underlines a fundamental difference between the two cultures in terms of relationships to land and sea. For Europeans, the map is more than just an object of practical use: it represents a form of domination and control. The ability to see the land in its entirety, from the perspective of a god, allows the viewer to lay claim to it, as we will see later in the propensity of European explorers to leave their names, and the names of their sponsors, strewn across the landscapes they mapped. By way of contrast, Inuit maps are designed to be held in the hand and felt, and represent a more tactile relationship with the landscape, one in which humans and their bodies are in contact and collaboration with the land. As a result, these maps are slightly abstracted to the eye (although no less authoritative) and do not offer the sense of visual control experienced when looking at European maps. Thus, they illustrate these two cultures' different perspectives in relation to the Arctic land: that of Europeans, which seeks to define, claim and dominate; and that of the Inuit, which seeks to relate, use and thrive.

These maps, facsimiles of which are held at the Scott Polar Research Institute, Cambridge, were carved by Kunit fra Umivik and collected by the Danish explorer Gustav Holm in the 1880s. As well as illustrating an important Inuit practice, they also evidence the dynamics of exchange that began to seep into Inuit relations with Europeans once explorers, traders and scientists started to work in the north (a subject discussed at greater length in the next chapter).

Ammassalik map carved
by Kunit fra Umivik.
Greenland National
Museum and Archive

A map of the Island of Thule,
by Arnold Mercator, 1558.

Maps c.2.cc.5

MYTHS OF THE NORTH

The fact that medieval Norse communities existed in the Arctic (see above) provides evidence that this region did not suddenly appear in the imagination of Europeans after the fifteenth century. Instead, like the central part of the African and Asian continents, the Arctic had long been known of and freighted with the baggage of historical imagination. While we do not know exactly how far back in history English, German or Norse awareness and imagining of the Arctic might go, we do know, for example, that the ancient Greeks were aware of the resources of the polar north and built it into their understandings of the world.

For the Greeks, the north was a source of riches, and its productive and mystical significance is mentioned as far back as *The Histories* of Herodotus, written in the fourth century BC. For Herodotus, 'Hyperborea' was a magical land beyond the north wind, with perfect terrain and twenty-four-hour sunshine (hence modern historians' suspicion that this region was, in fact, the Arctic). Hyperborea is just one of a number of visions of the north developed by classical cultures, the most enduring of which is probably that of 'Thule', put forward by the Greek explorer Pytheas after his expeditions of 330–20 BC.

Like the Greeks, people in later European cultures – even as late as that of Tudor England – imagined Hyperborea to be the source of some of their prized possessions, such as amber. This was also the case with Thule, with polar bear pelts, 'sea unicorn' (Narwhal) tusks and other forms of ivory joining a huge number of rare and precious artefacts understood to come from the Arctic. More specifically, they were understood as coming from 'Ultima Thule', 'beyond the borders of the known world', and a significant industry grew up, dedicated to describing and locating this place.

A map held at the British Library, is the only surviving example of a map showing the 'island' of Thule, and was engraved by the eldest son of the cartographer Gerard Mercator in 1558. It represents not just the continuing fascination with the Arctic and its riches, but also the blurring of modern, rational knowledge (Mercator's cartographical projections are still used to this day) with a world of fantasy and myth. Similarly, Mercator's studies of Arctic legends and his travel accounts were followed by British statesmen such as John Dee, who had a keen interest in the new world opening up before them and its potential resources.

Thule was therefore thought, even in the sixteenth century, to exist as a source of riches and opportunity. This meant that the search for trade routes such as the Northwest Passage was assumed to have the potential, not just to bring back riches from Cathay (modern-day China), but also to unlock the vast, imagined wealth of the lands of Thule. In short, even before explorers set off for the Arctic, their heads were filled with fantastic visions of the wonders and riches to be found.

DISCOVERING NORTH AMERICA WITH THE CABOT FAMILY

Into the mix of Arctic myths, imaginations and changing trade networks stepped the Cabot family – especially John Cabot and his son, Sebastian. Most likely born in Genoa, to a family originally hailing from Venice, John Cabot was the son of a spice merchant, and became obsessed with the possibility of finding shorter routes to Asia via the Atlantic. Cabot travelled to England in 1490, having heard of opportunities to undertake adventures under commission from Henry VII, and Columbus's 1492 discovery of land in the western Atlantic only made this an even more tempting possibility. Columbus, and those who listened to his initial reports, did not immediately think he had discovered a new set of lands but rather that he had encountered the eastern edges of Asia. Men such as Cabot (and monarchs such as Henry) were fired by a passion to stake their own claim on these new lands.

By 1494, the Treaty of Tordesillas, ratified by Pope Alexander VI, had divided the known world between the Spanish and the Portuguese, effectively giving these two nations control of the New World, its trade routes and the vast resource wealth to be found there. The true extent and value of the emerging Americas was still not known, nor how difficult trade with Asia might be, but the new horizons of the world, and access to trade routes west and south of Europe, were now dominated by these southern European powers; to monarchs like Henry VII, there seemed a very real danger of being marginalised in a globalising world of trade. In this context, men like Cabot, with the relevant skills and vision to see potential new routes across the Atlantic, were invaluable. As a result, by 1497, Cabot had been given command of the ship *Matthew* and instructed to set out across the northern Atlantic in an attempt to reach Japan. The theory was that a more northerly route could exist and would not be so restricted by the treaty.

Cabot would eventually encounter the region we now call Newfoundland, in Canada, and return to England carrying enough salted cod to cover his costs. A larger expedition set out the next year to seek another route further north but, it seems, was not heard from again. Although recent evidence suggests that Cabot may have made it home, the mission itself was a failure. In 1508, John's son Sebastian took up the mantle, departing to find a northerly route to Asia via the western Atlantic. Sebastian may have encountered what we now call Hudson Bay, in northeast Canada, which his crew refused to enter, before sailing down as far as Florida and then home. The mission had, again, been a failure, but Sebastian would not give up on Arctic trading routes and their promised riches, and he was later involved in the establishment of the Muscovy Company (see pp. 30–39), which monopolised trade between England and Russia.

The legacy of the Cabot family, especially John, is captured in a map from Richard Hakluyt's *Divers Voyages Touching the Discoverie of America…* (1582). The map notes where Cabot encountered Newfoundland in 1497, and was used by Sir Humphrey Gilbert in the sixteenth century to attract investors for his plan to colonise the land encountered by Cabot. By the time this map was produced, the area already housed a thriving English fishing port, St John's, which produced huge volumes of preserved cod for sale in England. Gilbert would later depart, with materials and colonists, to found a permanent settlement in St John's and, while the colony would have a rocky existence, it was one of the earliest English settlements abroad. The search for Arctic trade routes, its accidental discoveries and the material evidence resulting from it had formed the foundation of what would, eventually, become the British Empire.

Oriens

70 60 50 40 30

N.A.Kena

Groenlandt

Frisland

Scotia
Anglia
Hibernia
Gallia
Hispania
Maiorca
Fefte
Moroc.

Barbariæ pars.

Brasil

C.S.Finfte
C.S.Vincé
C.Boiador

Madera
Canaria

Frobyfher
Coxves
la borador
S.Brandam
Depona
Mare
Veide
Azores.

R.Elizabeth
Sama bara
Corterecal.
Aues
Cozo
C.Britou
S.Johan
Iean Steuen
Garsa
Canar

Tropicus

Grad bay
Accarier
1535
Norombega
I.Gabot. 1497
Aredonig

Claudia

S.anno

Bermuda
Sept Cités

350 340 330 320 310 360 20 25 30 35 40 45 50 55

Meridies. 310

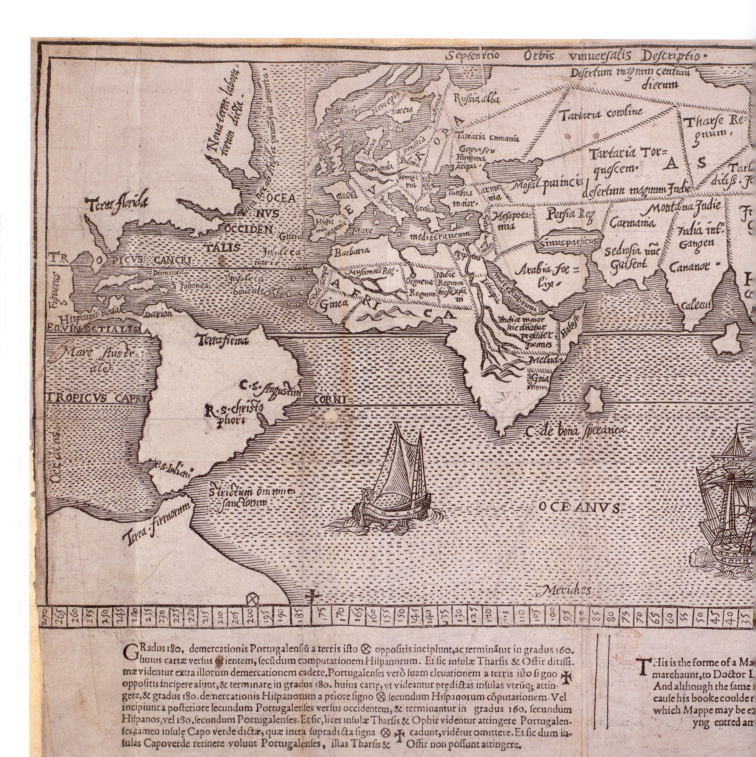

Not all eyes turned west, however. The discovery of the Americas, complete with new ways of reaching Cathay and profiting in-between, had created new enthusiasm in Europe for the exploration of routes through the Arctic to the lands of the east. As the examples of Thule and Hyperborea show, people were already prepared to believe riches could be gained by exploring the north, but a new impetus now drove the desire to explore.

The English trader Robert Thorne, seeing both danger and opportunity, was another early advocate of polar exploration as a way for England to avoid being closed out of a rapidly globalising trade network after the signing of the Treaty of Tordesillas. While he was largely ignored during his lifetime (Henry VIII being preoccupied with domestic politics), Thorne's lobbying was important in informing the later fitting-out of various Arctic voyages, and he set out some of the early arguments for a channel leading, via the Arctic, to the east. The main logic governing this assertion was that such a channel existed to the south, so a similar one must exist to the north.

Thorne's focus, however, was on trade routes via the North Pole and Northeast Passage. A world map of 1582, based on Thorne's 1527 prototype, shows no way to the Indies via the Northwest Passage, as the continent impedes progress, presenting Thorne's view that an eastern route must exist. Such an opinion also had the advocacy of the Muscovy Company, and thus support for the Northwest Passage was stifled for a number of years.

While the Northeast Passage expeditions inspired by Thorne failed and enthusiasm for attempting a Northwest Passage would grow as a result, his belief in open polar seas was the germ of an idea that persists into the present day. In Thorne's time, it was believed that an open sea existed at the pole, housing a giant magnetic rock – the reason compasses pointed to the pole. While our ideas about an open polar sea have developed, with climate change now the determining ideology, Thorne's thesis shows that the modern idea of an ice-free, navigable North Pole is far from new.

ALL THE RICHES OF RUSSIA

The Muscovy Company is largely forgotten in the popular history of English private interests in foreign trading; the Hudson's Bay Company and East India Company inhabit that niche very comfortably. However, this company was one of the first mercantile ventures undertaken as England sought to expand and globalise its trade horizons. First established as the Company of Merchant Adventurers to New Lands, led by Richard Chancellor, Sebastian Cabot (see above) and Hugh Willoughby, the enterprise initially sought trading ventures in Asia – aiming to use the Northeast Passage as a way around Spanish and Portuguese interests, not to mention the dangers posed by a long journey around the Cape of Good Hope. Willoughby led the first expedition in 1553, although he had no experience as a navigator; he had made his name as a defender of English land and strategic points against the Scots.

The expedition and its ships soon encountered trouble with ice. Once stuck in the ice they were well supplied with goods and garments, including those intended for trade, but it became apparent that this Northeast Passage would not provide a viable trading route. Willoughby struck out north, encountering Spitsbergen – an island in the Svalbard archipelago, north of Norway – and Novaya Zemlya, while Chancellor, separated from the other ships in the expedition, undertook a 1,000-kilometre journey across snow and ice to reach Moscow. By undertaking trade with the Czar and returning to England with letters of permission to open trade with Russia across the sea, Chancellor was able to lobby for a monopoly of trade; once granted, this meant the company could be rebranded the Muscovy Company, in 1555. It went on to become the cornerstone of English and Russian relations for many years, with a monopoly that could expand to new areas and new products.

An illustration published in 1625 in *Purchas His Pilgrims*, a compendium of exploration narratives drawing from the work of Hakluyt, depicts the whale fishery of 'Greenland' – which is to say, in fact, Spitsbergen. Willoughby had encountered these islands before his death. The later account, also published in *Purchas*, written by Thomas Edge under the title 'A Brief Discouerie of the Muscovite Merchants of seas, coasts, and countries delivered as they were hopefully begun, and have ever since happily beene continued by the singular industry and charge of the Worshipfull Society of Muscovite Merchants of London', is a lengthy description of the company's growing monopoly on northern trade and goods production. In spite of the failure to find the Northeast Passage, Chancellor and Willoughby's actions had opened up trade with Russia and charted new whaling and hunting grounds, where precious commodities could be gathered.

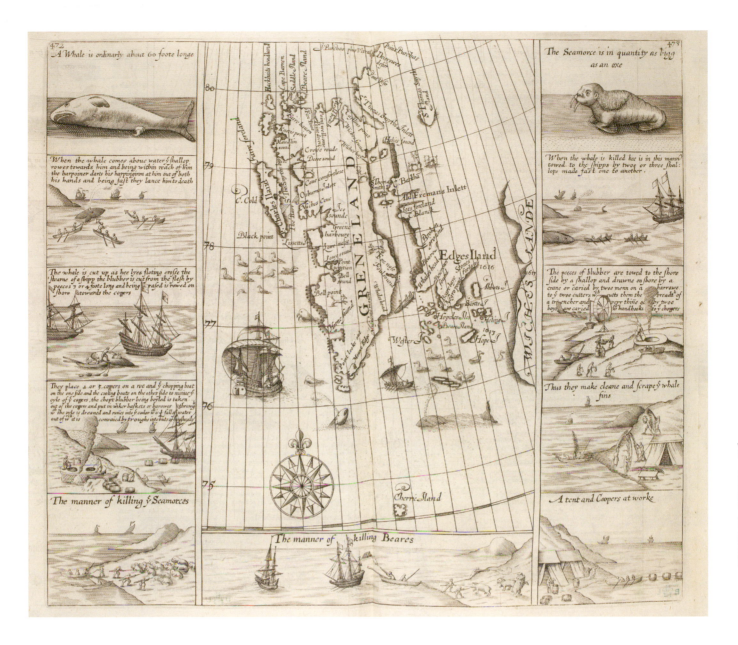

While keen to attribute the achievements of various sailors, not least Willoughby, Edge's account also highlights the bounty of the whale, including the products that could be derived from it. Discussing the various parts of the animal, as well as its prodigious size, he finds the most notable aspect is blubber, 'which yields Oyle'. Over the coming centuries, London's lighting and fashion trades, to name just two, would become hugely dependent on the whaling industry for a continuous supply of products. As we will see, the strain on whaling communities was immense, leading to a symbiotic relationship between whalers and explorers, with the latter continually opening up new grounds for the former to exploit. The search for the Northeast Passage had shown that failed expeditions could still be hugely productive for traders, though destructive for natural environments, establishing a pattern that would run well into the twentieth century. Wherever explorers went, the natural world could not be the same again.

The process of whale hunting, as depicted in *Purchas His Pilgrims* (1625).
G.6840

EXPLORATION AND
THE REFORMATION

The many expeditions in search of the Northwest Passage and other trade routes to Asia were, as discussed above, not sporadic, single ventures but part of a concerted campaign to break Spanish and Portuguese trading monopolies and develop England's role on the world stage. This was particularly the case during the reign (1558–1603) of Elizabeth I, whose survival as a monarch and ability to develop a dynasty depended not just upon her conceiving an heir (an important issue, with its own politics and social context) but also on developing the nation's ability to finance its state and wars at the same level as other great powers of the age. The articulation of all this – the importance of developing England's trading base and the possible significance of Arctic trading routes – was masterfully achieved by Richard Hakluyt, whose reputation still looms large in the history of exploration, geography and cartography.

Hakluyt was born in 1553 into a family of high social standing hailing from the Welsh Marches; the family was also already in possession of one geographer, Hakluyt's cousin once-removed (also Richard Hakluyt). These family networks and an education at Westminster School and Christ Church, Oxford, developed the young Hakluyt's geographical sensibilities before he took holy orders. Now indulging his enthusiasm for all the accounts of explorers that came his way, Hakluyt also made the acquaintance of many of the period's notable seafarers, using these connections as a way of finding information about new voyages and discoveries.

To the present-day reader, such activities may seem a distraction from Hakluyt's role as defined by his holy orders, but they can in fact be understood as an attempt to defend the faith, and examining Hakluyt's role in the church underlines the relationship between faith, politics and exploration in this period. Protestant England, threatened on all sides by Catholic nations incensed by the dissent of Elizabeth I and her father, Henry VIII, needed to gain an advantage in the new trade networks with Asia and make the most of discoveries in the New World if it was to be able to fund its own survival and the future of the Protestant faith. In this context, Hakluyt's research, publications and advocacy can be seen as mutually entwined with his priestly role.

Hakluyt is remembered for one particular publication produced as part of this research, *The Principall Navigations, voiages and discoveries of the English nation, etc.* (1589). This was a compendium of various geographical discoveries from English expeditions of the sixteenth century and paid particular attention to searches for the Northwest Passage (in the hope that it might yet yield a productive trade route to Asia and a source of wealth, in spite of previous disappointments). The second edition of Hakluyt's publication (1599) featured an early version of the map shown here, which was produced by the English mathematician and cartographer Edward Wright using Mercator's innovative new projection for mapping the whole globe (the version reproduced here was published later, in 1657, 41 years after Hakluyt's death, and has been modified by John Moxton).

Mercator, assumed by many to be a Protestant, had developed his projection in 1569 and it represented a way of viewing the world as accurately as possible on a flat sheet of paper. By using this new projection of the world, Wright and Hakluyt were underscoring that theirs was a rational, Protestant view of the world – a world in which Protestant traders could remake the balance of trade and break southern European monopolies. Hakluyt, then, was heavily involved in advocating the use of Arctic trade routes to achieve these goals and, in doing so, articulated how his world looked, was understood and would develop in the ensuing centuries.

A PLAT of all the
WORLD.

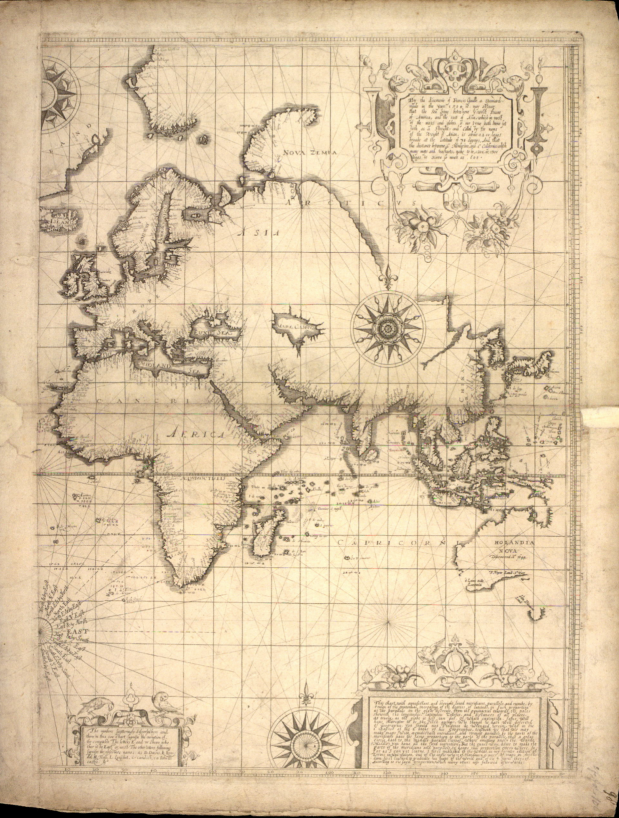

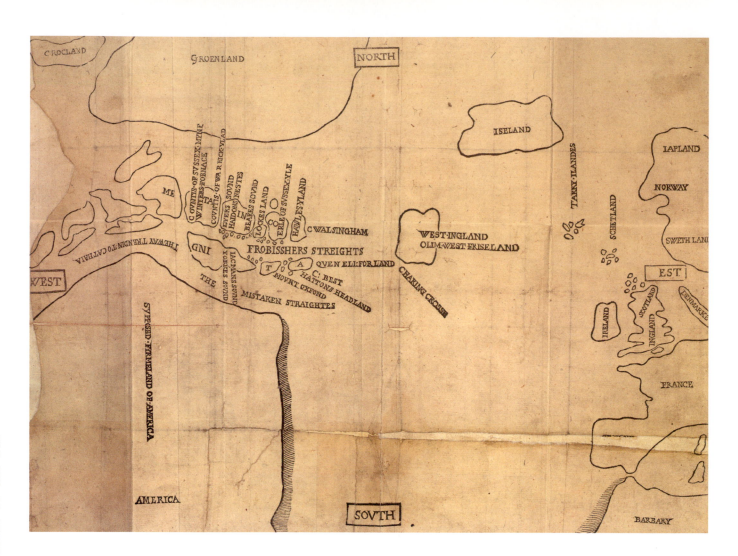

A map of the entrance to the Northwest Passage
from George Beste's, *A true discourse of the
late voyages of discouerie, for the finding of
a passage to Cathaya, by the Northweast, vnder
the conduct of Martin Frobisher Generall* (1578).
C.13.a.9.(1)

FAME AND FORTUNE?

John Cabot's 1497 voyage to the north had inaugurated English exploration of the Arctic during a period of political and economic change in Europe. The failure of attempts to find routes via the North Pole and the Northeast Passage, however, meant that England either needed to abandon hopes of establishing its own trade route to the east or find an alternative, possibly to the west.

Even in the face of the failure to find viable trade routes to the east, however, vested interests had still grown up around the exploration of, and other trade opportunities found in, northern waters. The most powerful interested party, the Muscovy Company, was a significant impediment to proposed exploration of the Northwest Passage, seeing any routes, resources or trade opportunities discovered as presenting a threat to its monopoly. The company was still at the mercy of prevailing geopolitical pressures, however, and eventually had to yield to continuing calls for further exploration to the west.

The result of all of this was the appointment, in 1576, of the English seaman Martin Frobisher to undertake the first major expedition to the Northwest Passage since the late-fifteenth-century endeavours of John Cabot. Martin Frobisher was one of a number of English explorers who would set out to find the Northwest Passage but he was arguably in a different mould from those later understood as 'polar explorers'. An adventurer and privateer, Frobisher had made his name preying on French shipping routes in the English Channel, under an English licence. Later on, he would continue to develop this reputation through his exploits in repelling the Spanish Armada, the feat for which he was most celebrated during his life (he was knighted as a result).

Despite lacking skills as an explorer, Frobisher was a skilled seaman and also understood the ebb and flow of politics and trade in the sixteenth century. He recognised the importance of a trade route via the Northwest Passage, the significance of any resources that might be found on it and the crucial role of public support in making sure expeditions could go ahead. The maps shown here were printed in the wake of Frobisher's 1576 voyage, as part of an attempt to drum up enthusiasm for a return journey to the Northwest Passage; Frobisher was convinced he had found an entrance to the Passage and huge resources of gold too.

In reality, the maps show the proportion of fantasy still present in European imaginings of the north (note the open sea and obelisk at the North Pole), as well as Frobisher's failings as a chart maker. The opening shown is not, in fact, an entrance to the Northwest Passage but, instead, what we now call Frobisher Bay, in northeast Canada. Despite this inaccuracy, the map helped set the stage for over four hundred years of British interest in the Arctic, which proved to be a continual temptation for polar and armchair explorers alike. As for the gold Frobisher claimed to have found, despite his returning to mine huge quantities at the expense of many lives, and instigating the construction of a huge smelting complex in Dartford, England, the gold turned out to be worthless iron pyrite, or 'fool's gold'. In the end it was used as building material around the town; it can still be seen in the external walls of Henry VIII's manor house.

A map of the world showing open polar
seas and an obelisk at the North Pole,
in George Beste's, *A true discourse of
the late voyages of discouerie…* (1578).

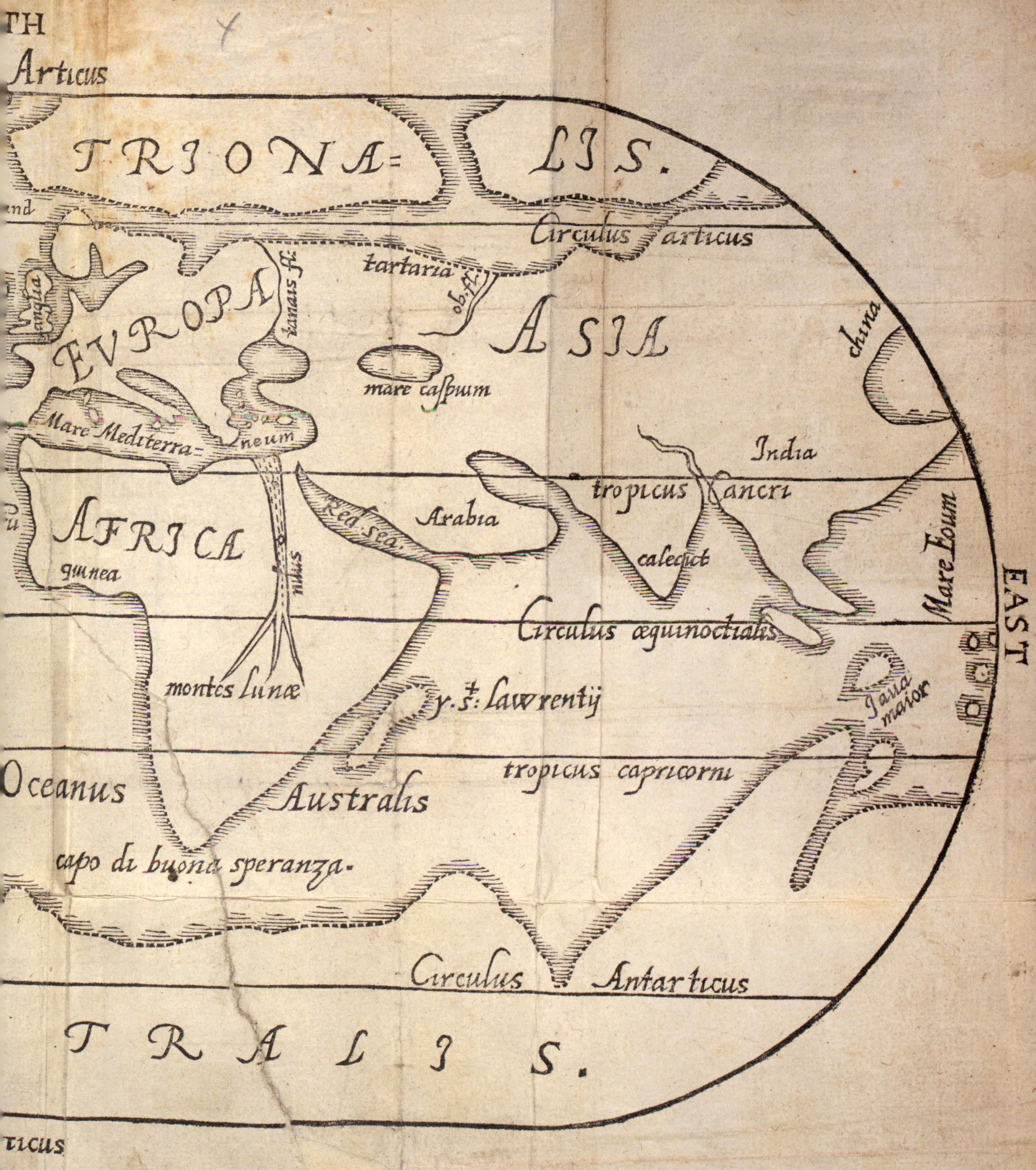
TH
Articus
TRIONA=
LIS.
Circulus articus
tartaria
ob fl.
tanais fl.
EVROPA
anglia
ASIA
china
mare caspium
Mare Mediterra=
neum
India
tropicus cancri
AFRICA
Red sea
Arabia
calecut
Mare Eoum
EAST
guinea
nilus
Circulus æquinoctialis
montes lunæ
y. s. lawrentij
Iaua maior
Oceanus
Australis
tropicus capricorni
capo di buona speranza.
Circulus
Antarticus
TRALIS.
ticus

RESISTING THE EXPLORERS

Focusing on the politics and financial pressures that drove Frobisher runs the risk of obscuring the fact that his exploits did not occur in European seas or against a European landscape. Instead, Frobisher's explorations were undertaken in the lands of various Inuit groups, with their own cultural and political contexts, within which we should understand and deal with the arrival of his ship.

Frobisher made extensive contact with the Inuit of Greenland and what would become northern Canada as an inevitable consequence of his exploration, but also of his invasive inland activities, as he attempted to mine the 'gold' coveted back in England. Some of this engagement was mutually productive, with useful goods traded for manufactured wares. Such wares were often made of metal, which was of incredible value to the Inuit, who had no way of producing the high temperatures required for metal work. However, the image shown opposite, based on a drawing by the artist John White, shows that Frobisher's interactions with the Inuit were otherwise fraught and ended in conflict.

Unlike later captains, who often tried to manage relationships with local cultures by reaching out to them, as well as overlooking or indirectly reprimanding what were understood as breaches of conduct (such as petty theft), Frobisher insisted on harsh punishment and retribution. On his first expedition, five of Frobisher's men disappeared, suspicions arising that local Inuit had captured and killed them. Thus began a cycle of conflict and retribution in which Frobisher and his crew kidnapped Inuit individuals and, on his second voyage of 1577, engaged in battle with some groups. The most significant of these engagements was the battle at Bloody Point – the likely subject of this illustration –where as many as forty men from Frobisher's crew attacked a group of less than twenty Inuit.

Such encounters, in which Inuit communities collaborated with, resisted and fought Arctic explorers, underlines the fact that this land was neither empty nor the Inuit within it passive in response to the arrival of explorers. They would protect their interests, seek to improve their lives and resist events they saw as posing a threat. The dynamics are similar to those set forth in the *Kalâdlit Okalluktualliait*, discussed above, and would persist over the coming centuries of colonial exploration, evolving and changing as greater numbers of Europeans and Americans arrived in the Arctic, for an increasing range of reasons.

Another link between that nineteenth-century chronicle of Inuit life and Frobisher's encounter with indigenous peoples is the survival in record, from an Inuit perspective, of the experience and history of European explorers and colonists. Three hundred years later, when the American explorer Charles Francis Hall collected testimonies from Baffin Island Inuit about gold mining *kabloona* (white people), he found that stories about Frobisher had survived among the Inuit of Iqaluit (the capital of Baffin Island) – a testament to the strength of oral tradition (see p. 161). Stories also endure today, suggesting that the five men who disappeared on Frobisher's first expedition lived in the community for a number of years before attempting to sail back to England in a makeshift boat.

The English in Queen Elizabeth's Reign discover GRONELAND, land there & are oppos'd by y Nativ.

A manuscript depiction of Frobisher's conflict with Greenland Inuit, most likely battle at Bloody Point. From the manuscripts of Sir Hans Sloane.

Add 5253 f.8

A Woman of GRONELAND *with her Child.*

INUIT CAPTIVES

Frobisher's attempts at retribution for the suspected capture of his men not only resulted in open conflict with the Inuit but also the taking of captives, who were forced to travel back with the expedition to England. The bringing back of captives or guests from territories encountered by Europeans was relatively common even before the discovery of the Americas; indeed, so-called 'guests' were often captives – important members of indigenous societies who were brought back to Europe as collateral, to underpin agreements or to assert the power of explorers and traders. The individuals seen in illustrations produced between 1585 and 1593, in particular the woman and child opposite, were most likely taken captive after the battle at Bloody Point.

These captives were used to instantiate the findings of the expedition and, as with other individuals brought back from the New World, caused a stir in English society. While in Bristol, the male captive, Kalicho, displayed his kayaking and hunting skills, killing two ducks on the River Avon with his darts. These displays were put on for a number of groups; local dignitaries, including the mayor, turned out to see the Inuit – evidence of the fascination that Frobisher's captives (and the New World in general) held for the English public.

The example set by interactions such as Frobisher's, combined with an enthusiasm to learn about the peoples of the rest of the world, meant that explorers brought back a number of indigenous peoples, including other Inuit, to London over the coming centuries. As a result, there are numerous local histories of displays (such as that of Kalicho), as well as records of what English scholars tried to learn about the Inuit and their habits and society. Often, relatively superficial habits (such as the eating of raw or undercooked meat), had a disproportionate impact on the English imagination, as did the desire to teach visitors English words, habits and manners. This was often achieved successfully, even within the short amount of time available.

Death usually awaited captives and visitors from the New World. Unused to the European climate, and with no immunity to European diseases, all of the Inuit brought to England by Frobisher eventually succumbed to illness. Thus began the creation of a sad geography in parts of England and the rest of the British Isles, as the graves of indigenous peoples from around the world began to appear. While Frobisher and his men had no understanding of the effects disease, combined with lack of immunity, would have on the indigenous Arctic people they brought back to England, these were the first hints of the devastation of such people that would be wrought. Over the coming years, as contact between explorers, traders and hunters and the Inuit increased, various diseases and infections, not least those that were sexually transmitted, would have a disastrous effect on Inuit communities.

Manuscript illustration of an Inuit woman and child brought to England as captives by Frobisher. From the manuscripts of Sir Hans Sloane. Add 5253 f.9-11.

THE HERO AND
THE PASSAGE

Martin Frobisher did not have a monopoly on Elizabethan derring-do on the high seas, nor even, perhaps, heroic attempts on the Northwest Passage. Frobisher's expeditions overlapped with the English seaman Francis Drake's epic voyage to the Pacific Ocean and, indeed, around the world. This voyage took place in the same context as Frobisher's attempts to forge a Northwest Passage from the Atlantic side: England's position on the world stage as threatened by, especially, Catholic Spain. To understand the significance of access to the Pacific, and particularly an audacious raid like that Drake was about to undertake, it is important to keep in mind that Spain had sole control of the western edge of the Americas, not for a few years or even a couple of decades, but for two generations. As a result, all the resources of the western Americas and the possibilities for trade with Asia were easily within Spain's control. Drake's voyage was an attempt to upset this financially profitable apple cart.

Drake set out from England with six ships in 1577, himself aboard the *Pelican*, to navigate south of the Americas and into the Pacific. The astounding loss of men and material sustained on the journey was another reminder as to why England needed an easier passage to Asia; by the time Drake reached the Pacific Ocean only the *Pelican* (now re-named *Golden Hind*) was left. Drake began to plunder the Spanish coast of South America and his luck now changed dramatically. While the long years of Spanish control here caused broader geopolitical headaches for England, it also meant that the Spanish felt unassailable, with captains, governors and others in charge believing themselves to be too far away from European traffic to face any threat from foreign powers. Having acquired not just bullion but also better charts, Drake headed to the coast of North America in March 1579, soon after his most successful acquisition, the Spanish galleon *Nuestra Señora de la Concepción* (nicknamed *Cacafuego*).

Interestingly, the surviving records from Drake's expedition become very sparse at this point. In the 1628 *The World Encompassed by Sir Francis Drake*, the record jumps from 16 April 1579 to 5 June 1579 with just a single entry. In this, Drake writes vaguely about entering 'the frozen Zone' and experiencing frigid temperatures, as well as encountering a mysterious, 'unnatural, congealed and frozen substance'. This vague account has led a number of researchers to suggest that Drake left England with a secret set of instructions from Elizabeth I. It is possible that any such instructions directed Drake to try to find a western entrance to the Passage – in the same way, later, the Admiralty also secretly instructed James Cook to search for the Passage on his third voyage to the Pacific (see pp. 84–5) – and that Drake actually sailed much further up the North American coast than Whale Cove, Oregon (*Portus Novae Albionis* to Drake), the traditionally accepted northernmost point of the expedition.

The map provided in *The World Encompassed by Sir Francis Drake* provides few clues, possibly because of the strict embargo that was put on the dissemination of information from Drake's voyage. Indeed, we must assume that the map's suggestion that the Northwest Passage does not exist did not match Drake's own thoughts, as we know he was in disagreement with the way in which the map displays *Terra Australis*. Having been driven south by storms after June 1579, Drake concluded, correctly, that the southern continent did not exist and was instead an assortment of islands and smaller continents, as modern maps of Oceania show. Drake's story, and, to some extent, this map, both indicate how important routes and knowledge were in the geopolitical games of the early modern period, and also suggest that one of England's greatest heroes was bound up in the hunt for the Northwest Passage.

FIRE

AYRE

Sr Francis Drake.

Ferdinando Magellanus

NORTH

The Artik circle

Groen land

Baffins Bay

Frisland

Hudsons Straits

Davios straits

Buttons Bay

New Brittayne

New found land

THE

SEA

NORTH AMERICA

Hudsons B.

New England

N. France

Westerne Iles

OR Nova

MEXICANA

Virginia

THE

California

New Gra nada

Sumer Iles

Iapan Il.

The Gulf of

Mexico

NORTH

Lanu blada

C S Lucas

Mexico

Hispaniola

P. Rico

S Bernardo

Los Iardinos

Of Coralos Of Pazaros

S Petro

Nico

Iamaica

Palo mas

Gui ana

SEA

Nadadores

Q Barbudos

I S Cruz

Quito

Parte

Lake Parime

R Grande

The Æquinoctiall Line

Cy Ocean

Peru

of Amazones

Parnam Butos

Hoornse Iles

Coco I.

Flies Ne

Waterland

Dogs Iland without ground

ZVR

V

THO

Il. of good hope

Itraytors I.

In Il.

America

Bra sile

Potosi

Ciudad real

of Peru

OR PERV

The Pacificke Sea

Anita

S Fe

R Ianeiro

Twise in our age hath these straights beene passed by Englishmen, the first was by Sr Francis Drake Añ 1578 the second by Mr Thomas Cavendish in the yeare 1586

Patagonum C. Blanco R of Plate chica

The straits of Magelan La Moire straits

The Antarttike Circle

MAGALLANICA

SOVTH

The Eclipse of the Sunne

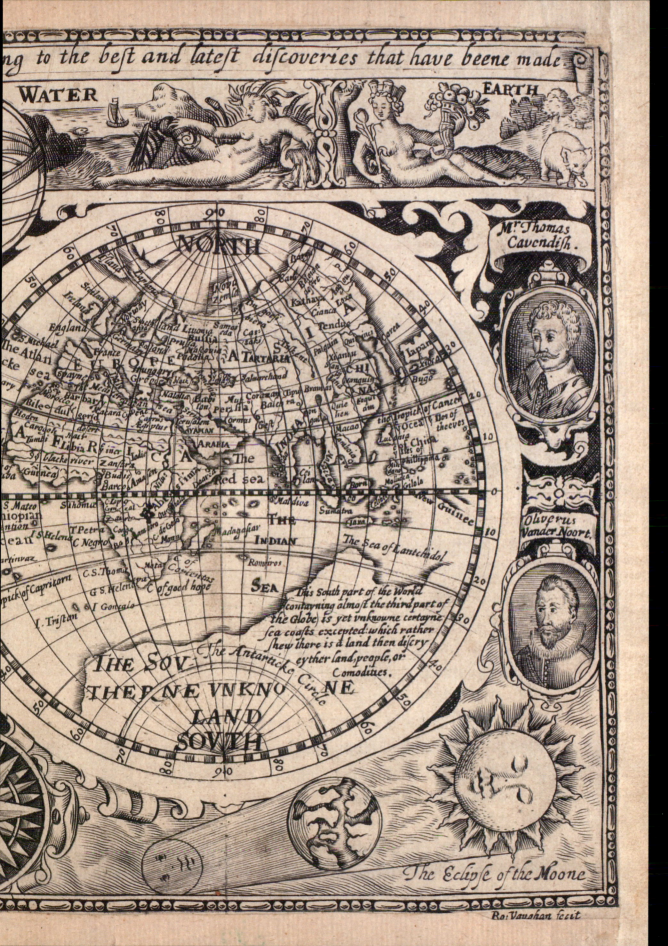

THE NAVIGATOR AND THE PASSAGE

Another Elizabethan bound up in the search for the Northwest Passage was John Davis, a sailor and extraordinary navigator. Well known to his contemporaries, liked and respected, Davis found support for his search for the Northwest Passage in the person of Elizabeth I's principal secretary, Sir Francis Walsingham. Davis's desire to search for the Passage was underpinned by his abilities as a navigator, his belief (in spite of Frobisher's failures) that a passage must exist, and his patriotic desire to further England's cause in competing against Spain. As a result of Walsingham's backing, Davis was able to undertake three voyages in search of the Passage between 1585 and 1587, during which he would lay the groundwork for numerous future explorers.

Davis's expeditions mainly traversed the seas running north along the west coast of Greenland, the reason this area (the Davis Strait) bears his name to this day. His first expedition, in the *Sunneshine* and the *Mooneshine*, was only a modest success in terms of acquiring information about the Passage, but Davis did make contact with Greenland, which had slipped out of the reach of European knowledge since the decline of the Norse colonies described in the *Kaládlit Okalluktualliait*, and in Aron Kangek's historic woodcuts. Returning convinced that the Passage lay further north, Davis lobbied for a further expedition. Ice, and weather less accommodating than that of the previous year, turned back the expedition of 1586 (not the last time capricious weather would affect an expedition), but 1587's voyage was more successful. Setting out with the *Sunneshine*, the *Elizabeth* and the *Ellen*, two of which were to focus on fishing for cod in the bountiful fisheries discovered previously, Davis would eventually reach latitude 72°92° N before being forced by winds to alter course. While Davis charted the Baffin Island, Greenland and Labrador coasts, and also noted the entrance to what was later named Hudson Bay, the expedition returned having discovered no further evidence of the Passage.

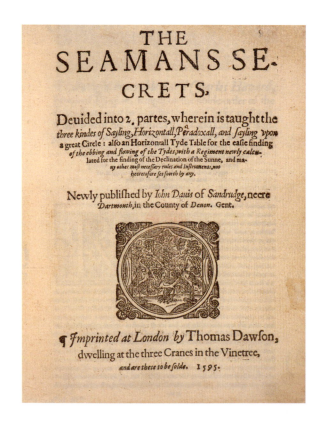

Title page and instructional illustrations from John Davis's *The Seamans Secrets* (1595).
C.54.bb.33

Nonetheless, Davis's belief in the Passage was undiminished. In his 1595 account of seafaring discoveries around the world, *The worldes hydrographical discription, etc.*, the frontispiece reads: 'Wherein is proued … that the worlde in all his zones, clymats and places, is habitable and inhabited, and the seas likewise vniuersally nauigable without any naturall anoyance'. Despite this, Davis would not voyage to the Arctic successfully again. A subsequent attempt to reach the Arctic via the west coast of the Americas was unsuccessful and Davis died in 1605, fighting Japanese pirates in the East Indies. Davis's legacy extends beyond his discoveries and the names he left on a map, however, as he was also a prodigious navigator with a flair for teaching. His 1595 publication, *The Seamans Secrets*, is an instructional account long revered as a source for learning the secrets of navigation. The style, which revolves around answering questions posed rhetorically to the reader, is similar to that of today's instructional books and it contains numerous details as to the use of navigational tools, such as the Davis quadrant (or backstaff), which he invented.

After 1587, the English conflict with Spain reached crisis levels, with the Armada departing one year later, and Walsingham, who had championed Davis's expeditions, passed away in 1590, removing an important voice at the Privy Council. In this context, Davis's skills were redeployed elsewhere, hence his eventual death far from home. The age of empire, in which men could be consistently deployed on the same venture of Arctic exploration, was some way off; these were days of pragmatism. Davis was of use in searching for Arctic trade routes when finance, politics and war allowed, but was otherwise sent to the places in which his expertise was needed most. His career illustrates the talent of those involved in the search for the Passage and, at the same time, the global game in which their efforts were bound up.

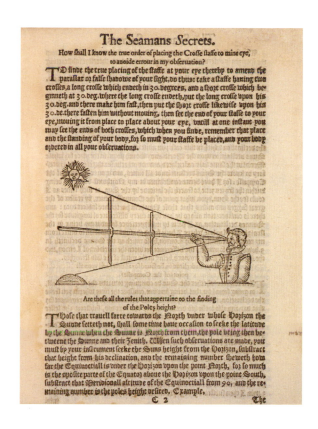

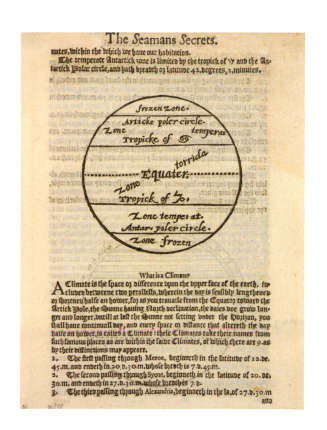

A EUROPEAN PROJECT

William Barents's expeditions were depicted in Gerrit de Veer's *Waerachtighe Beschrijvinghe van drie seylagien...* (1598).

C.133.e.34

England was not the only nation interested in the political and economic potential of northern routes, nor, as we have seen, was the Northwest Passage the only possibility. During the sixteenth century, the Dutch were caught up in the same geopolitical game as England; indeed the Netherlands (as we now know them) were on the front line. In 1568, the Eighty Years' War for Dutch independence from Philip II of Spain had begun; a result of the escalating religious conflicts born of the Reformation. This religious revolution would reshape Europe, redrawing its political boundaries and having a profound effect on European empires of the coming centuries; it was not just a religious conflict, therefore, but a political one.

The ultimate success of the Netherlands was determined not by the size of the nation nor by the resources at its immediate disposal; rather, trade and finance were significant weapons of war. The Dutch East India Company, which had a monopoly on Dutch spice trade in Asia, not only provided capital and resources for

the relatively small nation – profits from the company and its investments provided the copious funds needed for the war – but was also actively involved in open conflict. Despite this mercantile and military success, Dutch traders and investors constantly needed to look for new opportunities, markets and routes. As they had among the English, eyes eventually turned to the Arctic.

It was within this context of global tension and national strife that the Dutch explorer William Barents attempted to organise his expeditions to the Arctic. Barents was a student of Petrus Plancius, a Dutch Reformed Church minister and cartographer who believed the Arctic would yield a route to the Americas, specifically via a Northeast Passage. Having generated excitement and funds to try to find the Passage, Barents was able to undertake three journeys in total: in 1594, 1595 and 1596.

The first two expeditions had little success but, while the States General of the Netherlands refused to fund a further expedition, a prize was promised to whoever could find the Passage. The council of Amsterdam thus paid to outfit two ships and Barents was able to undertake his third expedition. Barents and his men first explored Novaya Zemlya – an archipelago in the Arctic Ocean, north of Russia – achieving 81°N before sailing east into what they thought was the beginning of a navigable Northeast Passage. By November, the ships were trapped in ice and the crew were forced to make their way back to Novaya Zemlya to build a shelter. Despite trouble with polar bears and diminishing supplies, the crew were in high spirits for a long time, calling themselves the 'Burghers of Novaya Zemlya'. Things changed rapidly, however, as the men became ill, and Barents eventually died of scurvy, leaving the men to dig a channel through the ice to escape in small boats. The tragic end of Barents's last expedition caused many to give up on the Northeast Passage, meaning that the Netherlands needed to look to other areas for new trade routes and resources to support the war with Spain.

Various depictions
of the challenges
and events faced by
Barents's crews,
from de Veer's,
*Waerachtighe
Beschrijvinghe van
drie seylagien.*
C.133.e.34

PUTTING HUDSON ON THE MAP

The English explorer Henry Hudson left his name on some of North America's iconic landmarks and charted waters, in the form of Hudson Bay and the Hudson River, both of which were indispensable to the trading future of the continent. What is often forgotten, given the later financial productivity of both of these areas, is that in discovering these locations, Hudson was failing to find what he was actually looking for; he too was bound up in the search for trade routes via the Arctic. At various times, Hudson was instructed to find routes via the North Pole, Northeast Passage and Northwest Passage, and his employers were a diverse group; he worked for the Muscovy Company, the Dutch East India Company and the British Crown during his career. Hudson is, therefore, yet another example of how the quest for Arctic trading routes was one shared by various European nations attempting to gain an advantage in the globalised world of sixteenth- and seventeenth-century trade.

After two unsuccessful expeditions for the Muscovy Company, in 1607 and 1608, the Dutch East India Company commissioned Hudson

to undertake another mission to the Northeast Passage in 1609. Setting sail in the ship *Halve Maen* (Half Moon), Hudson once again found his path blocked by the ice and, acting under his own instruction, turned to see if western routes fared better. This expedition led him to the coast of today's New York state and what is now called the Hudson River, precipitating later Dutch settlement in the area.

It was on his return journey that he would discover Hudson Bay. Hudson put into port in England and was detained by officials, most likely in the hope that they might gain access to his logs and other information. While he still managed to dispatch information back to the Netherlands, his next expedition was to be in the service of the English. Setting sail in search of the Northwest Passage, Hudson and his crew eventually sailed into a bay they believed to be the Pacific. A map of 1612 shows the outcome of the resulting exploration and bears a Latin inscription, which translates as 'A long voyage, over too wide a sea, separates us from China and in my heart I cannot endure so great a delay.' Thus spoke Hudson, and intrepid, he set course from the West Indies to seek a shortcut.' However, the map was not published under Hudson's instruction: he had been left behind in the Arctic after his crew mutinied and banished him to a small boat with his son and a few loyal men. Hudson was not heard of again, except in a very few Inuit oral histories relating to a white man and boy marooned in a boat, which may or may not be about Hudson.

'This, then, is the map of a mutineer, published under the instruction of a ringleader, Abacuk Pricket, and plainly seeking to justify the decision to throw Hudson from his own ship. The notes continue: 'And he had already begun to conquer the unexplored strip, to promise success to the King, but to neglect his men, when the crew put a stop to his great enterprise', before suggesting that Hudson still lives in the Arctic, merrily continuing his work for the Crown, rather than perishing in the terrible conditions. As well as being a justification for the mutiny, the map also notes where the crew overwintered in 1611 (shown in the bottom-left corner of the map) and contains some of the first information about Hudson Bay, which was to become a great trading interest for English merchants. Here begins the story of one of the many unintended consequences of exploration of the Northwest Passage. Hudson had set out to find routes to Asia, but instead encountered the site of what would become a major trading port, and charted an area that would go on to be of major importance to the hugely lucrative English fur trade. Such incidents are common in the history of Arctic exploration: the information uncovered, even in the context of 'unsuccessful' expeditions, is invaluable, for example, to fur traders, whalers and many others who see an opportunity to make profit from the resources of the north.

Tabula Nautica, qua repraesentãtur orae maritimae, meatus. ac freta, noviter a H. Hudsono Anglo ad Caurum supra Novam Franciam, Indagata [sic]. Anno 1612.
Maps 70095(1)

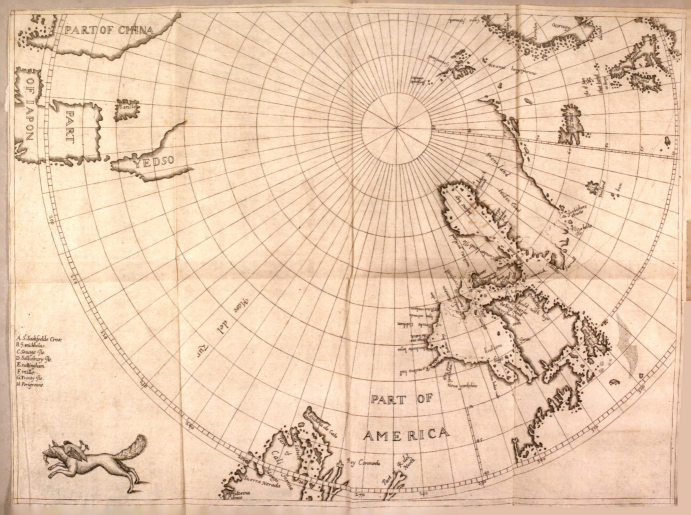

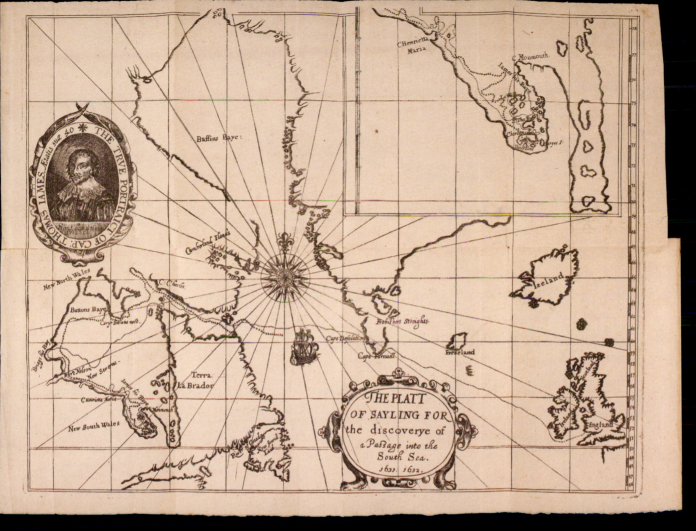

A chart of Hudson Bay and the route
of Thomas James, from his account,
*The Strange and Dangerous Voyage
of Captaine Thomas James in his
intended Discovery of the Northwest
Passage into the South-Sea* (1633).

THE 'NORTH-WEST FOX'

Successive failures to locate a passage or find new information about it led to a brief pause in exploration at the start of the seventeenth century. However, the Muscovy Company, now fantastically successful, continued to stoke the desire of private investors and adventurers to find similarly profitable investments in other parts of the Arctic. The hiatus came to a halt following the lobbying of two adventurers: Luke Foxe, sponsored by a group of London investors (then known as 'adventurers'), and Thomas James, sponsored by a group of Bristol investors. Foxe had faced disappointment in arranging his Arctic expedition as one of his backers, Henry Briggs, died, placing the expedition in jeopardy until a rival venture, led by Thomas James, stimulated the interest of Bristol's merchants. Both Foxe's and James's expeditions would take up Hudson's mantle and head for Hudson Bay, in the hope that this huge body of water would yield a passage to the Pacific. The question was whether the bay was large enough to accommodate the desires and egos of two English adventurers.

Having gained the support of various patrons, not least Charles I, Foxe departed London in April 1631 on board the *Charles*. His voyage was marked by a spat with James in Hudson Bay (of which more later) and, in spite of charting the western coast of the bay, little evidence of a passage was found. Foxe maintained that Roes Welcome Sound – a long channel at the far northwest of the bay – was a promising place for further investigation, but his limited finds and early return dampened enthusiasm for further searches. The account *North-west Fox, etc.* (1635), however, showcases Foxe's most notable achievement, the charting of a small channel leading north of Hudson Bay, marking a new furthest north in the exploration of the area. Unnamed here, it was later marked as Foxe Channel by William Edward Parry, the nineteenth-century naval officer who also sailed there (see p. 109).

North-west Fox, etc. is a notable entry in the history of expedition literature, situating Foxe's own exploits within a detailed description of the history of English Arctic exploration thus far. It also begins with a rather wonderful deprecation of the author's skill: 'Gentle Reader, expect not here any flourishing Phrases or Eloquent tearmes, for this Child of mine begot in the North-wests cold climate, (where they breed no Schollers,) is not able to digest the sweet milk of Rethorick, that's food for them.' The account also deals with Foxe's decision not to overwinter, made on account of the health of his crew: he felt it would lead to deaths and impede any further meaningful exploration. The danger and potential waste of investors' money meant Foxe determined to return home, reaching England in October with little to show for the expedition but no deaths under his command.

Hudson Bay would one day yield the profits sought by investors, albeit under very different circumstances, but Luke Foxe had failed to find the evidence that would unlock them and the London adventurers would not see much from their investment. Meanwhile, their Bristol counterparts' hopes rested with Thomas James. James would indeed have a different experience of Hudson Bay and the relationship between the two explorers shows competition for Arctic trade routes and resources heating up.

THOMAS JAMES'S PERILOUS WINTER

Thomas James could not have been more different from Foxe: James was an academic and a refined man while Foxe, as he noted in his own account, was a rougher, more decisive character, lacking James's polished intellect. Despite this, the two of them were now bound up in what amounted to a competitive joint venture. After lobbying Charles I on behalf of his Bristol-based investors, James had agreed to undertake an expedition at the same time as Foxe and split any profits between them, according to who made the more significant geographical and financial discoveries. Since Foxe had already acquired the King's name as the title for his ship, James and his crew set out from Bristol in the *Henrietta Maria*, named after the King's wife.

Foxe and James encountered one another in Hudson Bay towards the end of August 1631. James's account, published in 1633 and incorporating a map of the region, plays down the meeting, noting that they had some difficulty boarding each other due to contrary winds but that, once this was done, they shared food and information between them. Foxe's account, published two years later, offers a slightly different perspective on the encounter and criticises James and his 'discourse of Arte, as observations, calculations, and the like … [he] showed me many Instruments, so that I did perceive him to be a practitioner in the Mathematiks', but 'no Sea-man'. It is possible that Foxe notes this in order to contextualise an apparent slight by James, who left his colours flying while Foxe was on board the *Henrietta Maria*. The two clashing personalities took leave from one another without further incident but with James noting that the August weather was 'as cold, as at any time I have felt in England'. Despite this, James decided to overwinter on Charlton Island, to the south of Hudson Bay, where a tremendously arduous experience awaited him and his men.

Having sunk the *Henrietta Maria*, which he feared would be destroyed by the expanding ice if left afloat, James and his crew spent the winter in shacks constructed on the shore. His account focuses on the 'miseries' of the winter, during which four men died of scurvy and the rest were bitterly cold and hungry. They then had to work through plagues of mosquitos to re-float the ship once the weather improved. The account is an epic of endurance and suffering that was widely read and inspired many later authors. Most notably, it is suggested that James's account inspired Samuel Taylor Coleridge in his depiction of the frigid environments of *The Rime of the Ancient Mariner* (though, in the poem, published in 1798, the mariner's purgatory is endured in Antarctica). Despite its resulting in a classic account of English exploration – an account that greatly enriched English writing and perceptions of the northern polar world – it is safe to say that James's decision to overwinter was a disaster. Needless to say, Foxe could not resist the opportunity to say 'I told you so' in his own published account.

Foxe was certainly correct in one respect: James was undoubtedly a man with a scientific mind. His own account of the expedition details the various instruments taken on it and provides various notes on longitude, tidal flows and the variations in compass reading taken during the time in Hudson Bay. All of this he turns to his advantage in arguing that the Northwest Passage does not exist and, even if it did, would be a useless avenue for trade. This latter proved to be true, but it did not stop many more trying.

A MAP
of the
NORTH-POLE
and the
PARTS ADIOINING.

OXON
At the THEATER
MDCLXXX

PART   PARTS   UNKNOWN

OF

AME

RICA

Briggs Bay
former Hubberts Hope   NEW DENMARK
Port Nelson   Hope Inlet   Sr. Philips
                     Winter harbour   Hincks

BUTTONS BAY   Ne ultra

NEW   NEW
SOUTH   New Severn   NORTH
WALES.   WALES.

C. Southampton
Cap Swans ness

Henrietta Maria
C. Pembrock   Mare
                     Christianum
JAMES'S BAY
              Mare   Mansfield   Nottingham I
              Novum   Nochitz I   Diggs I   Charles
         HUDSONS BAY   Salsbury I

Mare Maison nuestred
         an 1611

Bay of Gods Deliverance

NOVA
BRITAN-
NIA

Port Nelson
                    I. of Gods
Salvage Ile   mercies
                    E. Elizabeth

HUDSONS
STRAITS

Resolution I

Button I.

To the Right Hon.ble Charles Fitz Charles Earle of
Plymouth Viscount Totnes and Baron Dartmouth
This Map is Humbly Dedicated
by M. Pitt.

St.Ba. Lancasters
-Sound

BAFFINS BAY

St. Thomas
Smiths Bay

Nochitz I.

DAVIS STRAITS

FORBISHERS STRAITS

C. Desolation

GREENLAND

C. Christ

C. Bisford

Desolation
hope
Whites C.

C. Borell

C. Spagia

FREESLAND

THE DEUCAL

NOVA ZEMBLA

Sinus dulcis

In the Philosophicall Transactions of a° 1674 n 101, there is set down a Description of Nova Zembla as it was sent to the Royall Society from a Russia Merchant and discovered by order of the Grand Czaar, but there being not joyned to it either Longitude Latitude or other measure, we thought it better to follow the two newest Laps, one printed at Amsterdam a° 1678 the other at Nuremberg 1679 and to place this by it selfe, which shews it not an Iland but joyned with the Continent at the letter

TAR
TA
RY

PART

OCEAN

NORTHERN OCEAN

MUSCO

Vologda

Vologda.

CÆREMIS TARTARS
LUGOW

PERMIA

PETZORA

OBDORA

MOLGOM
ZAIA

LEUCOMORIA

CARELIA

THE WHITE SEA

LAPLAND

FINMARK

Bellamoreskoy Leporico

Schetland I.

AMAZING MAPS AND
POOR THEORIES

Once attempts to explore the Arctic for trade routes began, its lands and seascapes were shown in numerous, and varied, printed polar hemisphere maps from the mid-sixteenth century. A map by Moses Pitt, from Charles II's own copy of Pitt's 1680 atlas (previous pages), removes various erroneous islands. The difference in quality between this map and those accompanying the works of Frobisher, and even Thorne (pp. 28–29), illustrates not just improving knowledge of the Arctic but also the huge developments in British cartography over this hundred-year period.

Not only is Pitt's atlas technically impressive, utilising the techniques prevalent in Dutch cartography at the time, it is also an opulent piece of work. The maps in Pitt's atlas would have been time-consuming to create in the first instance, but are also heavily embellished with colour and gold detailing, meaning that they were extremely costly to produce. The run of volumes was never actually completed as a result of escalating costs and Pitt bankrupted himself in the process of making them.

Luckily, Pitt completed the most northerly part of the globe first, leaving us with this view of how the English understood the Arctic in the late seventeenth century. It gives a sense of the resources thought to be useful at this point and illustrates the continuing fascination with, and emerging geographical understanding of, this supposedly blank land. Interest in the indigenous cultures of the Arctic can be seen in the map shown here, with the kayak and Inuit figures bearing a resemblance to those drawn by John White (see p. 41), possibly as a result of Pitt's familiarity with White's work in the manuscript volume held by the Irish-born English physician and collector Sir Hans Sloane (see below). The opposite side of the inset illustration shows some of the bounty of the Arctic: whales and, possibly, furs. Notably, the outline of Hudson Bay had been refined by this point. It was, in 1680, a fully fledged trading interest, incorporated by a royal charter ratified by Charles II ten years before. However, contrary to what the map suggests, North America is in fact connected to Greenland, which shows how much further the charting of this area had to go.

Progress in scientific knowledge would also have to be made before a better understanding of the formation of this part of the world could be achieved. As well as owning this atlas, Charles II employed the hydrographer Joseph Moxon, a significant proponent of the theory that open sea ice could not freeze, on account of its motion and salinity. Moxon wrote many treatises on the subject and turned it into a popularly held theory that would continue to inspire explorers for over 150 years – all the way up until the mid-nineteenth century.

THE ARCTIC AND THE RENAISSANCE WORLD

On the pages directly following the pan-Arctic map produced in Pitt's impressive atlas, is a depiction of 'Lapp' – or, more accurately, Sami – cultural practices, which represents the way in which Europeans saw the Sami people at a particular point in their history. The Sami live in the European Arctic, predominantly in the northern parts of Norway, Sweden, Finland, and in northeastern parts of Russia. They have been caught up in European land-use politics, dynastic conflicts, religious strife and population pressures for centuries and still form a unique part of European culture today.

The print in Pitt's atlas is not the only version of this illustration held at the British Library. An original manuscript of this work is held in a set of manuscript volumes that also contains the depictions of Arctic Inuit brought to England by Martin Frobisher (see p. 43) and of the battle at Bloody Point, discussed above. These manuscripts, originally owned by Sir Hans Sloane and made available to specially introduced researchers in his private library, were produced by various artists and widely known in seventeenth-century London. The 'Sami' manuscript is an original work by Sylvester Brounower, dating from the sixteenth century, from which this later printed edition is copied. Originally sent to Locke by William Allestree in 1673, 'Lives and Manners of the Laplanders' depicts what are believed to be various habits of the Sami as they vary across the seasons.

In both versions held at the British Library, the scene is divided into winter and summer with numerous parts of the illustrations being numbered, showing Sami practices at various times of the year. In the winter scene, item number 9 depicts someone castrating a reindeer, while number 10 possibly illustrates an element of Sami shamanistic practice. However, by the time the viewer reaches number 11, the illustrator is getting

rather fantastical. Sami are shown communicating directly with reindeer, while a reindeer walking on its back legs is possibly the weirdest part. Things are a little less odd in summer, where people are shown carrying out butchery and (in 10) the milking of reindeer, although that assertion rather depends on exactly what is going on in illustrations 17 and 19.

Apart from showing how significant reindeer are to Sami life in a roundabout way, the work is far from being an accurate and considered depiction of Sami life and culture. What it does display, perhaps, is a British instance of the European fascination with nearby Arctic neighbours in the wake of the wars that accompanied the Reformation. In particular, the military successes of Gustav II Adolf (ruler of the Swedish Empire, 1611–32) in support of the Protestant cause and during the Thirty Years' War were attributed in contemporary writings to his use of 'Lappish' wizards, who harnessed the weather to his advantage. This is one of a number of ways the Arctic figured in the popular imagination and in politics of the seventeenth century, and it is possible that such imaginations are still at play in these illustrations.

By 1673, just forty-one years after Adolf's last and most significant intervention in European religious politics, at the Battle of Lützen, the original Brounower work would inspire the production of these prints. Charles II sat on the English throne, monarch of a Protestant country who converted to Catholicism on his deathbed after a reign marked by religious intrigue. We can only speculate as to what Moses Pitt intended by including the work in an atlas dedicated to a king of ambiguous religious standing; what is clear from the image is that the Arctic was not just influenced by Europe but had the power, at least in imagination, to influence Europe in turn.

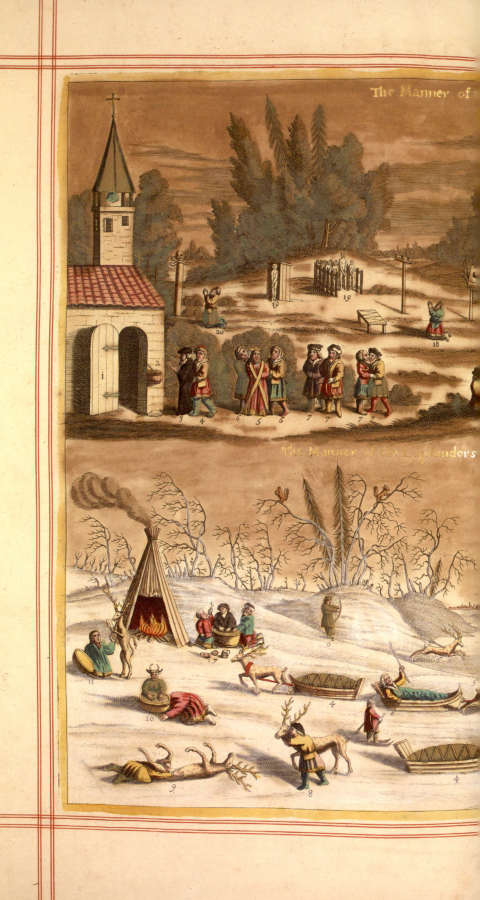

The Manner of the Laplanders

Sweden Page:11

Rt HONble ANTONY EARLE of SHAFTSBVRY

F.H. Van Houe. Sculp.

An illustration of the summer and winter activities of the 'Lapps', from Moses Pitt's, *The English Atlas, Vol. 1* (1680). Maps 1.Tab.16

A FAILED FRIENDSHIP

Christopher Middleton, an experienced sailor, took part in a series of voyages to Hudson Bay in the 1740s, over the course of which he also measured the variation of the needle of the compass. This variation, caused by the proximity of these journeys to the Magnetic North Pole (as opposed to the Geographic North Pole), was analysed and later published by Middleton through the Royal Society's journal *Philosophical Transactions*, in a paper titled 'A New and Exact Table, Collected from Several Observations, Taken in Four Voyages to Hudson's Bay … Shewing the Variation of the Magnetical Needle …' (1753). The paper was to change Middleton's life.

The article attracted the attention of Arthur Dobbs, an Irish-born parliamentarian with significant interests in trade and a fascination with the Northwest Passage. Dobbs and Middleton quickly formed a bond, with Middleton passing information to Dobbs from inside the Hudson's Bay Company so that it could be used to lobby Parliament and set up an expedition. Middleton had acquired a powerful friend who promised to further the young company man's interests and provide him with an opportunity to explore and conduct further science in the Arctic. For someone who had achieved so much already, not least his recognition as a bright scientific mind, such promises were hard to ignore.

In the end, Middleton was awarded command of HMS *Furnace* and *Discovery*. Planning was poor, the men assigned substandard and the Hudson's Bay Company (on whom Middleton was to rely for support while overwintering) only grudgingly supportive, but, on 8 June 1741, he set sail to locate the Northwest Passage via Hudson's Bay. A map published in 1746 shows the route taken by Middleton, as well as the site of his overwintering at the Hudson Bay post Churchill. A miserable winter ensued (it was such a trial to Middleton and his crew that Dobbs later suggested it had undermined the resolve of the men and the expedition).

Striking north from Churchill, Middleton was instructed to look for the passage around 65°N. He made a number of geographical discoveries, naming Wager Bay and Cape Dobbs. Beyond this, however, the news was negative. Middleton assumed, correctly as it turned out, that Wager Bay was closed and that the various other avenues explored would not yield a passage. Indeed, he concluded that such a route could not exist

Chart of the Seas, Straits, &c. thro' which his Majesty's Sloop 'Furnace' pass'd for discovering a Passage from Hudson's Bay to the South Sea (1746).
Maps 70095(7)

and, once again, that even if it did, it would not be practicable. This, however, was not the news Dobbs wanted to hear. Perhaps Middleton should have seen this coming – after all, he had already been party to Dobbs's determined and tenacious nature when he gave him information about the Hudson's Bay Company – but the ferocity of the attack would no doubt have surprised him. Dobbs accused Middleton of deceit: he brought forward men who attested that he was deliberately concealing his discovery of the Passage, and engaged in a lengthy pamphlet war with Middleton over the veracity of charges laid against him.

The map reproduced here was part of this dispute, providing details on Wager Bay and outlining the failings of Middleton's exploration and reasons why a passage could be considered to lie there, including the presence of whales. But why were Dobbs and others engaged in a campaign to destroy the reputation of a man with significant scientific and navigational achievements under his belt? What could they hope to gain from undermining Middleton's account? The answer lies in a book published by Arthur Dobbs two years previously.

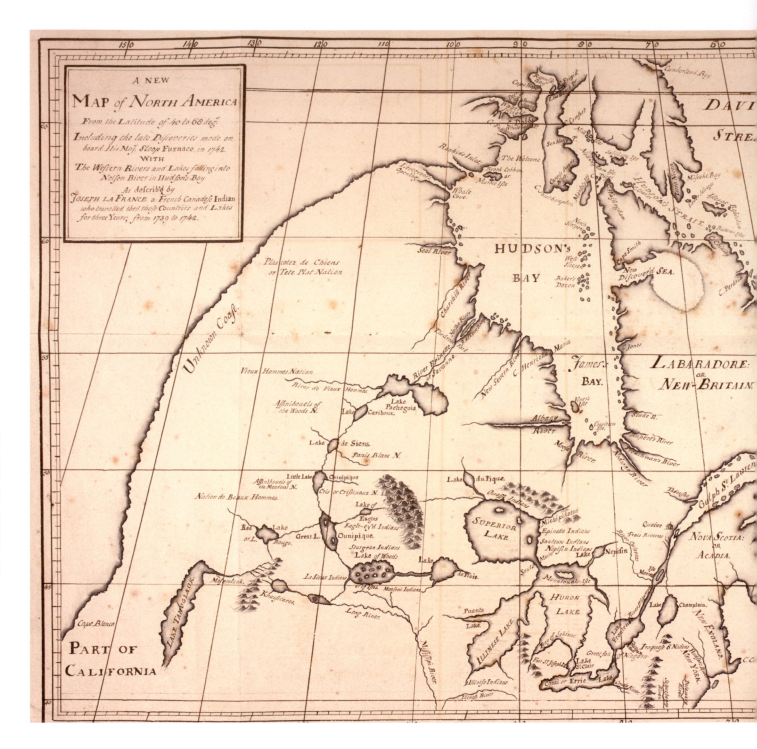

The suspect chart published
as part of Arthur Dobbs's
*An Account of the Countries
Adjoining to Hudson's Bay* (1744).
G.14612

PARLIAMENTARY EVIDENCE

Arthur Dobbs was a Member of Parliament with an eye for the developing British role in a world of settlers and empires. He owned land in North Carolina, which, by 1745, totalled over 160,000 hectares. As a result, Dobbs began to believe that Britain was destined to have a key role in the colonial future of North America; to do so, it needed access to its own trade route.

The eighteenth century had brought brisk trade from the Arctic to Britain, especially from the Hudson's Bay Company and whaling fleets. In both these areas, though, exploration was not necessarily financially productive: it cost money to outfit expeditions, and profits could be made by servicing the same areas time and again, or even by staying in or close to company factories and waiting for materials to be supplied. These had been the main productive avenues opened up by the efforts of Cabot, Frobisher, Foxe et al., over the previous 200 years of interest in the Passage, meaning that speculative investor interest in further exploration had waned. Dobbs would change this state of affairs and set the scene for years of exploration to come.

Dobbs knew that the discovery of the Passage and the pushing back of colonial frontiers could not be left to chartered companies and traders, as he recognised the financial constraints under which they operated. Instead, he needed to find ways of stimulating broader interest, and his treatise *An Account of the Countries Adjoining to Hudson's Bay* (1744) was his main tool. The map published in this account was an attempt to provide evidence that the Northwest Passage was real and attainable. Patched together from contemporary maps, and with a liberal interpretation of First Nations testimony regarding the size and shape of North America, it was used by Dobbs to argue for continued exploration.

To our eyes, the problems are obvious. North America drops away beyond Hudson Bay, making a passage seem easy but overlooking the huge expanse of land that would later be recognised as Alaska and northwest Canada. It therefore manifests a prevalent European fantasy that North America was, in fact, much smaller than it is, a fantasy inspired by the desire to find passable trade routes to the Far East. So powerful was this desire, that this rather spurious map convinced Parliament to award a £20,000 prize for the discovery of the Passage.

Men such as Dobbs, while they never set sail for the Arctic themselves, are crucially important to our understanding of this continuous need to explore, open up and exploit the Arctic. They recognised the wider geopolitical pressures of the changing world around them and were prepared to gamble on cobbled-together 'facts' if it meant British interests could be furthered.

SEEKING ROUTES AND
EXCHANGING KNOWLEDGE

One of the most significant Arctic discoveries of the eighteenth century (and not directly connected to efforts to find the Northwest Passage) was that of Vitus Bering. A Danish navigator working for the Russians in much the same way as the later English explorer Joseph Billings (see pp. 87–7). Bering finally found that there was a passage between eastern Eurasia and western North America. The Bering Strait was discovered during voyages that stretched from 1728 to 1741 and culminated in Bering's landings in Alaska with his lieutenant Alexei Chirikov. However, Bering's findings were not published and so crucial information about the Pacific ends of the Northeast and Northwest Passages remained unknown, leaving the door open to others. The French astronomer and cartographer Joseph-Nicolas Delisle, while based in St Petersburg, had helped advise Bering, but on his return to Paris in 1747 took various items and information with him; these found their way into the hands of Philippe Buache.

Buache was one of the most renowned geographers in the world at this point, occupying the post of royal geographer at the French court, and was a frequent speaker at the Academy of Sciences. He had already displayed an active interest in the northern and southern poles and was intensely interested in the possibilities of finding a Northwest Passage across North America. When Delisle returned to Paris with his Russian documents, France was still in control of its North American possessions – the area of Quebec or 'New France' – and so northern sea routes were of great interest to the French colonial effort. Buache used the information provided by Delisle to produce various maps, which were reproduced in a 1753 publication, *Considerations Geographiques, etc.*, after maps and papers had been presented to scholars in Paris.

The maps are an exercise in filling blank spaces with informed conjecture – 'best guesses', if you will. While some cartographers left blank space on maps where the placement of landmarks could not be certain, others, like Buache, used the spaces to undertake mental exercises based on the best available sources of information at the time. It was like making a jigsaw out of pieces from various different boxes. The detailed map produced by Buache is the most interesting and provides instances in which conjecture worked well and others where it failed completely. Buache shows the Alaskan part of the North American continent sweeping down to the southwest, a decent approximation of the fractured landmass that would vex and frustrate Cook on his third expedition in 1776–9. The geographer also, however, detailed some fabulous flights of fancy: the Chinese colony of 'Fousang', believed to have been on North America for centuries, and various inland waterways, which were fancifully shown stretching from the northeast of the continent to the west coast, as far south as British Columbia and California.

The Arctic was not the only site of Buache's conjecture. In the 1730s he had also produced a map of the 'Great Southern Continent' (a combination of our Antarctica and Oceania). On this map, too, you can see areas that are almost correct – he shows the continent to be ice-covered and capable of calving huge icebergs. Other elements, however, are wide of the mark – for instance, New Zealand is charted as the northernmost extremity of the continent. In the realms of both Arctic and Antarctic exploration, Buache and his ideas were to have longevity beyond the life of their maker. Arthur Dobbs used Buache's maps to bolster his arguments for the existence of a Northwest Passage, while also dismissing his closing off of Hudson Bay from these routes as propaganda from the French, who were seeking to steal a march on the British. This was despite Buache's being a member of the loosely defined 'scientific republic' in which Sir Joseph Banks (see below) was a strong believer; the group was dedicated to the development and exchange of knowledge across borders and outside of politics. Similarly, when Cook was sent to look for the Great Southern Continent in subsequent decades, Buache's maps were part of the reason that senior administrative figures believed the landmass to even exist.

In Buache's work, we see an exemplar of the practice of filling in cartographic 'blanks' through conjecture, as well as how these hypotheses were developed through international exchanges of information and influenced the thinking of various administrators and explorers for years to come. Buache, with his French maps, influenced by Russian exploration and heavily debated by British explorers, reminds us that the desire to explore the Arctic and open its trade routes was a pan-European adventure in a globalising age.

A chart showing the location of 'Fou-Sang', one of a number of imaginative geographies published by Philippe Buache in *Considerations Geographiques* (1753).
215.a.24

CARTE DES NOU
entre la partie Orient.le d
Avec des Vuës sur la Gr.de T
et sur la Mer de l'Ouest
Dressée par Phil. B
Présentée à l'Acad.
et approuvée
du 6. Sep

Publiée sous le Privilege de l'Acad. des Sciences

Lieuës Marines de France.
100.   200.   300.

Lieuës Marines d'Espagne.
100.   200.   300.

s DÉCOUVERTES
t l'Occid.le de l'AMERIQUE
onnuë par les Russes en 1741.
s communications de Mers.
er Geographe du Roi,
ciences le 9. Août 1752
on Assemblée
suivan.

Groenland

Detroit de Davis

Baye de Baffin

Cap Farewel

Gr. Banc

Montes de Glaces

B.e de Cumberland

80
300

300

Lac d'eau douce

290
280
270
260
250
240

Lac Empasto

CTIQUE

B.e de Repulse

C. Smith

Det. d'Hudson

Elisabeth
I. de Resolution
Chidley

Terre Neuve

Bel Isle

B.e de Wager

Chesterfield

Terre de Labrador

Quebec

Louisbourg

I. Royale

Acadie

Lac de Fonte

Polaire

Eau de Wager

Baye d'Hudson

FRANC

de Valasco

Riv. de Parmentier

Whale cove

Nelson

Charchil

FLeuve St Laurent Et. Golfe

310

Cercle

Lac Belle

Conasset Ville

Rio los Reyes

Minhausset

Port de l'Irena

Grande Eau

Lac des 2. Charges

CANADA

Lac Superior

Lac Huron

Lac Ontario

300

Haro Riv.

On soupçonne qu'il y a en cet endroit quelques communications de la Mer à la Grande Eau

R. Bourbon

L. des Forts

Antis quagia gamon

NOUV.

Lac Michilina kinak

Lac Michigan

Renards

Miamis L. Erie

Fortes. reconnuës par les Russes

Fou-sang des Chinois

Mer DE L'OUEST

L. Bourbon

L. Ouinpigon

R. de Poscoyac

L. des Prairies

Villes pour Le la

Illinois

200

Archipel de St Lazave

Côte Merid.le indiquée par Guill. Delisle

Ouachpouanes

Sioux

Moingona R.

Missouri R.

El. du Moscorito

Retour des

Panis

Missouri

Akansas

Nouv.lle Orleans

Entrée de Fuca

Quivira

Teguaio

Sta Fé

Lou is i a n

Entrée d'Aguilar

Cap Blanc

Cap Mendocin

B. de Pinos

California

Nouveau Méxique

Rio del Coral

Rio del Norte

Golfe du Mexique

LA MER DU SUD

P.te de Monterey

280

Mer Vermeille

MEXIQUE ou NOUVELLE ESPAGNE

NDE MER

Canal S.te Barbe

I. S.t Clement

C. d'Enganno

I. de Paxaros

C. Abel

B. de la Madelene

C. S.t Lucas

les S. Marier

I. de Chamilli Coriente

Lieues Communes de France.
100. 200. 300. 375.

250

Verstes de Russie de 105. au Degré.

500. 1000. 1500. 1800.

ÆPARIS sur le Quay de l'Horloge du Palais

SAMUEL HEARNE
AND THE HUDSON'S
BAY COMPANY

In the 1770s, Samuel Hearne, veteran sailor turned fur trader, was caught up in the Hudson's Bay Company's attempts to explore the northern parts of its territory. The granting of a trade monopoly in the area, as we have seen, had come with certain other responsibilities, not least the continued exploration of the region and support for the finding of the Northwest Passage, but the company had attracted criticism in this regard. Profits were good, but exploration was expensive and the opening of frontiers risky, so the company had not invested much time and energy in these activities. The directors in London came under increasing pressure for this to change; and thus Samuel Hearne comes into the account.

Young, fit and well known for his snowshoeing, Hearne had developed a reputation for diligence and hard work since joining the company in 1766 on the sloop *Churchill*. Between 1769 and 1772, Hearne would conduct three expeditions inland from the Hudson's Bay Company's main territories. The aim was to examine reports of copper deposits in the interior, as well as to search for a route to the Northwest Passage or, even better, a navigable waterway running from east to west across the continent. Hearne's expeditions were a disappointment in this respect, as the main rivers were impassable and ran too far north to provide a useful route (although Herne's plotting of the mouth of the Coppermine River did place it much too far to the north).

The expeditions do tell us much, however, about how First Nations groups interacted with traders, and about the violent politics of interactions between First Nations and Inuit groups. Matonabbee, a Chipewyan born in the area of Prince of Wales Fort near Churchill, Manitoba, became involved in Hearne's third expedition, in 1770, and successfully led him up the Coppermine River to the Arctic Ocean. The Chipewyan were vicious rivals of local Inuit, as Hearne found out when he became involved in a raid on an Inuit group encountered by Matonabbee's band. This rapidly turned into a massacre at a location Hearne named 'Bloody Falls', and the account of the incident, published in his book *A Journey from Prince of Wales Fort in Hudson's Bay to the Northern Ocean* (1795?), became so well known that the later explorer John Franklin passed comment on it when he encountered the location during his nineteenth-century overland expeditions.

Hearne's book, written during his retirement and published soon after his death in 1792, became an authoritative account on the landscape, biology and cultures encountered in the areas that now comprise the Northwest Territories of Canada. The British Library copy, published in 1795, contains a bookplate-cum-library stamp found frequently throughout the Library's collections. '[*Jos:Banks*]' is one of a number of marks denoting publications that used to belong to the library of Sir Joseph Banks, a scientist, explorer, trustee of the British Museum and much more besides. Banks had a deep interest in the exploration of North America and its arctic regions, but this book also reflects a more general enthusiasm for information about the Arctic in metropolitan London. As part of Banks's extensive library at his Soho Square house, Hearne's work would have been consulted by the many visitors to the collection, especially individuals who were planning further exploration, business ventures or study. The account contains many notes and illustrations, such as the above-discussed, on the material culture of Inuit and First Nations groups. This wealth of information made the book an important collection item for the likes of Banks, the British politician Thomas Grenville (who also donated a copy to the British Museum library), and many other collectors.

Prior to publication, Hearne's notes, maps and illustrations were also used by researchers such as the Welsh naturalist and traveller Thomas Pennant, and their value must have been extraordinary. Hearne's published work contains over a hundred pages of detail on Arctic flora and fauna, largely from a fur trader's point of view. Exemplary in this respect are Hearne's notes on the polar bear, which contain many astute observations as to the animal's behaviour (for instance, its disappearance to hunt on sea ice in the winter) but are mostly concerned with how to make the skins suitable for trade. Hearne's published reflections on the many bears he killed for their skins also reminds us how damaging the fur trade was to Arctic ecologies.

The stamp of Sir Joseph Banks, found in many books originating from his personal collection, including this copy of Hearne's work.
454.f.20

Plate II   To face Page 98

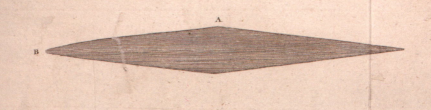

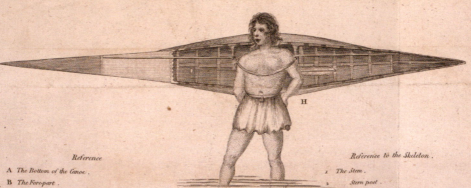

Reference

A The Bottom of the Canoe.

B The Forepart.

C The Frame, compleat.

D A Set of Timbers bent and lashed in their proper
   shape for drying.

E A Canoe compleat.

F A Paddle.

G A Spear to kill Deer with in the Water.

H The method of carrying the Canoe in Summer.

Reference to the Skeleton.

1 The Stem.

2 Stern post.

3 3 Two forked Sticks, supporting the Stem & Stern.

4 The Gunwalls.

5 Small Rods, placed between the Timbers, & the Birchrind.

6 The Timbers.

7 The Kelsin.

8 Large Stones, to keep the Bottom steady, till the Sides
   are sewed to.

J.H. delin.   London, Published Jan.ᵗ 1ˢᵗ 1795, by Cadell & Davies Strand.   Neele sculp. 352 Strand

Plate V.

At the end

Fig. 1.   A Bow

See Pages 79 & 124

Fig. 2.   An Arrow

Fig. 3.

A left foot Snowshoe 4¾ feet long

& 13 Inches broad.   See Page 325

Fig. 4.   A Sledge   See Page 324

Fig. 5.

A kettle made of Birch rinde

See Pages 250 & 316

S. H. delin.

London, Published Jan.ʳ 1ˢᵗ 1795, by Cadell & Davies, Strand.

Neele sculp.ᵗ 352 Strand.

AN ARCTIC ZOOLOGY

Another book containing Banks's stamp is that of Pennant himself: his *Arctic Zoology* (1784–5). Pennant did not undertake the extensive northern travels that Hearnes or Banks did. Instead, his book is very much a work of research, much of it built on Banks's collections. Indeed, the beginning of the book contains a fulsome tribute to his generosity, with Pennant stating that access to these books, plates and manuscripts was central to the publication of his own book. Banks's own interest in North America was stimulated at an early stage by his travelling and botanical career. In 1766, he travelled to Newfoundland and Labrador on a ship captained by his friend Constantine John Phipps and spent the summer exploring and botanising. Having already built a significant reference library ahead of the trip, Banks returned with various specimens and illustrations of the flora and fauna he encountered.

Such collections were a huge boon to men like Pennant, who sought to produce authoritative publications but perhaps lacked the means to carry out all of the first-hand research required. Despite access to Banks's collections, the publication of this research had its own troubled passage. As Pennant notes in his introduction, Arctic zoology was not originally intended as the focus of the work. Instead, Pennant had wished to produce a work on American zoology, which would be of research value and interest to London scholars as well as, in Pennant's words, acting as a testament to the union between Britain and its prospering

colony on the other side of the Atlantic Ocean. During the research and writing, however, the good feeling and prosperity offered by the colony foundered and the American Revolution began.

In the aftermath of the American War of Independence, Pennant felt that he was not able to complete the work as initially framed, presumably because the remaining areas of British North America did not provide enough unique fauna to furnish the book. However, the rest of Canada presented Pennant with a viable alternative: turn his work into a study of Arctic zoology. Having hit upon this idea, Pennant set about furnishing the book with material on the Orkney islands, Svalbard and so on, making extensive use of Banks's collections, especially those from his 1766 expedition. Perhaps unsurprisingly, and in spite of the tributes offered, this eventually led to acrimony. Pennant certainly received a lot more than he gave and, eventually, Banks's enthusiasm for his work and projects was withdrawn, albeit after the publication of *Arctic Zoology*.

Pennant's work fed a developing enthusiasm for published research about the Arctic and its environs. Such books were undoubtedly saleable but also part of a growing trend, as shown by Hearne's contributions, for taking a scientific approach to the polar regions. In subsequent years, scientific endeavour would underpin many Arctic expeditions, providing both a lens through which to see the space and a way of displaying prowess, power and, eventually, ownership.

Thomas Pennant's *Arctic Zoology* (1784-85).
G. 2807 and G. 2808

IV

G. Low del.

P. Mazell sc.

BIRD CATCHING at ORKNEY.

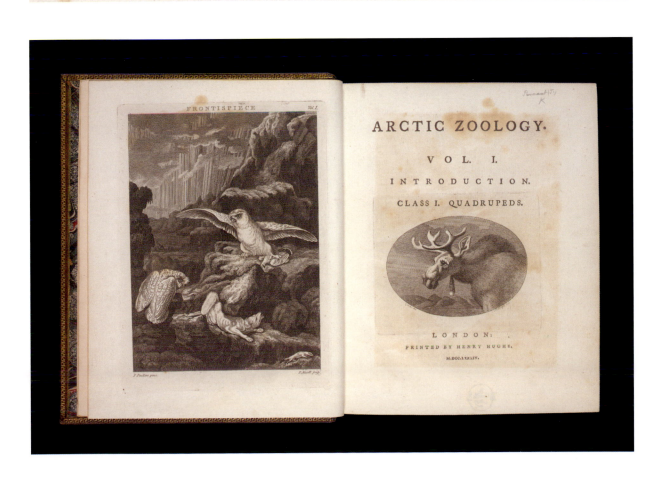

FRONTISPIECE

Vol. I.

ARCTIC ZOOLOGY.

VOL. I.

INTRODUCTION.

CLASS I. QUADRUPEDS.

LONDON:
PRINTED BY HENRY HUGHS.
M.DCC.LXXXIV.

P. Paillou pinx.

P. Mazell sculp.

NELSON'S CONFLICT WITH A BEAR JULY, 1773.

Painted by R. Westall, R.A.　　London Published by Cadell & Davies, Strand 1809.　　Engraved by J. Landseer.

Resurgent interest in the Northwest Passage did not occur in isolation. In June 1773, Captain Constantine John Phipps, 2nd Baron Mulgrave (the same who had captained Banks to Newfoundland and Labrador in 1766), was tasked with taking the bomb ketches HMS *Racehorse* and *Carcass* in search of a passage to India via the northeastern Arctic. An MP for Lincoln since 1766 who had seen service in the Seven Years' War and American War of Independence, Phipps was typical of the diligent servants of Empire who would be drawn into the search for the Arctic.

Britain's role in the world had changed since the expeditions of Frobisher and other sixteenth- and seventeenth-century explorers. It was no longer a group of nations wracked by division, hard-pressed by European religious politics and in the grip of major political upheaval. Rather, a more unified state had asserted itself on the global stage and was on the way to developing a major global empire. Phipps's expedition set out in the final years of Britain's dominion over North America, and the desire for better trade links with India would only become more important towards the end of the century. This particular Arctic expedition, then, suggests that the quest to claim Arctic trade routes and resources was switching from one of desperation, as perhaps was the case in the hard-pressed times of Frobisher, to that of cultivating as many options and developing as wide a power base as possible for a fledgling global empire.

Key characters in this developing global empire were also present on Phipps's expedition; most famously, a young Horatio Nelson, who was serving on the *Carcass*. Despite men (or rather, boys: he was fourteen years old at the time of departure) of his age being barred from the expedition, Nelson believed he was worth a man's place and worked his way onto the crew of the *Carcass*, under Captain Skeffington Lutwidge. Such self-belief was put to the test when both boats became trapped in ice off Spitsbergen on 30 July. Nelson volunteered to command and navigate a cutter to safety and permission was granted, although, in the end, the ice broke up on 8 August.

The more important story from this expedition, however, is illustrated by an image from Nelson's 1859 biography. This well-known account states that Nelson set off to hunt a polar bear, only for his gun to jam, thus requiring the *Carcass* to intervene by firing its gun to keep the young midshipman safe. Accompanying the tale was this suitably heroic illustration of Nelson, smartly (and inappropriately) dressed, which has fixed the story in national memory and given rise to the idea that, had the polar bear been closer, the British would by now be speaking French. Unfortunately, there can be no way that events unfolded in quite such close quarters as this, and there is reason to believe that much of this account is embellished.

A depiction of Nelson's supposed encounter with a polar bear from *The life of Admiral Lord Nelson, K.B.: from his Lordship's manuscripts* (1809). 1859.c.5

A portrait of Olaudah Equiano from
his work, *The Interesting Narrative
of the Life of O. Equiano* (1789).
615.d.8

ALL THE WORLD IS DRAWN NORTH

There is another, much less spurious, story that emerges from the 1773 expedition commanded by Phipps and it is one of the many fascinating parts of *The Interesting Narrative of the Life of Olaudah Equiano, etc.* (1789). For Equiano, as for Nelson, the Arctic is a small footnote to a life full of travel, incident and achievement. Nonetheless, Equiano's presence here tells us something about the worlds he navigated, as well as reiterating the significance of the Arctic in an era of intensifying globalisation.

Olaudah Equiano, or Gustavus Vassa, spent his early life bound by the slave trade in west Africa. He was not only enslaved at a young age but also worked in the trade itself before he was given the opportunity to buy his own freedom. Equiano had been taught to read and write by an earlier master, and when Robert King, an American merchant and Quaker trading in the Caribbean, bought him on account of his useful word and numeracy skills, it was agreed that Equiano could buy his freedom for the price of £40. Prodigiously industrious, and able to pick himself up from disastrous setbacks, Equiano eventually managed to raise the capital to purchase his freedom in 1767. King had made the offer in 1765.

As a freeman, Equiano continued to work at sea and eventually found his way to England, where he entered the paid service of Dr Charles Irving, as a hairdresser. Irving seems to have been keen on allowing Equiano to further develop his education and other skills, earning the affection and loyalty of his employee. Irving was a renowned scientist, who developed an 'apparatus for making sea water fresh' and, as a result, was encouraged to be part of Phipps's 1773 expedition and sail on the *Racehorse*. Agreeing to take part in the expedition, Irving desired Equiano to accompany him, even though Equiano himself took a rather dim view of the endeavour; he later wrote in his published account that the purpose of the journey was 'to find, towards the north pole, what our Creator never intended we should, a passage to India'.

Any misgivings Equiano displayed gave way, as almost a whole chapter of his narrative is concerned with the many events of the journey. Alongside details of the workings of Irving's apparatus, and anecdotes concerning animal hunts and a major fire, the event Equiano relates in most detail is the fastening of the ships in ice. While Nelson's recollections (detailed above) focus on his own determination to lead, and disappointment when this does not come about, Equiano concentrates on the spiritual effects of his experience. By this point a godly man, Equiano often dwells on how the stresses of seafaring life turn crews to God, only for their faith to slip away once danger passes. Equiano's account therefore shows us two unique things about Arctic exploration in the eighteenth century. First, the effect its stresses and strains had on the large crews involved. Second and perhaps most importantly, Equiano's very presence reminds us that the search for Arctic trade routes was part of a global, political game that drew people from across the world to risk it all after being 'roused by the sound of fame', as Equiano wrote.

THE DEFEAT OF CAPTAIN COOK

John Webber's *The Resolution beating
through the Ice with Discovery in the most
eminent Danger in the Distance* (1787-92).
Maps 7.TAB.74

I. Webber R.A. fecit

The Resolution beating through the Ice, with the Discovery in the most eminent danger in the dis...

London Publish'd Aug.ᵗ 1. 1792 by I. Webber. Nᵒ. 312 Oxford Street.

The work of Arthur Dobbs had an enduring legacy in eighteenth-century British exploration. Not only were successive expeditions around the world instructed to try to find Arctic trade routes, but even some of the boldest and most expansive voyages of exploration included some form of search for the Northwest Passage. It was in these circumstances that the greatest explorer of the age was ordered to try to locate the route. By 1776, Captain James Cook had already been on two epic journeys and charted a huge swathe of the globe, including parts of Antarctica. Cook's third journey (1776–9), arranged in more of a hurry than his previous expeditions, was important for the charting of western Canada, but he was also tasked, via secret instructions from the Admiralty, with finding the western exit of the Northwest Passage.

While Cook is often remembered for his phenomenal work in the charting of the lands we now call Australia and New Zealand, he also had a significant role in charting parts of Canada. He made his reputation surveying the Saint Lawrence River during the Seven Years' War, during which his charts were used to bring an armada of 200 British ships through the 'Traverse' – a narrow, navigable channel of the river that cuts abruptly from its north to south side. Similarly, on his third voyage of discovery, Cook's exploration of the coasts of British Columbia and Alaska was undertaken in the context of expanding Spanish and Russian influence in these areas. By charting the shorelines here, the Admiralty hoped Cook would ascertain the usefulness of the coast to the Empire and its traders, as well as discerning its important strategic positions.

The key to this work was the secret instruction Cook received to find the western entrance to the Northwest Passage and, if possible, chart it through and return to England via the Atlantic. However, Cook was to be disappointed: not only was the northwestern part of the North American continent much larger than expected, but none of the many inlets and coves he found showed any sign of being an entrance to the Passage.

The Resolution beating through the Ice with Discovery in the Most Eminent Danger in the Distance (1787–92), part of the collection of George III, shows the *Discovery* in danger while a group of walruses look on. As supplies for the expedition ran low, Cook's crew refused to eat the meat that could be obtained by hunting, particularly that of the walrus; as a result, Cook, now furious with his crew, was eventually beaten back by the ice at 'Icy Cape' in 1778. With this began a chain of events that would lead to his death in Hawaii in February 1779. The Northwest Passage had not only defeated the greatest explorer of the eighteenth century but it had also, in its reluctance to relinquish the route so desired by Dobbs and his contemporaries, indirectly contributed to his death. With that, and the war with France that was to come, British interest in the passage faded for over thirty years.

MEN OF INTERNATIONAL REPUTE

While British interest in the discovery of polar trade routes faded at the end of the eighteenth century, other nations had plenty of reasons to keep probing Arctic coasts for trade routes and political advantage. During the reign of Catherine the Great (1762–96), the Russians took particular interest in Arctic exploration and the potential of northern sea routes. Catherine's rule saw Russia expand its territories along many of its borders, through conquest and diplomacy, not least into the North American territory now known as Alaska.

In contrast to the pattern of Britain's colonial expansion (and that of many other European nations), Russia's dominions were chiefly determined by geographical proximity, with a huge expanse of the northern Eurasian continent falling under its control before trading expansion even began in North America. Nonetheless, as with all empires, routes of communication and trade were essential in connecting these colonial spaces and generating the finances required to make the expansion of control worthwhile. Furthermore, this period of colonial expansion coincided with the flowering of Russia's Enlightenment, with Catherine's court supporting the arts and sciences, and constructing a grand new infrastructure to support this intellectual endeavour. Exploration, colonial expansion and geographical, anthropological and zoological study often ended up going hand in hand during these years.

It was in this context that one of Russia's major expeditions departed, tasked with adding detail to charts of the Northeast Passage almost 200 years after William Barents's expedition foundered on Novaya Zemlya. Tasked with accurately charting the coasts between the Kamchatka Peninsula and the North American coast, the *Slava-Rossii* (Glory of Russia) expedition would last from 1785 to 1794 and was captained by an Englishman – Joseph Billings. Billings had served under Captain Cook on his final voyage (see above), beginning the journey as an able seaman on the *Discovery* before training as assistant astronomer and transferring to the expedition flagship, HMS *Resolution*. It was this experience of working on a major voyage of exploration that no doubt qualified him to undertake such an important Russian voyage.

Over the next nine years, supported by his second officer and hydrographer, Gavril Saychev, Billings would undertake a monumental programme of mapping and charting, as well as making detailed zoological and anthropological studies of the environments and cultures encountered. As a result, the expedition's publication, is not just a work of exploration and mapping but a significant study of the peoples who were now finding themselves, at least nominally, under Russian rule. The expedition led by Billings therefore encapsulated all of the crucial elements of eighteenth-century Russian colonial expansion in its Enlightenment era.

Billings's Arctic skills and experience, acquired under Cook, were appropriated by a foreign nation to further its own polar goals. Subsequently, Billings's journals and records, published in Russia and the rest of Europe in multiple translations, disseminated his findings and experiences widely, influencing future Russian explorers and those from further afield. The horizons of Arctic exploration were expanding, driven by the increasing demands of European colonial and political endeavours, and the world of knowledge and skills produced was also broadening its reach.

Нарта съ упряжкою собакъ употребляемая въ окрестностяхъ города ОХОТСКА.

A plate from G. A. Sarychev's account *Puteshestvie flota kapitana Sarycheva po severo-vostochnoĭ chasti Sibiri, Ledovitomu moriu i Vostochnomu okeanu, v prodolzhenie os'mi let, pri Geograficheskoi i astronomicheskoi morskoi ekspeditsii, byvshei pod nachal'stvom flota kapitana Billingsa s 1785 po 1793 god.* (Travelling of captain Sarychev's fleet around the north-eastern part of Siberia, the Arctic sea and the Eastern ocean that happened over eight years, as part of the geographical and astronomic expedition led by captain Billing in 1785-1793; 1802)

792.1.12

THE 'ANCIENT MARINER' AND THE ARCTIC

Coleridge's *Rime of the Ancient Mariner* is, for many, the quintessential articulation of the grandeur and terror of adventure on the high seas. It also bears the marks of inspiration drawn from the exploration of the Antarctic and the Arctic. Published in 1798, it sits in a quieter moment in British interest in polar exploration, following Cook's death in Hawaii and his discovery that the Great Southern Continent could only be an icy, wind-blasted space around the southern pole. Nonetheless, Cook's polar work, as well as that of many earlier Arctic explorers and ocean voyagers, provided a vast amount of material for Coleridge to draw on.

While the narrative of the poem plays out in many places – the mariner's ship being exposed to numerous extreme locations as part of his purgatorial voyage – it is the southern sea and the Antarctic that provide some of the most evocative imagery. The albatross shot by the mariner and the extreme cold and ice experienced soon afterwards are mostly drawn from accounts of exploration in the southern oceans. William Wordsworth, friend and collaborator of Coleridge, remembered later in life discussing the early form and narrative points of Coleridge's poem and recommending works that could provide source material and imagery. Notable among these was an account of sailing in the southern seas, George Shelvocke's *A Voyage round the World by the way of the great South Sea* (1726), which included notes on the southern species of albatross. The dramatic description of the bird and its majestic flight inspired its use as an emblem of the fate of the ship's crew.

Shelvocke's account is not the only source of inspiration for Coleridge's epic poem and *The Rime of the Ancient Mariner* may also be inspired by Arctic voyages. Thomas James's ill-fated Arctic voyage of 1631 (see p. 59) may also have had an impact on the narrative. Having been trapped in the ice and subjected to the threat of magnificent and gigantic icebergs, James later described the terrible beauty of the Arctic landscape in the published account of his expedition. It has always been suspected that the striking imagery provided by James also inspired the evocative scenes created by Coleridge, which often endure in readers' imaginations and have led to the production of wonderful illustrations, such as those from the 1875 edition by Gustave Doré.

Since the publication of Coleridge's poem, the albatross has been associated with bringing ships luck until they come to harm, at which point they become a harbinger of terrible bad luck. This idea has filtered into maritime and popular culture in the succeeding centuries and provided a number of memorable lines in theatrical works and films such as Joss Whedon's *Serenity* (2005). However, it appears that before the publication of Coleridge's tale, mariners and explorers had no such superstition about the harming of an albatross. During the 1768–71 expedition of HMS *Endeavour* (captained by James Cook), Sir Joseph Banks made a habit of shooting any albatross encountered to take home as a specimen. Given how far the expedition was from home, with much to do and no back-up ship, it seems unlikely the crew would have let Banks carry out such an act if they were wracked with superstition.

The shooting of the albatross,
illustrated by Gustav Doré in
The Ancient Mariner (1877).
1875.b.5

TWO

ONE WARM LINE

SEEKING AN ARCTIC PASSAGE

Despite the efforts of James Cook and many others, the Northwest Passage had not become a new silk road of the oceans. Instead, the search had frustrated some of the greatest navigators of the age. However, it provided unexpected opportunities, which were taken advantage of by, among others, the Hudson's Bay Company. Greater contact with the Arctic had also stimulated artistic and literary creativity in the nations of explorers, while instigating a period of dramatic and destructive change for Arctic peoples.

Success and stimulation aside, interest in the Arctic had faded by the end of the eighteenth century. Disappointed hopes were not the main reason; rather, it was global war that was responsible for turning attention away from the Arctic. Years of conflict against revolutionary France – which led, in turn, to the wars against Napoleon – drained the manpower and resources required for speculative expeditions in Europe. But the end of the war presented the British, in particular, with many reasons to go back to the Arctic; a surplus of men and ships was one of many factors on the side of exploration.

In this chapter, we will follow the revival of Arctic exploration in the nineteenth century. Britain goes from being a nation under pressure to the dominant colonial power of the age, and the search for the Northwest Passage becomes a crucial way of displaying this new-found status. For the explorers to come, such as John Ross and John Franklin, the aim was not to earn wealth but to assert Britain's dominance, by filling in one of the last blank spaces on the map.

Icescapes encountered by
Captain John Ross, published
in *A Voyage of Discovery,
made under the orders of the
Admiralty, in his Majesty's
ships* Isabella *and* Alexander
*for the purpose of exploring
Baffin's Bay, and enquiring
into the possibility of a
North-West Passage* (1819).

G.7399

BRITAIN'S COMMAND OF THE OCEANS

After a pause in attempts to forge a Northwest Passage, caused by the failure of the greatest navigator of the age, James Cook, and the long, bitter hostilities of the Napoleonic Wars, 1818 saw renewed vigour in the search for Arctic shipping routes. The search was largely driven by one man, and his reasons for seeking the passage were slightly different from those of enthusiastic predecessors such as Arthur Dobbs. Sir John Barrow, Second Secretary to the Admiralty and in a position to wield significant influence on the actions of the Royal Navy, was obsessed with Arctic exploration and Britain's – as he saw it, inevitable – role in the discovery and mastery of various Arctic sea routes.

In researching his compendium of the history of Arctic exploration (*A Chronological History of Voyages into the Arctic Regions*, 1818), Barrow became convinced that routes for shipping and trade via the Arctic existed and that the time had come to discover them. Not only did Barrow think the shipping technology was available, he also believed the Navy was in possession of the best men and had a manifest destiny to discover one or many Arctic passages. This destiny, as he saw it, was underpinned by Britain's naval superiority in the wake of the Napoleonic wars – Britain had been completely dominant at sea throughout the conflicts – and the final victory, after bloody land campaigns. Barrow thought that, in the wake of such victories, Britain was due to take charge of the oceans.

Barrow's lobbying paid off in 1817, when the Navy began to fit out two expeditions bound for the Arctic. One, under David Buchan, with a young Franklin serving as a lieutenant, was to explore towards the North Pole, looking for a passage directly through the north; the other, under John Ross, was to search for the fabled Northwest Passage. Ross seemed a good choice for the role – he was a veteran and competent sailor with a strong interest in science – and he took a good crew with him, including the likes of William Edward Parry, who would captain later expeditions to search for the passage (see p. 109).

Ross was of a scientific cast of mind and had a great interest in the flora, fauna and people he would likely encounter on his journey. This is clear from the published account of the expedition, which focuses heavily on the landscapes, animals and cultures met with, especially the 'Arctic Highlanders', a group of Inuit from northeastern Greenland, who were known to Europeans only through rumour. In the end, Ross was to turn back from exploring the Passage, declaring that he had seen the channel he and his crew were navigating drawing to an end during a short break in foggy weather. With the summer season drawing to a close, Ross decided to return to London, to the dismay of some of his crew and the fury of Barrow. Barrow, in various anonymous reviews of Ross's book, declared that he had not tried hard enough, showing too much interest in research and not enough grit as a navigator. To Barrow, this was a great disappointment: his first throw of the dice at displaying British prowess in the Arctic had ended in failure and acrimony. Ross's career would suffer from his decision, even though, with hindsight, most would say it was a sensible one. Other members of his crew, like Parry, would, however, benefit from Barrow's disappointment, fury and continuing zeal.

THIS PAGE & OVERLEAF

Ross was fascinated by the Inuit peoples he encountered during the expedition, much to the chagrin of Sir John Barrow. These illustrations come from *A Voyage of Discovery, made under the orders of the Admiralty, in his Majesty's ships Isabella and Alexander for the purpose of exploring Baffin's Bay, and enquiring into the possibility of a North-West Passage* (1819).

G.7399

Drawn by A.M. Skene.

HEAD of a WHITE BEA[R]

London, Published Feb.ʳ 2, 1819, by Iohn Murray, Albemarle

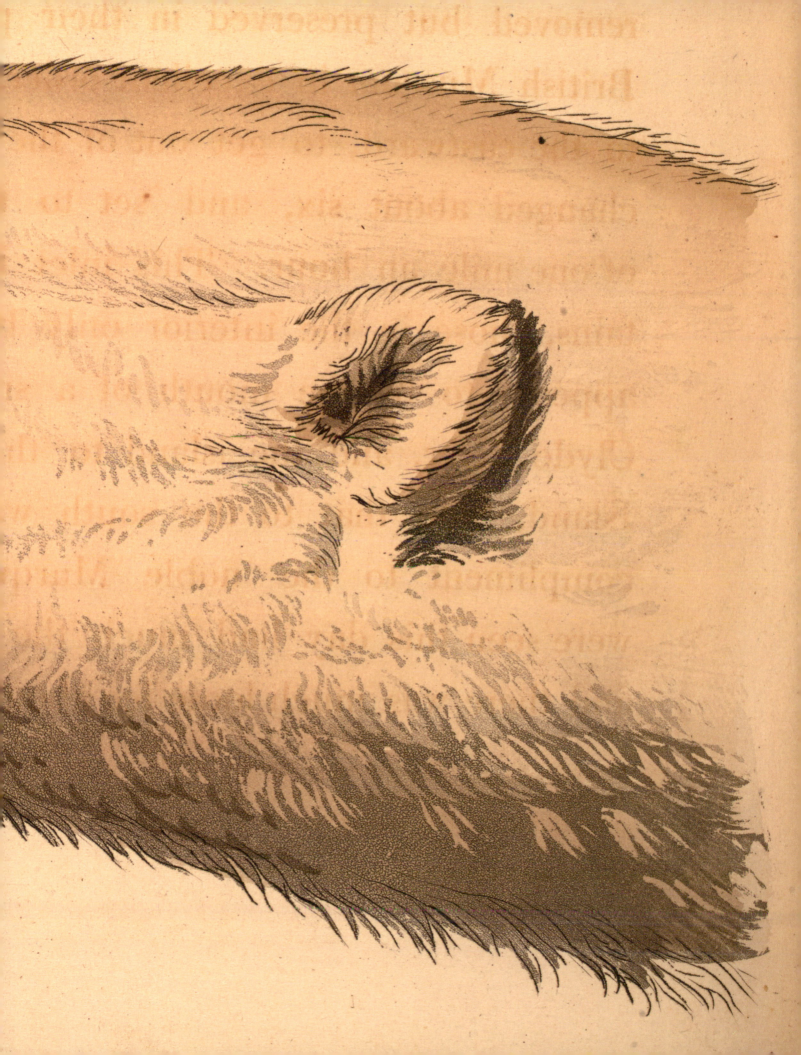

THE EXCITEMENT OF THE ARCTIC

Description of a view of the North coast of Spitzbergen, now exhibiting in the large rotunda of Henry Aston Barker's Panorama, Leicester-Square; painted from drawings taken by Lieut. Beechey, who accompanied the Polar expedition in 1818 (1819).
C.126.g.9(5).

The Ross and Buchan expeditions generated great excitement among the British public. Previous generations of Arctic explorers had operated in secret, in order to maximise the advantage of any route discovered. After all, the benefit for the British of finding a trade route through the north would have been minimal had the Dutch or, even worse, the Spanish, known about it too. Under Barrow's regime the benefit of a trade route was secondary – a display of imperial soft power only worked if others heard of you making it.

So, while Ross and Buchan prepared for and eventually departed on their respective voyages, the newspapers were awash with stories about the expeditions, and London's notables were free to visit and promenade upon the ships as they prepared for departure. The result was a deep interest in the progress of HMS *Dorothea* and *Trent* (on Buchan's expedition), and a desire to know as much as possible about the results and experiences of the expedition when the ships returned home. By the early nineteenth century, newspapers and books were not the only means by which this information could be transmitted to the public. New modes of mass entertainment were continually being developed.

One particular innovation in this area was the production of panoramas: vast, realistic landscape artworks, which surrounded the visitor, in an attempt to convince them that they stood in the scene depicted, and which were viewed from a central platform. There were a number installed across London but the most noteworthy, that of Henry Ashton Barker, was based in Leicester Square. Barker's panorama hosted a great variety of scenes, but the Arctic promised to be particularly popular and so, on Buchan's return, and with access to accounts of the journey, it was transformed to depict the expedition's time in the ice near Spitsbergen. Small-scale reproductions of the panorama were provided as a guide to and keepsake of the show, and these highlight the main attractions. The activities of the crew are foregrounded, as are notable flora and fauna; of particular interest in this scene are the great auks, now extinct, which look rather like penguins.

Arctic panoramas would continue to be big business from this time onwards, and many captains who led expeditions worked directly with various producers to put the shows on display, not only in Leicester Square but in places such as Vauxhall Gardens in south London. The public enthusiasm for the panoramas shows just how willing people were to buy in to Barrow's performance of British mastery of the waves. This enthusiasm would endure, even through the most trying tragedies, into the mid-nineteenth century. Displays such as Barker's could not sate the public appetite for news of heroic Arctic deeds (which spilled out into books, newspapers, pamphlets, songs and more), and there was also a desire for stories of the darker side of exploration.

TERROR IN
THE ARCTIC

In 1818, Mary Shelley's novel *Frankenstein* – later to become a classic, not just of gothic horror but of nineteenth-century literature in general – caused a sensation. The years leading up to the (at the time, anonymous) publication of the book had seen unusually bleak weather – caused, we now know, by the eruption of Mount Tambora in Indonesia, in April 1815 – and, in the particularly dismal summer of 1816, a group of friends gathered together in the Villa Diodati, on Lake Geneva, to tell unsettling and frightful stories. This attempt to while away a few hours gave rise to Shelley's iconic tale and also John Polidori's *The Vampyre* (1819), which would go on to inspire Bram Stoker's *Dracula* (1897).

The young Shelley's story captured a sense of trepidation at the scientific and technical innovations of the early nineteenth century. It is to this that the book's subtitle, *The Modern Prometheus*, refers, alluding to the myth of a Greek titan who stole fire from the gods (to give to humankind) and was subsequently punished for his actions. The field of Arctic exploration was a crucial target of Shelley's critique as the Arctic provided the setting for the beginning and end of the book and, therefore, the backdrop against which the key characters perceive their hubris.

Shelley's narrative begins in the voice of a young sea captain, Robert Walton, writing to a relative about his current journey. He hopes to bring 'inestimable benefit to all mankind' through the discovery of a 'passage by the pole' to the riches of the east. (It is worth noting that Shelley's character is not a Naval Officer, as would be recognised by John Barrow; instead, the young captain harks back to the endeavours of Cook,

Luke Foxe, Martin Frobisher and others.) While trying to navigate the ice, the captain and his crew witness a giant man sledding across the ice and then, later, come across an exhausted Victor Frankenstein. Frankenstein tells the captain that the man he saw was his quarry, and proceeds to tell the story of his 'Adam'. While listening to Frankenstein's shocking tale of hubris, the captain's realisation of his own folly begins to close in around him. He and his crew become locked in the ice: both he and Frankenstein have overreached themselves.

Shelley's use of the Arctic and its capricious ice as a dramatic device illustrates the other side of popular fascination with the Arctic. Despite believing in Britain's ability to conquer the world, people were also thrilled by the inherent danger of the project at hand. Significantly, Shelley's tale was published at a point of renewed enthusiasm for the Arctic, something the Lake Geneva storytellers probably could not have foretold in 1816, but which affects our present-day perspective on the book. It is hard to know whether Shelley was especially prescient, or whether the Arctic ice simply provided a useful (and terrifying) backdrop for the book, but her take on Arctic exploration would turn out, over the next half century, to be remarkably accurate. Ross, Buchan, Franklin and many others all became, to a greater or lesser extent, endangered by the ice they sought to conquer, as weather conditions overwhelmed their expeditions. Some, like Franklin, his crew and many who went to look for them, would be defeated, trapped and undone by the element they sought to control and master.

frankenstein

or The Modern Prometheus

by MARY WOLLSTONECRAFT

SHELLEY · *with engravings on wood*

by LYND WARD · *New York* · 1934

HARRISON SMITH AND ROBERT HAAS

---

many, many, months, perhaps years, will pass before you and I may meet. If I fail, you will see me again soon, or never.

Farewell, my dear, excellent Margaret. Heaven shower down blessings on you, and save me, that I may again and again testify my gratitude for all your love and kindness. — Your affectionate brother,

R. WALTON.

Letter Two: to Mrs. Saville, England
ARCHANGEL, *March 28th, 17—.*

How slowly the time passes here, encompassed as I am by frost and snow! yet a second step is taken towards my enterprise. I have hired a vessel, and am occupied in collecting my sailors; those whom I have already engaged appear to be men on whom I can depend, and are certainly possessed of dauntless courage.

But I have one want which I have never yet been able to satisfy; and the absence of the object of which I now feel as a most severe evil. I have no friend, Margaret: when I am glowing with the enthusiasm of success, there will be none

5

---

and then I shall repose in peace. I understand your feeling," continued he, perceiving that I wished to interrupt him; "but you are mistaken, my friend, if thus you will allow me to name you; nothing can alter my destiny: listen to my history, and you will perceive how irrevocably it is determined."

He then told me that he would commence his narrative the next day when I should be at leisure. This promise drew from me the warmest thanks. I have resolved every night, when I am not imperatively occupied by my duties, to record, as nearly as possible in his own words, what he has related during the day. If I should be engaged, I will at least make notes. This manuscript will doubtless afford you the greatest pleasure; but to me, who know him, and who hear it from his own lips, with what interest and sympathy shall I read it in some future day! Even now, as I commence my task, his full-toned voice swells in my ears; his lustrous eyes dwell on me with all their melancholy sweetness; I see his thin hand raised in animation, while the lineaments of his face are irradiated by the soul within. Strange and harrowing must be his story; frightful the storm which embraced the gallant vessel on its course, and wrecked it — thus!

20

Adieu, my dear Margaret. Be assured that for my own sake, as well as yours, I will not rashly encounter danger. I will be cool, persevering, and prudent.

But success *shall* crown my endeavours. Wherefore not? Thus far I have gone, tracing a secure way over the pathless seas: the very stars themselves being witnesses and testimonies of my triumph. Why not still proceed over the untamed yet obedient element? What can stop the determined heart and resolved will of man?

My swelling heart involuntarily pours itself out thus. But I must finish. Heaven bless my beloved sister!

R. W.

Letter Four: to Mrs. Saville, England
August 5th, 17—.

So strange an accident has happened to us that I cannot forbear recording it, although it is very probable that you will see me before these papers can come into your possession.

Last Monday (July 31st), we were nearly surrounded by ice, which closed in the ship on all sides, scarcely leaving

11

A WHALER'S VIEW

The search for the Northwest Passage had not yet uncovered a viable trade route, never mind a route to Asia, but it had benefited other segments of the English and European economies. In particular, it had benefited the whalers. The whaling industry was big business, providing a constant stream of products for nineteenth-century London, especially. By now, the city was totally dependent upon the whaling trade, with mechanical lubricants, oil for lighting, and whalebone for fashion items such as corsets all being sourced from the bodies of whales. This meant that whale fishing was a vastly profitable industry and huge pressures were put on European stocks. Whalers were, therefore, constantly on the lookout for new opportunities. These were often provided by explorers, who frequently stumbled across rich areas of the oceans while failing to find a navigable Northwest Passage or route across the North Pole. Whalers moved into these areas and, in turn, became experts in navigating Arctic seas and avoiding the dangers of the ice. With these skills, many whalers ended up working as ships' masters on voyages of exploration, while others became recognised experts in their own trade, and in navigation and the sciences more generally.

One such was William Scoresby, an experienced whaling captain and author of *An account of the Arctic Regions* (1820). Scoresby's book is a formidable history of the Greenland whaling industry as well as an exceptional work of science; the appendices to each of the two constituent volumes contain multiple zoological illustrations, as well as depictions of different forms of ice crystal and snowflake. Scoresby was such a respected figure in these areas that he maintained correspondence with the greatest scientific minds of the day, including the President of the Royal Society, Sir Joseph Banks (see p. 75). Such respect and acceptance of Scoresby's research would suggest that one of his most significant arguments – that sea water would freeze when the temperature reached a low enough point, irrespective of depth, movement or salinity – might be heeded in London's political and administrative circles, despite of Scoresby's low social rank and form of employ.

Barrow, however, was an ardent believer in the theory that open water existed at the Pole, and espoused it in various publications and meetings, against all evidence to the contrary. This brought him into conflict with Scoresby's opinions and, in spite of the strength of his argument and the many members of England's scientific community who respected Scoresby, Barrow would not budge from his own firm belief. In this respect, perhaps, we see the seeds of disaster being sown for Barrow's future expeditions. As Shelley's narrative showed, hubris is a particularly dangerous thing when men venture into realms once thought to be inhabited by gods, and Barrow's insistence that the ice must disappear somewhere in the Arctic region would lead to the loss of many ships and men. Scoresby, meanwhile, lives on in literature as the template for Philip Pullman's Texan aeronaut, Lee Scoresby, in the *His Dark Materials* trilogy (1995–2000).

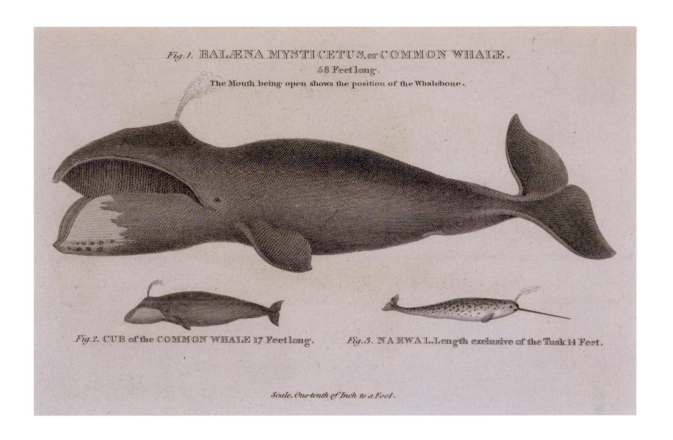

Illustrations from
William Scoresby's
*An Account of the
Arctic Regions* (1820).
G.2602 and G.2603

Fig. 49. r. ⁷/10.

Fig. 50. s. ⁴/10.

Fig. 51. r. ⁷/15.

Fig. 52. r. ⁴/10.

Fig. 53. r. ⁴/20.

Fig. 54. r. ²/15.

Fig. 55. s. ⁷/8.

Fig. 56. s. ⁷/8.

Fig. 57. s. ⁷/8.

Fig. 58. s. ⁷/12.

Fig. 59. s. ⁷/8.

Fig. 60. s. ⁷/8.

Fig. 61. s. ²/10.

Fig. 62. s. ⁷/8.

Fig. 63. s. ⁴/10.

Fig. 64. s. ⁴/10.

Fig. 65. s. ⁴/8.

Fig. 66. s. ⁴/10.

Fig. 67. s. ⁷/8.

Fig. 68. s. ⁴/15.

Fig. 69. s. ⁴/6.

Fig. 70. s. ³/10.

Fig. 71. s. ⁴/20.

Fig. 72. s. ³/10.

Drawn by W. Scoresby Jun.ʳ

Edinburgh, Published by Constable & Cº 1820.

W. & D. Lizars Sculpt.

Fig. 73. l. ⅛.

Fig. 74. m. ¹⁄30.

Fig. 75. m. ⁴⁄35.

Fig. 76. m. ²⁄25.

Fig. 77. m. ²⁄15.

Fig. 78. l. ⁴⁄10.

Fig. 79. n. ²⁄15.

Fig. 80. m. ¹⁄20.

Fig. 81. o. ⁴⁄15.

Fig. 82. o. ⁴⁄20.

Fig. 83. o. ¹⁄20.

Fig. 84. o. ⅛.

Fig. 85. o. ⁴⁄25.

Fig. 86. p. ⁴⁄10.

Fig. 87. n. ¹⁄30.

Fig. 88. n. ⁴⁄30.

Fig. 89. p. ⁴⁄15.

Fig. 90. o. ¹⁄20.

Fig. 91. n. ⁴⁄10.

Fig. 92. o. ⁴⁄10.

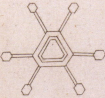

Fig. 93. s. ⁴⁄10.

Fig. 94.

Fig. 95. o. ⁴⁄15.

Fig. 96. g. ¹⁄20.

Drawn by W. Scoresby Jun.ʳ   Edinburgh Published by Constable & Cº 1820.   W. & D. Lizars Sculp.ᵗ

ENCOUNTERS ON THE PASSAGE

Barrow's rekindling of British enthusiasm for the Arctic had consequences for the peoples of the region itself. As with the 1818 expedition of John Ross, the attempts of British explorers to push into different areas of the Arctic brought them into contact with groups of Inuit who had had little or no previous contact with explorers, traders or settlers from Europe and North America.

The upheaval this caused should not be underestimated. Community relationships, cultural histories and economies of trade were now open to rapid and dramatic change, especially in those circumstances where European and North American ships remained in place for a long period – if overwintering, for instance. There was the small matter of the explorers' dress and appearance, which was completely unlike that of the Inuit, and their travelling in ships beyond the scale of any construction undertaken by indigenous Arctic communities. On top of this, the explorers brought with them a wealth of materials: wood was a rare and precious commodity among many indigenous communities, but more significant was the sudden availability of decorative glass and metal. For communities used to basing their tools on stone and ivory, metal was a revelation: keen cutting blades and low-weight metal tools were highly desirable to Inuit hunters.

As a result of these dramatic changes, contact is remembered, not just by Western explorers, but by indigenous communities too. In recent years, as a new wave of Western encroachment onto the Inuit way of life has threatened to erode cultures, histories and memories, much work has been conducted in order to record Inuit oral history and preserve it for posterity. The results are a testament to the enduring power and longevity of this tradition of oral history, as accounts still exist of the arrival of explorers such as Ross. Dorothy Harley Eber's twentieth-century work with communities in Nunavut, Canada, documented in *Encounters on the Passage: Inuit meet the explorers* (2008) and stored as recordings in the Canadian Museum of History, reveals numerous stories of, for example, how local Inuit interacted with explorers such as Parry, whose long residences provoked extensive cultural interaction and economic exchange.

These accounts capture how profound the encounters were for Inuit groups, who describe Navy ships as moving mountains and express the overwhelming power of European weaponry, whether it was being used to hunt or directly intimidate. They also provide a robust historical record, often correlating with the published accounts left by Western explorers. Some of these explorers, such as John Ross, realised how authoritative Inuit knowledge was and used it to improve their expeditions: they recognised its importance for making a success of polar travel. Many others, however, neglected and ignored such knowledge and historical testimony, to the detriment of their expeditions. Inuit knowledge, experience and recollection have an integral role to play in our understanding of the last 500 years of Arctic history.

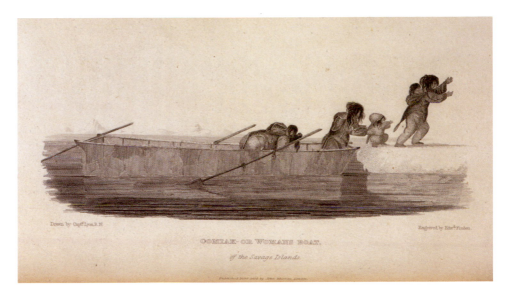

COMIAK OR WOMANS BOAT,
of the Savage Islands.

SNOW VILLAGE OF THE ESKIMAUX,
Winter Island.

ESKIMAUX MAN DANCING.

George Francis Lyon was captain of the
Hecla on Parry's second expedition and
left a detailed visual record of time
spent with the Inuit in *The Private Journal
of Captain George Francis Lyon* (1824).

304.k.23

PLANNING FOR
AN EXPEDITION

Sir Joseph Banks is perhaps best remembered for his contribution to Cook's *Endeavour* expedition of 1768–71, yet, as discussed in chapter one, he had a keen interest in the Arctic. Two of his other voyages, first to Newfoundland and Labrador in 1766 and, later, to Iceland, in 1776, took place close to Arctic environments. Moreover, Banks's good friend Constantine John Phipps was a polar explorer, leading the 1773 expedition on which Horatio Nelson and Equiano travelled (see pp. 80–83). As a result, Banks's famous library, held at his house in Soho Square, contained numerous items relating to the polar regions, and particularly a map collection. His was an active research collection, which he often used, and it travelled with him on his early voyages (books on botany, today held at the British Library, travelled with Banks on HMS *Endeavour*). Now bound into four volumes, covering the Americas, Asia, Europe and (a much smaller volume) Denmark, the collection of hundreds of maps is global in scope, though, reflecting Banks's own interests, the South Pacific and Atlantic Arctic feature prominently.

These collections were not solely for Banks's own use, however. As for Thomas Pennant, when researching his *Arctic Zoology* (1784–5, see pp. 78–9), they were open to a wide public of scientific and critical minds, irrespective of social rank, for use in developing the sum of the world's knowledge. By the nineteenth century, a now elderly Banks, no longer travelling but with a huge appetite for facilitating the development of knowledge, enthusiastically welcomed those wishing to learn to use his collections. Researchers came from all walks of life and with all sorts of interests, so it is not surprising that, mixed in among them, were young polar explorers seeking to further their chances of successful commission by researching their subject of interest in advance.

One of these men was William Edward Parry. Parry was due to travel with Ross on his 1818 expedition and was therefore keen to develop his own knowledge about the area of the Northwest Passage before departure. He was also known in London society and reasonably well connected, and so Banks took Parry under his wing. A letter from Parry to his parents, written in 1817, tells us that, having breakfasted together, the pair had then made use of Banks's library, with Banks showing the young Parry a map of the changing ice mass of Greenland. Parry states: '[e]verybody has remarked, in the common vague way, that the seasons have altered lately, and Sir Joseph very confidently attributes this to the breaking up of the Greenland ices.' The exact map with which Banks illustrated his point is not held at the British Library, but the various illustrations of North America and Greenland in the collection were no doubt also covered by Banks and Parry, ahead of the young officer's voyage.

Parry's letter provides a number of interesting details that develop our understanding of his later expeditions. The fact of his extensive planning itself shows us a man who would undoubtedly lead expeditions in the future, while his exchange with Banks on the changing ice structures of Greenland explains why Parry was so sure that Ross had turned back too early in 1818: he believed a channel through the passage was going to open up. Finally, Banks's statement also suggests the beginnings of a global perspective on climate and some understanding of the elements of climatic change. While ideas of the complex causes and effects of climate change did not gain significant attention until the twentieth century, here Banks hypothesises that changes to substantial bodies of ice in the Arctic could have an impact on weather patterns further to the south. In short, the exploration of the Arctic and its enthusiasts, men like Banks, were beginning to shape our knowledge of the weather and the world around us.

OVERLEAF
One of the maps from the collection of Sir Joseph Banks, illustrating the incomplete Arctic coastline of North America. Banks's maps were used extensively by future expedition leaders, such as Parry, in planning their journeys.
Maps 181.m.1

THE COMFORTS OF HOME

Parry's planning and determination to succeed meant that his expedition of 1819 would end up being one of the most successful westward attempts on the Passage for a long time. Clearly marked by Ross's decision making, but also keen to learn how to better provide for his crew, Parry undertook major adaptations to the practices and methods used in sea-going expeditions to the Arctic. His main aim was to make the arduous process of overwintering more hospitable to a crew – a particularly important investment, since Ross's expedition, Parry's only previous Arctic experience, had not been able to endure the Arctic winter.

As well as taking action to ward off the ever-present danger of scurvy, Parry also innovated in order to keep his crew as warm and comfortable as possible in winter. While the usual methods – covering ships in tarpaulin and constructing snow

walls around the vessels – were used to keep heat in, the temperature could also now be raised using a boiler-driven heating system. Parry had worked with designers and engineers to develop what was effectively an early central-heating system, with water heated by a stove and run through pipes to provide heat and comfort for the sailors.

The idea was inspired, and worked well in terms of providing heat for the crew. However, it also made them uncomfortably wet. Ships overwintering in the Arctic are tremendously damp places as a result of the natural humidity in the air, not to mention the tremendous volume of water vapour produced by a large number of men living, cooking and cleaning in close proximity to each other. This resulted in relatively cold water vapour condensing on the central-heating pipes and then dripping on the men as they went about

Illustrations from Parry's chronicle of the 1821-23 expedition. Note the men playing cricket while the ships winter over, locked in the Arctic sea ice. Parry's vivid account was published as *Journal of a second voyage for the discovery of a North-West Passage from the Atlantic to the Pacific; performed in the years 1821-22-23, in His Majesty's Ships Fury and Hecla, under the orders of Captain William Edward Parry* (1824). G.7394

their daily business and, most uncomfortably, as they tried to sleep. On later voyages led by Parry, the problem was fixed by wrapping wool around the pipes, to soak up the condensed vapour.

Parry's refinements and innovations worked to keep the crew relatively comfortable and safe. Their mental health, always at risk because of the boredom and constraints imposed by the long winter darkness, was supported through the publication of on-board papers and the performance of plays (more on both entertainments later) and the crew were suitably supplied, in order to make HMS *Fury* and *Hecla* merry versions of England on the ice. This state of affairs is best illustrated by the frontispiece of Parry's book on the 1821–23 expedition (opposite above), which shows the ships in winter quarters with the crew going about their business outside.

Alongside shooting and maintenance work, members of the crew are also playing a game of cricket on the ice; it is as if to say, you can take the men out of England, but you cannot take England out of the men.

As well as keeping his men healthy, Parry would record a number of other achievements on his expeditions. An 1819 expedition disproved Ross's assertion that he had seen the end of Lancaster Sound, and Parry also managed to push his way to a furthest west that would long endure as a benchmark in Arctic exploration. Perhaps most importantly, though, Parry's expedition is an illustration of the importance of scientific and technical innovation to the practice of Arctic exploration.

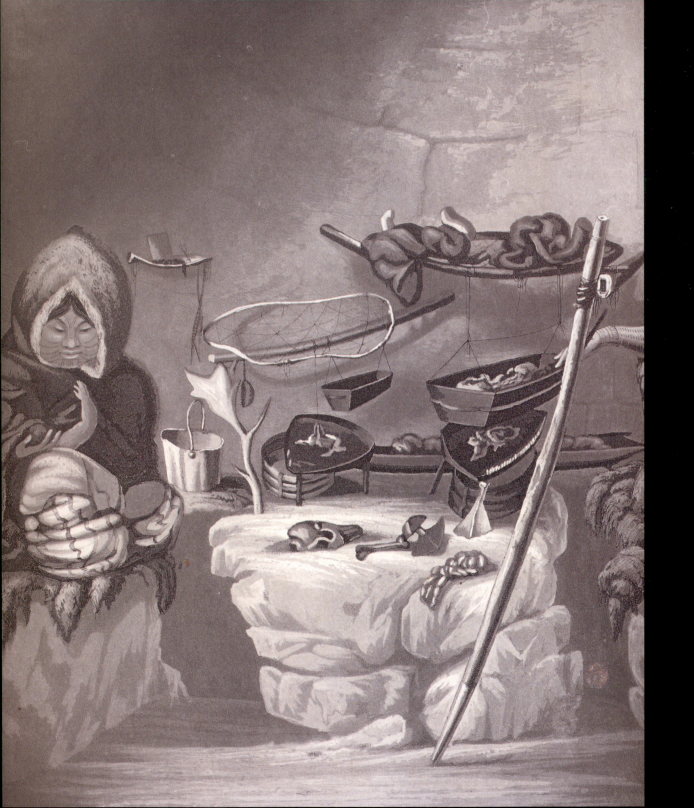

A WINTER'S ENTERTAINMENT

Arctic publishing began with the expeditions of Parry; the writing and illustration of the *North Georgia Gazette* were designed to keep the men working on productive tasks during a time of year when they were trapped inside the ship by the dark and unpredictable weather. Men of lower rank were often given an education during the winter months and the newspaper's production also aimed to contribute to this. Parry's expeditions, as discussed above, were impressively successful in terms of the health of his men and the lack of acrimony on the overwintering ships, so it is no surprise that his success should have been mimicked on later voyages of exploration.

Parry's experiments originated a long history of polar publication and, later, printing, which has left a unique record of Arctic exploration for subsequent generations. This has ranged through the *Illustrated Arctic News* of the mid-nineteenth-century (produced on Edward Belcher's multi-ship expedition of 1852), right up to the printing activities of Robert Falcon Scott's and Ernest Shackleton's Antarctic expeditions, which produced the *South Polar Times* (opposite) and *The Antarctic Book*. Belcher's voyage, led by HMS *Assistance* and also including HMS *Resolute* and the steamer *Pioneer*, was fraught with problems and compromised by poor leadership, but the newspaper acted as a bond between crew and officers during the winter months. The illustrations reproduced overleaf are from a facsimile edition, published on the ships' return to England. It reflects the insatiable appetite for information about the Arctic (and the search for Franklin's lost crew) back in London; the Arctic mania surrounding the early Navy expeditions was clearly enduring.

Polar publishing and printing did not exist solely to bond crews and entertain London readers, however, even though these were important functions. Shackleton's *Nimrod* expedition to the Antarctic, from 1908 to 1909, included a large printing press for the publication and printing of the book *Aurora Australis*. The book entertained the crew and helped pass the winter months but also played a part in supporting the British claim to Antarctic sovereignty. Historically, the place of publication, usually reflected on the title page of a book, has been used to express claims of settlement and development, as illustrated by the provision of British printing presses to Quebec when it was conquered in the eighteenth century. Shackleton's *Aurora Australis*, listed as 'published at the winter quarters of the British Antarctic Expedition', acted as a way of making the same claim on the Antarctic landscape. This hostile environment, devoid of human life and populated only by a few hardy animals and plants, was now subjected to a very British form of settlement and development. Polar publishing and printing had become an important mechanism in expressing control over these inhospitable environments, as well as having a role in developing skills and keeping crew members healthy.

The *South Polar Times* was produced during Scott's two journeys to Antarctica: the *Discovery* expedition of 1901-04, and the *Terra Nova* expedition of 1910-13. The pages below were issued in 1911.

Add. MS. 51040

The *Illustrated Arctic News* was published as a facsimile when Belcher's expedition returned to London. It provides insights into how sailors passed the time. Plays and balls are described, in which male members of the crew performed female roles.

1875.c.19.

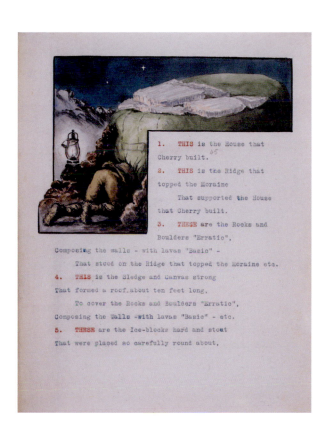

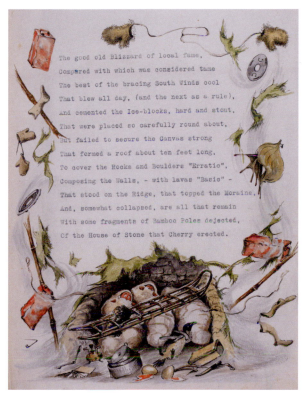

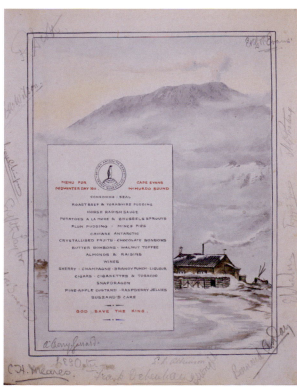

21

THE
ILLUSTRATED ARCTIC NEWS.

Nº III.   "TUTO ET SINE METU."   DECR. 31. 1850.

CHRISTMAS day in Latitude 74° North! At any rate, it has the merit of being a novelty although we must plead guilty to being like most other people, sufficiently old fashioned, to prefer spending it at Home!—

A rare occurrence by the bye, for we "Mariners of England"— and we shall have to do in 1850, as we have done before; namely, spend a merry Christmas and a happy New Year, amongst those jolly mortals called Shipmates.

It is true, no gentle hand rests on ours; no laughing child clambers on our knee. We have not to smile at the vivacity of three-score, nor rejoice in the unfaded beauty of her 'who never spoke a word unkind'.— Such can only be found in that one bright spot— an Englishman's Home!— Yet our Chair will be there, and our name will not be forgotten.— God be thanked we have each our consolation. We rejoice in the hope that they are happy; they gladden with the thought that we are doing our duty.

And so we will, gallant Friends! Thanks to Her Majesty's Roast Beef, and Plum-pudding; — our Christmas in spite of Emperor Zero, must be a jovial one, and we can best insure a happy entrance to the Coming Year; by drawing still closer the bonds of friendship, which unite us to our Brother Arctic Navigators.

ARCTIC SKETCHES

FASHIONS FOR THE MONTH.
ARCTIC LITERATURE.
THE AURORA BOREALIS.

On the 15th inst. the 'Aurora Borealis'— we allude to the interesting Paper so called— again made its appearance, and in defiance of Nature, bids us hope that Summer is rapidly advancing if we are permitted to judge by the great increase to its leaves.—

Like its predecessors, this Nº contains a great diversity of matter, combining useful information, with lighter articles — and we sincerely wish that the Editor's Box of the 'Illustrated Arctic News', was in as flourishing a condition, as that of our cotemporary.

Our Box intended originally for literary purposes, produces only pipe lights, and half smoked Cigars.

GRAND BAL MASQUE

H.M.S. RESOLUTE. DEC. 5. 1850.

RESTAURANT

WELCOME

---

feelings of gratification by all concerned and whilst we in our humble capacity have attempted however badly to denote the scenes which occurred; we feel convinced that our friends in England will be delighted to know that every individual in the Expedition enjoyed himself heartily and rationally on this memorable occasion.

AN ARCTIC CHRISTMAS SONG.
Air "Oh! nothing in life can sadden us"

I delight, I confess in a snug Christmas party,
Where mirth, wit and humour combined for the night,
Dispel all our sorrows, and make us quite hearty,
Where friendship and fun in a family unite—
Where the old folks from their fire-side corner,
Look joyfully on at the company there,
Whilst young fellows, under the Mistletoe—warmer,
Are made by kissing the Maidens so fair.

Since the Bergs have not done so, don't let care upset us,
Nor allow it the flow of your spirits to nip,
For though we are absent, our Friends don't forget us,
But are drinking our healths in a frume of Flip!
Our Parents the friends of our earliest childhood,
Are thinking of us, who to them are so dear;
And our Sweethearts and Wives, could they see us, they smile would,
And dash from their eyes the sensitive tear.

For here, where stern Nature in darkness doth reign,
Where the Mountains & hills, with snow are all crown'd,
Sweet Memory will ever convey us in thought again,
To our Homes, where Happiness only is found—
Let us hope for the best, and in sorrow not ponder,
But partake with kind feelings our bounteful cheer,
Fill to those whose hearts by absence grow fonder,
A right merry Christmas, and happy New Year!

THE OLD YEAR GOING OUT, AND THE NEW YEAR COMING IN.

EDITORS PORTFOLIO.

JANUARY, 1851 has gone by, the first milestone in our journey towards another Christmas, that it has passed quickly and pleasantly, all the squadron could attest, and nothing perhaps has conduced more to throw cheerfulness around us, than the daily perceptible increase of daylight. How delightful it has been to observe with every fresh day some distant point of land reborn again to view, after having been hidden in obscurity for weeks, how interesting to hear daily each individual expecting some feat which proved satisfactorily to his own mind that the days were indeed lengthening.

From New Years eve to Twelfth night we were under the impression that we nearly lived at the hospitable board of the gallant leader of our Expedition, hospitality which (we are merely the voice of the public in proclaiming it) seems only to be limited by the number of Chairs in the Resolute and the size of the Cabin.

On such occasion was pledged with sincerity, the health of Her Majesty

ROYAL ARCTIC THEATRE.
Scene from "Bombastes Furioso."

the Queen: Her consort and Ministers the Admiralty; and those at home who had officially and privately had tended so much to the success of our enterprise, our safety, & our comfort.

Absent Friends would they could have heard the cheer that followed it told volumes for the health and happiness of those upon whom the happiness of the absent depend. last but not least we pledged our brother sailors now wintering within the Arctic Circle. God send that they have spent as equally happy winter, and if those who entered by Behrings Straits have received the gallant men we came to seek, pleasing indeed for us, as well as them, will be the recollection in after years of the Winter 1850.

Scenes from Franklin's
*Narrative of a Journey to the
Shores of the Polar Sea, in the
years 1819, 20, 21 and 22* (1824).
G.7397

THE MAN WHO ATE HIS BOOTS

Parry was not the only one to have returned from the Ross expeditions of 1818 disappointed, nor was he the only junior officer to subsequently lead a major Arctic expedition. Indeed, John Franklin (who served as lieutenant on David Buchan's voyage) was entrusted with opening up an entirely new front. The John Franklin most of us imagine when we think of this notable explorer is the man captured in a daguerrotype produced shortly before the departure of his fateful 1845 expedition on HMS *Erebus* and *Terror*. This is the image of a man past his prime, bulging at the seams of his uniform and most definitely not in the best shape to undertake an Arctic expedition, especially since we now understand the importance of youth and fitness to the successful execution of arduous feats of travel and exploration. However, the Franklin who set out on his own 1819 expedition was very different.

Franklin was, by this point, not just an experienced polar explorer but also a veteran of some of the most deadly naval conflicts of the Napoleonic Wars. Proven in combat, he was a man of determined resolve and certainly not easy to fluster. He was powerfully built and a notable presence on deck, capable of impressive feats of endurance. While Parry was entrusted with forging a path west, Franklin was given the even more challenging task of taking a small team of men overland to locate the northern shore of North America and then explore this as a baseline for the charting of the Northwest Passage. This is now known as the 'Coppermine Expedition'. It was expected that he would be so successful in this endeavour that he would even be able to meet up with Parry to exchange information and confirm that the areas charted connected to one another.

Even today such a plan would be difficult to execute, and that it was even attempted says much about the belief invested in the Navy. In reality, the expedition was to be one of the most arduous undertaken by the Navy, with those who survived doing so only through sheer force of will and a dose of good luck. The terrain Franklin faced in North America was difficult to navigate and challenging to travel over, even lightly. The difficulties faced were exacerbated, then, by the decision to travel heavy: as for the naval expeditions by sea, Franklin and his team took with them everything they thought they might conceivably need. However, the terrain and other factors – not least the all-out war raging between the Hudson's Bay Company and the North West Company, who were, in theory, meant to support Franklin and his party – arrayed against them and meant that even this prodigious supply was not enough.

The result was starvation. A plate from Franklin's expedition narrative (opposite bottom) shows one of the camps pitched by the party, where they cooked 'Tripe-de-roche' (Rock tripe), a moss that the men could collect and boil to form an unpalatable but just-about-nourishing meal. Things were to get much worse: unable to cross the Coppermine River and later finding their supply depot, Fort Enterprise, empty, the party resorted to boiling and eating their boots as they waited for supplies to be brought by local First Nations people. Worse still, after heavy weather and poor health forced the party to fragment, one of the voyageurs is suspected of resorting to cannibalism, killing his fellow men and, allegedly, feeding some of the meat to the officers he later met up with. Franklin's first overland expedition demonstrated his strength and determination, which were extensively noted at the time; the flaws of the expedition were not heeded, however, and would cost explorers dear in the rest of the nineteenth century.

SINGING AND SURVIVAL

The hardships of Franklin's overland expedition did not stop him tracking to the Arctic coast of North America again (he would lead another expedition there between 1825 and 1827). Nor did they divert the men under his command from noting some of the cultural highlights of Arctic overland travelling and North American culture. Then-midshipman George Back is rightly remembered as a hero of Franklin's first expedition, as it was he who tracked ahead, discovered that Fort Enterprise was empty and struck out to find Akaitcho and his band of Yellowknife First Nations people, who had been recruited by the North West Company to supply provisions and would eventually provide food for and tend to the survivors. Back was also the expedition artist, producing the famous plates found in Franklin's account, and had an interest in the arts and culture of others he encountered on his travels.

One outcome of this interest is the book *Canadian Airs* (1825), which was published upon Back's return to England. Back states that the book contains versions of songs enjoyed by the voyageurs (French-Canadian fur-trade employees), who were engaged by Franklin to canoe and portage material for the Coppermine Expedition. These were mostly sung in French, but Back translated them into English and set them to accompanying music. Modern critics view Back's work here with some scepticism, asserting that the transcriptions are gross corruptions of voyageur melodies and suggesting they may not, in fact, have been gathered from the expedition's voyageurs at all.

While the corruption is beyond doubt and the use of piano acoompaniment somewhere between the colonial appropriation of culture and, most likely, terrible taste, it is unlikely, given his close work with the expedition's voyageurs, that Back completely fabricated the melodies. This allows us to reflect on a difference between Back and his senior officer, Franklin. While Back took great interest in the voyageurs and First Nations people he encountered on the 1819 voyage (becoming besotted with Akaitcho's daughter, who was known as Green Stockings), Franklin's account of these groups is distinctly aloof. Indeed, his disdain for the voyageurs is palpable and a clear example of one of Franklin's genuine failings: a snobbery born of his own rank and a belief in the superiority of British politics, culture and values.

This failing, as well as a dogmatic adherence to the rules and methods of the Navy, were arguably factors contributing to Franklin's later undoing. His overbearing behaviour as Lieutenant-Governor of Van Diemen's Land (the country we now call Tasmania) may have played a part in his acrimonious departure from the colony in 1843, and his adherence to Navy principles certainly made the overland and, later, sea-borne expedition he led to the Arctic the perilous journeys that they were. It is also possible that, had Franklin had some of Back's ability to cooperate with and learn from other cultures, history might have turned out slightly differently.

While it may be easy to dismiss Back's book as cultural appropriation on the part of agents of empire, it is still important to consider why such a book was published and read in cities like London. Back's publication illustrates, once again, how great an enthusiasm there was back in Europe for news, information and even frivolities from the Arctic – the British Library's copy of this book came from one of its founder collectors, Thomas Grenville. Not solely an object evidencing cultural appropriation, it shows the refraction of British interest in landscapes and cultures vastly different from those found in London and the rest of the United Kingdom.

CANADIAN AIRS,

Collected by

CAPTAIN GEORGE BACK, R.N.

during the ARCTIC EXPEDITION under

CAPTAIN SIR JOHN FRANKLIN.

with Symphonies and Accompaniments
by
EDWARD KNIGHT JUNᴿ

The Words by

G. SOANE, A.B. and J.B. PLANCHE ESQ.ʳˢ

A bark Canoe going down a rapid.

Ent. at Sta. Hall.   Price 8/,

LONDON,

PUBLISHED BY J. POWER, 34, STRAND.

1836
3

Title page from *Canadian Airs,*
collected by Lieut. Back (1825).

G. 416

THE SCIENCE OF EXPLORATION

As Franklin was searching overland, Parry remained a crucial player in the efforts to locate the Northwest Passage by sea. Following his success in obtaining a marker of 'furthest west' on his first expedition, Parry's efforts were next directed at trying to find navigable channels further south. On his third expedition, undertaken between 1824 and 1825, this meant exploring Prince Regent Inlet in Nunavut, Canada, to see if it would yield a navigable waterway. Setting out with his trusty ships, HMS *Fury* and *Hecla*, Parry and his crew embarked on an expedition with a markedly scientific outlook.

As far back as Frobisher's voyages of the 1570s, Arctic exploration had contained an element of trying to understand more about the world, and its oceans, landscapes and peoples. Cook brought scientific methodology and a

technical approach to charting the Arctic and Antarctic, and explorers of the nineteenth century, such as Ross, were deeply interested in the flora and fauna of the Arctic. By the time of Parry's third attempt on the Northwest Passage, the practice of making scientific experiments and publishing their results had become an important aspect of Arctic exploration. On one level, this was pragmatism – these experiments had the potential to yield information and understanding that would make working in the Arctic an easier experience – but these practices were also about justifying further exploration.

In the context of empire, science was one of the myriad ways in which British expeditions and actions were justified. Parry's third account (1826) is an important instance of this and, despite the tremendous drama of

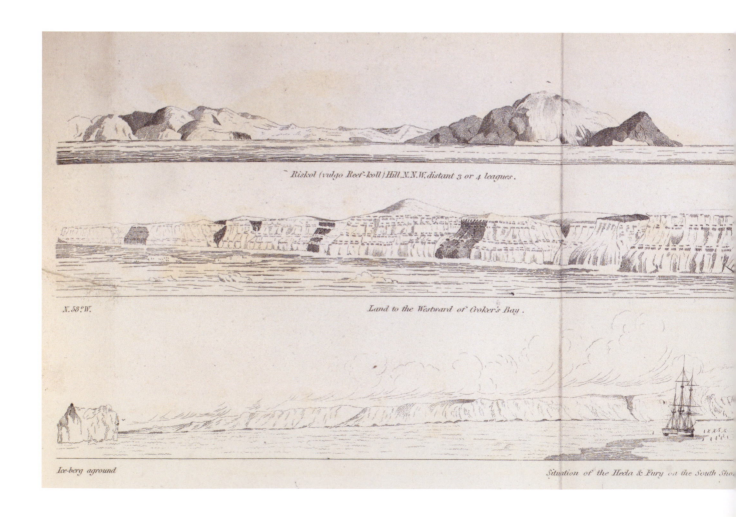

Riskol (vulgo Reef-koll) Hill. N.N.W. distant 3 or 4 leagues.

N. 58° W.

Land to the Westward of Croker's Bay.

Ice-berg aground

Situation of the Hecla & Fury on the South Shore

Coastal profiles published in Parry's
*Journal of a third voyage for the discovery
of the North-West Passage* (1826).
569.f.14

the third expedition – during which the *Fury* was abandoned along with a huge cache of material and supplies – it is still very much focused on reporting the scientific findings of the expedition. Latitude and longitude readings, meteorological data, botanical notes, zoological findings and much more are all present, as are substantial charts and coastal profile views, such as those illustrated here. The expedition was also a training ground for James Clark Ross, John Ross's nephew and already a man of substantial Arctic experience (he had served on Parry's two previous voyages), who would eventually lead his own expedition to the Antarctic. Ross's work here paved the way for his future research, into subjects including terrestrial magnetism. The results from the expedition were also of great interest to minds in European cities such as

London (Parry's journal was published with a 'Botanical Appendix' from William Hooker, future Director at Kew Gardens, London, who had a great interest in Arctic botany).

In short, Parry's third voyage was enmeshed in a complex network of scientific practices and actors, many of whom travelled with the expedition, while others observed at a distance. Arctic exploration was plugged into the globalised networks of scientific research, which had been nurtured in the previous century by men like Sir Joseph Banks and which continued to probe unknown areas of the globe. In turn, this provided a continual list of reasons and objectives for undertaking polar voyages, and a man like Sir John Barrow was always glad to have more reasons to send expeditions in search of the fabled trade route.

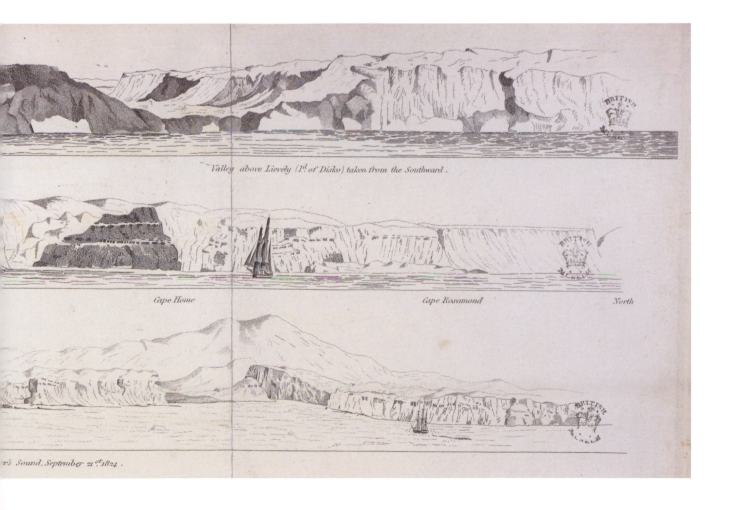

Valley above Lievely (I.ᵈ of Disko) taken from the Southward.

Cape Home   Cape Rosamond   North

r's Sound, September 21ˢᵗ 1824.

THE NEW TECHNOLOGY
OF EXPLORATION

NORTH HENDON.

Snow Cottages of the Boothians.

John Ross was not a man to take the perceived failure of his first expedition in 1818 lightly. Enduring the acrimony and the thinly veiled contempt of Barrow, Ross carved out a new life and interests in Scotland over the following decade. One of those new interests was the potential of steam as a means of driving ocean-going vessels. Ross published a treatise on the subject, arguing that, by the removal of dependence on the wind, trade and war at sea would be completely changed. He also sketched out some potential mechanisms for driving ships as well as for their possible structure as engines of war.

Such a publication was not enough for Ross and he was determined to prove his theories right by undertaking a voyage in a steam-powered vessel; if this vessel should depart for the Northwest Passage it would also help him to attempt to revive his reputation. Of course, Barrow was still in office at the Admiralty, and so an approach to that body to sponsor the expedition met with determined refusal. Ross was left to find other means whereby to develop his plan. Thankfully for Ross, the gin distiller Felix Booth was interested in Arctic exploration and aware of the promotional opportunities it could bring. Having witnessed the excitement generated by previous expeditions, Booth sponsored Ross, who was soon to depart on the small Liverpool steamer *Victory*.

The *Victory* and her crew left London on 23 May 1829, carrying John and his nephew, James Clark Ross. This was to be a scientific voyage in many ways: not just an innovative attempt to sail the passage in a steam-powered vessel, but also an opportunity for James to conduct various experiments. Once the *Victory* became stuck in the ice of the Boothia Peninsula, in September of that year, James set out on various expeditions with a view to developing readings to locate the Magnetic North Pole. The experiment in which he succeeded and the findings were published in the appendix to his uncle's account (1835).

After this initial success, things began to go wrong for the expedition. The ship had been a bad sailor from the off, lacking the necessary horsepower and propelling equipment to undertake a journey at sea, and now it made underwhelming progress against the ice. In his arguments for steam, Ross had suggested that the engines would provide a way of pushing through the ice. However, modern icebreakers still find this difficult and the underpowered engines of the *Victory* stood no chance. They were stuck in the ice for the next four winters. Supplies from Parry's abandoned ship, *Fury*, were invaluable to the crew's survival, but eventually they had to leave the *Victory*. Having somewhat improbably run into another ship, Ross found it was the *Isabella*, under his command during his previous expedition, and discovered that he had been assumed dead.

As it turned out, engineer John Braithwaite, who had supplied the *Victory*'s steam engine to Ross, probably wished the explorer had perished. Ross's published account was highly critical of the engine and Braithwaite's work, a condemnation Braithwaite felt to be unfair. He in turn published an account as to why Ross was wrong, including added attacks on his character, and so began a war of words which is bound into the back of the British Library's copy of the appendix. Braithwaite probably had a point: Ross showed himself to be unscrupulous when he tried to claim praise for his nephew's work on magnetism. Nonetheless, the cause of Arctic innovation and science had been greatly furthered and James had garnered experience that would support him through future voyages.

In spite of the mechanical difficulties Ross faced, his interest in Inuit culture and knowledge continued. *Narrative of a Second Voyage in Search of a North-west Passage, and of a Residence in the Arctic Regions during the Years 1829, 1830, 1831, 1832, 1833* (1835). 569.f.18

THE OTHER ROSS HEADS SOUTH

An iconic depiction of Mount Erebus from Ross's account *A Voyage of discovery and research in the Southern and Antarctic regions, during the years 1839-43* (1847). 2374.f.6.

J.E. Davis del. R. Carrick lith.

BEAUFORT ISLAND AND MOUNT EREBUS, DISCOVERED 28TH JAN

London, J. Murray, Albemarle Street.

Day & Haghe lith.rs to the Queen.

1841.

James learnt a great deal from his uncle, John, but he differed from him a great deal. Both were in possession of scientific minds and shared a passion for the Arctic but, where John showed himself to be a conservative explorer, his nephew pushed himself to the absolute limit. Not only did he commit to undertaking scientific research irrespective of the hardships, for instance, on Parry's Arctic expeditions, he also agreed to voyage to the southern oceans and explore the great polar mass of Antarctica. This expedition was set to depart in 1839 and it is worth remembering that this expedition's destination was the continent that had beaten Cook during his second voyage of exploration just over sixty years previously. Admittedly, Ross had the advantage of the intervening years' innovations in navigation, equipment and shipbuilding, but there is no doubt that his was still a task of prodigious difficulty.

Predominantly concerned with conducting scientific experiments regarding the earth's magnetic field, the expedition was also tasked with exploring the southern oceans, most notably the islands and continent south of the Antarctic Circle. Ross's pioneering work on magnetism meant he was the only man under consideration for the task, which also involved setting up stations for taking magnetic readings on the island of St Helena and on Van Diemen's Land. In this regard, the expedition is a prime example of how people and their skills were directed to the exploration of both poles. Often thought of in isolation, the histories of Arctic and Antarctic exploration are intertwined. Alongside Cook, Ross is a particularly notable individual, and the skills and methods he developed for Arctic magnetic surveying were later applied to research in the Antarctic.

Travelling with Ross as his second-in-command was Francis Crozier, who would later travel to the Arctic with Franklin. The ships, too, were also beginning a notable polar career: Ross took HMS *Erebus* and *Terror* – bomb vessels, whose construction was reinforced in order to absorb the recoil from volleying projectiles into enemy fortifications. It was thought that these two ships could be further adapted, to make them formidable vessels for polar exploration, and they worked so well that they would eventually be used for Franklin's 1845 Arctic expedition.

While Ross's account of the four-year voyage (1847) is very scientific in emphasis – with meteorological reports, magnetic readings, zoological accounts, charts and notes on currents included – it is also notable just how much exploration Ross and his crew were able to undertake. The result is an Antarctic landscape dotted with names more familiar from Arctic exploration, perhaps, as the illustration of Mount Erebus goes to show. Ross's Antarctic expedition, then, was not solely an opportunity for Arctic knowledge to be applied to Antarctic territories, it was also a proving ground for ships and officers. Such connections remind us that, while separated by vast distances – and despite being geographically and climatically distinct – the early history of exploration in the polar regions was one of interconnected aims, methods and stories.

HOOKER IN THE ANTARCTIC

Dr Joseph Dalton Hooker, Assistant-Surgeon on Ross's HMS *Erebus*, came from a distinguished scientific family. His father, William Hooker, was Director at Kew Gardens from 1841 to 1865 and also had experience in the polar regions (he was part of Parry's third journey to the Northwest Passage in 1824). Joseph Hooker joined Ross's 1839 expedition as both surgeon and naturalist, charged with the collection of notes and samples from the locations visited. Given the significance of the Antarctic to this voyage it may seem that opportunities were limited for a naturalist, and, although there were stops at St Helena, Van Diemen's Land and other, more promising, locations, these had been covered by botanists of previous years. However, participation in such a voyage, of exploration and botanical discovery, would develop Hooker's reputation as a scientist.

The initial, slim publication resulting from the expedition, was published by William Hooker, who seemed to acknowledge that his son had received a tough posting in the introduction. He states: '[w]hat, it may be asked, can be expected in the way of Botany, in those dreary regions of the extreme south, where the rigour and climate and the striking diminution of vegetation … appear to offer an effectual barrier to the very existence of plants?' It appears that Hooker senior's opening comments are something of a ruse, however, to soften up the reader and highlight Joseph's sacrifices, before he goes on to note some of the significant discoveries of the voyage.

One of the most significant outcomes was a set of notes on the biology and economic potential of tussock grasses. Growing in harsh weather and even swampy conditions, such grasses produce prodigious tufts of coarse, hardy vegetation, which, crucially, are digestible and nutritious to livestock. The existence of this vegetation meant that rearing livestock on British territories such as the Falkland Islands, annexed by the Empire again in 1833, became more economically practicable. The potential of the islands as a stocking and refuelling base for south sea expeditions, something the British sorely needed if continued exploration of Antarctica and its islands was to be a realistic possibility, was also developed.

The work of Joseph Hooker is yet another example of how families, people and products became bound up in imperial endeavours and the exploration of both poles. There are other products involved in this exchange of materials – hemp, wood, rum, sugar and India rubber to name a few – and Hooker's work, as well as his later role as Director at Kew Gardens (he followed his father into the role in 1865) attests to the globalised system in which the exploits of polar exploration were played out.

Dactylis caespitosa

An illustration of tussock grass from Sir
William Jackson Hooker's account, *Notes on
the botany of an Antarctic Voyage* (1843).
1424.h.3

EENOOLOOAPIK.

A portrait of Eenoolooapik
from the frontispiece of
Alexander Macdonald's *A
Narrative of some passages in
the history of Eenoolooapik,
a young Esquimaux* (1841).
10460.de.28

LEADING THE EXPLORERS

By the mid-nineteenth century, the majority of Inuit communities around the Northwest Passage knew of the *kabloona* (white men) and even took part in their activities. Since Frobisher's kidnap of Inuit during his sixteenth-century expeditions, relations between Inuit and white Arctic travellers had evolved significantly, with Inuit trading with, providing local knowledge to and often guiding explorers, traders, hunters and fishermen. By doing so, Inuit became bound up in a network of knowledge exchange that was common across the globalising world of empires: local experts would become bound up in the activities of explorers as they helped them to understand, navigate and report on new regions.

The Cumberland Sound Inuit of Nunavut remained outside these networks for many years, with explorers and their kin having little reason to travel to this part of the Arctic. From the late 1830s onwards, however, changing ice patterns and overfishing in other parts of the Arctic meant that the waters of Cumberland Sound became an enticing proposition for whalers. They were brought into contact with an Inuk called Eenoolooapik. An intelligent and adventurous man, who had heard of the *qallunaat* (white people), Eenoolooapik came into contact with the whaler William Penny in 1839; he had extensive knowledge of Cumberland Sound and was employed by Penny to provide information about the area.

Penny had heard a suggestion by James Clark Ross that whalers diversify their approach and so began scouting Cumberland Sound to find areas where he could winter in the north. For Penny, Eenoolooapik and his knowledge were invaluable in making the case for this expansion of frontiers and so Penny encouraged the young Inuk (only nineteen years old at the time) to travel back to Scotland with him. Eenoolooapik required little persuasion and boarded the ship *Neptune*, arriving in Aberdeen in November that year. He risked sickness and death by undertaking this journey to a world of new diseases, and indeed, soon fell ill, spending much of his time incapacitated. Nonetheless, he recovered and spent his time in Scotland socialising, learning (writing, especially), demonstrating the skills of the Inuit and participating in Penny's lobbying for a Cumberland Sound fishery.

By the time he returned to the Arctic in April 1840, Eenoolooapik had made a tremendous impression in Aberdeen. His life inspired a published account, which contained a facsimile of a letter written by him that relayed information about the habits of whales visiting the area. This letter and the map of Cumberland Sound he helped Penny produce made it abundantly clear that whalers needed to overwinter in order to hunt whales successfully in the Sound, something Penny and his peers later did with great success. This was not the end of Eenoolooapik and his family's work with the *qallunaat*, however. Other members of his family also visited London, where they were received by Queen Victoria, and worked with the explorer Charles Francis Hall.

Eenoolooapik and the many Inuit like him were an important part of the exploration of the North American Arctic and its exploitation for financial gain by Americans, Canadians, Europeans and Russians. They took huge risks in working with white adventurers, and contributed significant amounts of knowledge to these endeavours. These individuals are an example of how easily indigenous peoples could work with explorers, easily assimilating their manners and habits in order to better sustain relationships – an ability of Eenoolooapik's much remarked upon in Aberdeen. Inuit intermediaries were not alone here; individuals from across the world, in regions including Africa, Asia and the South Pacific, undertook the same responsibilities and displayed the same abilities as Eenoolooapik. These confident, adventurous and intelligent individuals made a mockery of the idea that non-European people were 'savages' of lesser potential than those who relied upon them.

A GRAND DEPARTURE

Planned to display the prowess of the British Empire (and burnish ageing reputations), the Arctic expedition of HMS *Erebus* and *Terror* led by Sir John Franklin was planned for 1845. With hindsight, it is easy to criticise the decision to send Franklin (knighted in 1829) to the Arctic. The historical record shows a man past his prime, and we also know that he had some failings – not least a hefty dose of personal and nationalistic pride. However, Franklin was also a distinguished veteran of the Napoleonic Wars, and had subsequently shown his capability in Arctic sea voyages, as well as his determination to survive the terrible odds of overland expeditions (see pp. 120–21). He served with distinction between 1830 and 1831 in the War of Greek Independence and his Lieutenant-Governorship in Van Diemen's Land did leave positive marks on the fledgling society; most notably, Lady Jane Franklin, née Griffin, was active in establishing a college and, possibly, in making the botanical gardens open to the public. He was a naval officer with a global body of experience.

Furthermore, in many ways, the 1845 expedition being planned by Sir John Barrow was a perfect fit for Franklin. After years of failures, this expedition was meant to be Barrow's last throw of the dice: an exhaustive attempt to crack open the Northwest Passage and salvage his reputation. Likewise, this was Franklin's final chance at a glorious command, to make sure that his difficult tenure south of Australia would not be the last mark made in his long career. Lastly, it seemed that Franklin's vast experience of naval expeditions would, surely, be more of a benefit that his deteriorating health would be a hindrance.

The expedition departed with everything the Navy thought it might need: not just rum, chocolate and supplies to ward off scurvy, but monogrammed cutlery, innovative tinned goods and a self-playing piano. These two ships and their crew were to be a floating display of British naval might bound for the Arctic, and the British public was to know all about it. The *Illustrated London News* gave the Franklin expedition a full-page report complete with illustrations of the ships (including some grand interior views) and their captain. The focus on the interior of the ships is a statement about how civilised the mission was intended be: filling in some of the last blanks on the world map in well-organised comfort was a very British endeavour. All of this celebration and expectation would, however, quickly sour. After stopping in the Orkney islands and making some contact on the Atlantic crossing, Franklin and his crew disappeared. Nothing was heard from the expedition once its crew set out from Baffin Bay for Lancaster Sound, and, after the summer of 1847, calls were made to send new expeditions out in search of Franklin. After all the pomp and ceremony of Franklin's departure, now began the greatest search in the history of polar exploration.

The departure of the *Erebus* and *Terror* depicted in the *Illustrated London News*, 24 May 1845.
P.P. 7611

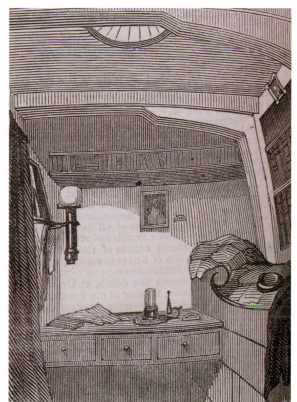

MAPPING A NORTHWEST PASSAGE

The long search for Franklin bred many diverse responses. Ingenuity, heroism, stoicism and patriotism were common, but others looked upon the search as an opportunity to inflate their own reputations and egos. One such man was Robert McClure, commander of HMS *Investigator* and second-in-command to Captain Richard Collinson, under his expedition's flagship, HMS *Enterprise*. Departing in 1850, five years after Franklin and his crew had left on their own Arctic expedition, Collinson and McClure were tasked with opening up an old front in Arctic exploration: taking a western approach to the Northwest Passage. Despite the fact that the route had defeated the likes of the great Cook, *Enterprise* and *Investigator* were to attempt a voyage through to the eastern side, hopefully encountering evidence of Franklin and his crew along the way.

Such an expedition would be challenging enough if undertaken by the most diligent of officers and crews. The selection of McClure and the interesting assortment of individuals that accompanied him probably meant, from the start, that the expedition would have some unexpected outcomes. McClure was more interested in the discovery of the passage than the search for Franklin, or even supporting his senior officer. HMS *Investigator* carried crewmembers equally interested in their own personal aims. Most notable was the ship's German translator and preacher, Johann Miertsching, who frequently clashed with McClure about the spiritual health of his crew and the Inuit they encountered.

McClure's aims became clear once his ship had reached the Pacific. Separated from the *Enterprise* and making contact with other naval personnel, before entering what was thought to be the western entrance to the passage, McClure was asked to consider waiting for his senior officer. McClure refused the request, however, taking the opportunity to forge ahead on his own and leaving a message for Collinson that he had gone ahead to look for the Franklin expedition. An argument could certainly have been made that, with Franklin's crew undoubtedly in a desperate situation by now, not a moment of the short Arctic summer season should be lost. These were not McClure's true intentions, however, and he struck out to try to breach the gap between the western entrance to the passage and Parry's furthest west of 1819.

A map published in 1853 (overleaf) shows McClure's progress, set against the expeditions of other polar explorers, and notes that he was successful. Having charted the coast of Banks Island (named after the botanist and bibliophile), in the Inuvik region, McClure found himself hemmed in by the ice and forced to overwinter at Investigator Cove. Eventually abandoning the ship in 1853, McClure and his crew struck out east and made contact with HMS *Resolute*, the search ship under the overall command of Sir Edward Belcher (of which, more below). Despite abandoning his superior and losing his ship, McClure had nevertheless forged the final link of the Northwest Passage, albeit by land. The contentious nature of his discovery would spawn much debate.

In 2010, Parks Canada, the body charged with protecting Canada's natural and cultural heritage, located the wreck of HMS *Investigator* using modern methods as well as the records left in McClure's publications. This was a highlight in Canada's archaeological work and own attempts to express its Arctic sovereignty and soft power by locating lost British expeditions.

Engraving of Commander Robert McClure in command of HMS Investigator as depicted in his published account The Discovery of the North-West Passage (1857).
10460.e.11.

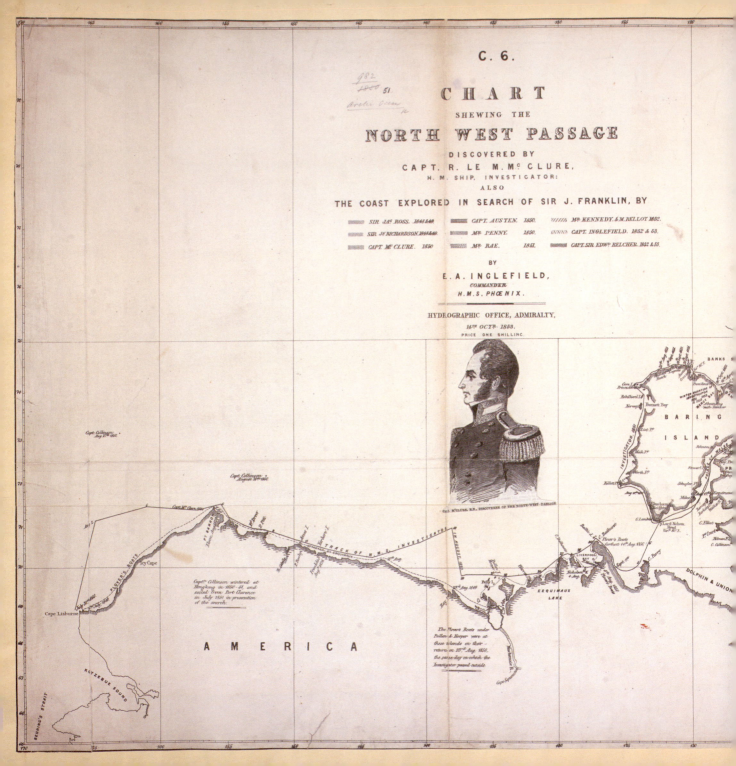

C. 6.

CHART

SHEWING THE

NORTH WEST PASSAGE

DISCOVERED BY

CAPT. R. LE M. McCLURE,
H. M. SHIP, INVESTIGATOR:

ALSO

THE COAST EXPLORED IN SEARCH OF SIR J. FRANKLIN, BY

SIR. JAS ROSS. 1848 & 49.	CAPT. AUSTEN. 1850.	Mr KENNEDY. & M. BELLOT 1852.
SIR. Jn RICHARDSON. 1848 & 49	Mr PENNY. 1850.	CAPT. INGLEFIELD. 1852 & 53.
CAPT. McCLURE. 1850.	Mr RAE. 1851.	CAPT. SIR EDWD BELCHER. 1852 & 53.

BY

E. A. INGLEFIELD,
COMMANDER
H. M. S. PHŒNIX.

HYDROGRAPHIC OFFICE, ADMIRALTY,
14TH OCTR. 1853.
PRICE ONE SHILLING.

Capt J. McCLURE, R.N. DISCOVERER OF THE NORTH-WEST PASSAGE

Capt. Collinson Aug 20th 1850.

Capt. Collinson August 5th 1850.

BANKS

BARING

ISLAND

AMERICA

KOTZEBUE SOUND

Cape Lisburne

Icy Cape

Capt. Collinson wintered at Hongkong in 1850-51, and sailed from Port Clarence in July 1851 in prosecution of the search.

The Plover's Boats under Pullen & Hooper were at these islands on their return on 23rd Aug. 1850, the same day on which the Investigators passed outside.

TRACK OF H.M.S. INVESTIGATOR

ESQUIMAUX LAKE

LIVERPOOL

DOLPHIN & UNION

BEHRING'S STRAIT

Chart shewing the Northwest Passage discovered
by Capt. Robert le M. M'Clure. Also the coast
explored in search of Sir John Franklin, by
Sir John Ross, 1848-49; Sir John Richardson,
1848-49; Capt. M'Clure, 1850; Capt. Austin, 1850;
Mr. Penny, 1850; Mr. Rae, 1851; Mr. Kennedy & M.
Bellot, 1852; Capt. Inglefield, 1852-53; Capt. Sir
E. Belcher, 1852-53 (1853).

SEARCHING FOR FRANKLIN, FINDING A PASSAGE

On returning to Europe, McClure lost no time in articulating his achievements. It is tempting to say that he was also covering himself against any potential court martial proceedings for abandoning his senior officer, but his letters give no sense of a man feeling the need to defend himself. Sir John Barrow had died in 1848, just two years before the Collinson-McClure departure. His role as Arctic advocate was taken over by his son, also John Barrow, who was Archivist to the Admiralty and, after his father's death, became the main official driving force behind continuing searches for Franklin and his crew. Barrow found himself on the receiving end of lobbying from Lady Franklin, as well as in receipt of claims and assertions made by the leaders and members of various search expeditions.

It was in this context that McClure sent Barrow a letter detailing his achievements in 1854, with reference to the advancements made by those who came before him, and making an audacious claim. Not only did McClure hope to have Barrow affirm his claim to discovering the Northwest Passage, he also hoped that Barrow would lobby Parliament to reinstate the prize of £20,000 for the discovery of the Passage, which had been repealed in 1828 due to repeated failures to chart a course between the Atlantic and Pacific Oceans. McClure had not exactly discovered the passage, connecting his own work with that of Parry's expeditions instead, and he certainly had not navigated it, having lost the *Investigator* and needing to be rescued by the crew of HMS *Resolute*.

McClure, however, was undaunted. He boldly confessed that he wished to 'solicit [Barrow's] influence' in Parliament, to 'obtain for the Officers and Crew of the "Investigator" that Reward which although they cannot legally claim, have arduously, equitably and virtually earned'. Having suggested, therefore, that

his intentions were for the good of his crew, McClure moved to assert their contribution to Britain, asserting that they had 'added to the Naval renown of this great Maritime Nation'. In this respect, McClure's letter is a masterful piece of propaganda, overstating his claims but only ever making them in relation to his crew and with reference to the benefits they had, in turn, brought to a nation he was trying to serve.

The plan worked and, in the end, Parliament titled McClure discoverer of a Northwest Passage and awarded him and his crew a prize of £10,000: not the whole sum, but still a substantial pot to add to an already large amount of hazard pay. Did McClure really seek to add glory to the nation and benefit his crew, or was he a man out to burnish his own reputation and avoid the threat of penalty for his own misconduct? The latter charge is hard to pin down, and in his letters, McClure at no point suggests that he thought what he did was wrong. Indeed, his acquittal at court martial (automatic upon the loss of a ship) suggests that he managed to convince others he was blameless. McClure was definitely out to further his own ends, however. Despite praising his crew in the letter to Barrow, McClure was not so generous with the crew that rescued him. Naval tradition dictated that prize money be shared among all those involved, but McClure maintained that he did not need rescue, and thus the crew of the *Resolute* were not due a share in the prize.

Both despite and because of his conduct, McClure is a grand example of the adventurous and daring men who were drawn to the search for the Passage. He may have had an odd relationship to the truth, and certainly held his actions in higher esteem than they deserved, but he had made great strides in British knowledge about the Passage.

15 Salisbury Street, Strand,
April 24. 1855.

Dear Sir,

I beg to enclose a letter from Ireland, also an Abstract of Arctic Voyages from the time of Henry VII, the first will explain that I wish to solicit your influence in advocating what may be considered a fair claim upon the Government, the other will shew the numerous unsuccessful attempts to accomplish that which has been the good fortune of the Officers and Crew of H. M. S. Investigator to achieve — vizt. The Discovery of the North West Passage between the Atlantic and Pacific Oceans, for which in the year 1745 during the Reign of George the Second a Reward of £20,000 was granted by Act of Parliament but in 1828 in consequence of the repeated failures of former times and the unsuccessful attempts of the well equipped Expeditions under Sir Edward Parry the solution of this Geographical problem was considered sceptical in the extreme, therefore Arctic discovery was abandoned and at the same time the Act for granting the Reward was repealed. —

In 1845 Arctic service was again revived under the auspices of the Admiralty and the Command of the Expedition given to Sir John Franklin but the repealing Act of 1828 was not cancelled which apparently in justice to those Employed upon that service should have been done so that those who traversed the Frozen regions of the North in these days might not be in a worse condition than the subjects of Geo: II. III. IV. —

It is now that the Discovery is actually completed that I indulge the hope of receiving your influence in Parliament to obtain for the Officers and Crew of the Investigator that Reward which although they cannot legally claim, have arduously, equitably, and virtually earned, and that those who have added to the Naval renown of this great Maritime Nation may feel that their services and deprivations have been appreciated and acknowledged. —

Trusting you will not think me unreasonable in advancing the claims of my Crew for the consideration of their Country

I remain, Dear Sir,
Yours very truly,

Robt. McClure.

The letter written by McClure to request
the reward of the prize for the discovery
of the Northwest Passage (1854).
Add.MS.35308 f69

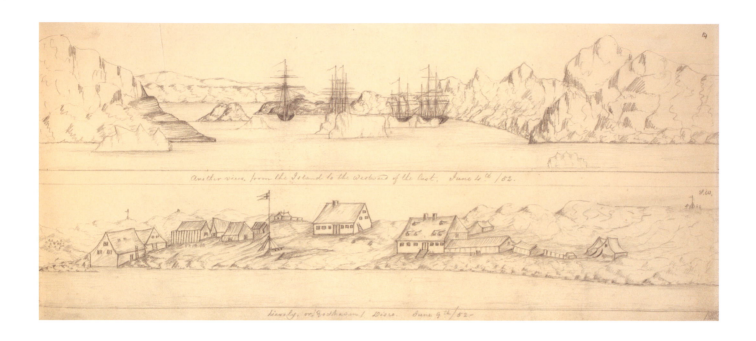

Another view. from the Island to the Westward of the last. June 4th/52.

Liévely, or Godthaven, Disco. June 9th/52—

SKETCHING THE PASSAGE

Robert McCormick had been a member of various Arctic
expeditions but has so far gone unmentioned in this book. In many
ways this sums up the character of his polar career: one defined
by diligent service and achievement, but often overlooked by his
superiors and the public in favour of those of more glamorous
explorers. Despite this, he left a beautiful record of his service as
a polar explorer in the form of publications, including *Voyages of
Discovery in the Arctic and Antarctic Seas, and Round the World* (1884),
and the manuscript illustrations shown here. These manuscripts
are held in a single, bound volume that was donated to Lieutenant-
Colonel John Barrow, the son of Sir John Barrow, with the tribute
'Presented to John Barrow Esq. with [illegible] McCormick's kindest
regards and best wishes for his health and happiness to continue his
able expeditions in the cause of Franklin and humanity.'

McCormick no doubt owed a debt to Barrow. A naturalist,
surgeon and experienced explorer, he had sailed on HMS *Beagle*
with Charles Darwin between 1831 and 1836, as well as serving as
zoologist and surgeon on James Clark Ross's voyage to Antarctica
in 1839. Yet, in spite of his diligent completion of complex duties,
McCormick was overlooked for promotion on his return, something
The Times mentioned pointedly in its 1890 obituary (pasted into
the front of this manuscript volume) – a possible dig at the Navy.
Despite this history of being overlooked, McCormick was one of the
first to raise the fate of Franklin with the Admiralty, in 1847, and to

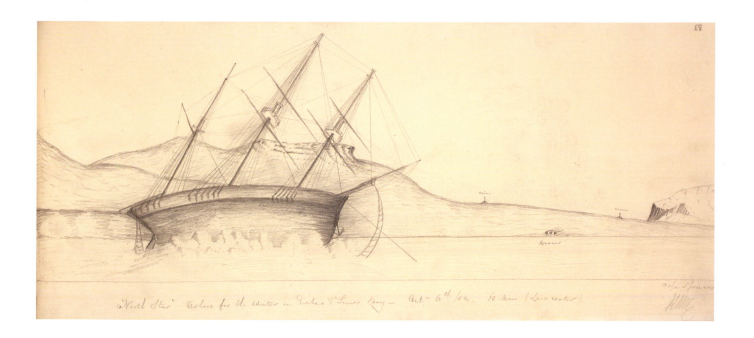

"North Star" Ashore for the Winter in Erebus & Terror Bay – Feb. 6th /02. 10 A.M. (Low water)

provide advice as to what form a potential search for the expedition might look like. By 1852, McCormick had been instructed with command of the pinnace *Forlorn Hope* by Barrow, and searched the area of the Wellington Channel alongside the lead ship, *North Star*.

This search for Franklin was a failure, covering an area too far north, but McCormick did manage to chart new waters and confirm that these were of no further use in the quest for a Northwest Passage. When not commanding the *Forlorn Hope*, McCormick served as surgeon on the *North Star*, and it was in this role that he made the sketches later given to John Barrow. These depict the landscapes encountered by the ship and its crew, as well as some of the tasks necessarily undertaken in order for the ship to survive the winter. The effort required is conveyed in McCormick's illustration of the *North Star* hauled ashore for the winter, where it would be relatively safe from the flows and pressure of the winter's sea ice.

The story of McCormick reminds us how many people were involved in these Arctic expeditions. We tend to remember just a few key names from the history of polar exploration, but more famous men were all supported by large crews of diligent officers and men. Some of the crew were no doubt careless, or trouble-making, but others were hard-working, talented individuals who, for whatever reason, did not receive the commendations, respect and remembrance they perhaps deserved. McCormick falls into this latter category.

Two illustrations from Robert McCormick's sketchbook, depicting Arctic landscapes, settlements and the effects of ice on ships.
Add.MS.33930 f.14 and f. 58

THE WINTER QUARTERS

HMS *Assistance* and the steamer *Pioneer*, shown in a print of 1855, were two of the vessels in a five-ship squadron led by Sir Edward Belcher in a search for Franklin and his crew that departed London in 1852. This was the largest single party sent in search of Franklin and the idea was to cover as much ground as possible, as well as providing plenty of back-up should any ships become stuck, damaged or run out of supplies. The expedition was far from successful, with the accompanying vessels HMS *Resolute* and *Intrepid* finding little other than the crew of McClure's now-abandoned *Investigator*, while the *Assistance* and *Pioneer* themselves became locked in the ice. What the ships did leave, however, was another vivid portrait of life on board them.

The *Illustrated Arctic News* (see p. 116) was published by ships on this expedition and the items seen here, a playbill from HMS *Assistance* and painting by Walter William May, are another part of a rich material record from the expedition. The playbill, in particular, is one of a number illustrated on-board the *Assistance*, which maintained a full programme of theatrical productions throughout the winter months. Keeping the men entertained, and therefore mentally fit and healthy, was an important part of the winter routine and required constant effort. The performance noted – 'Charles the Twelfth' – was one of the more serious entertainments, but this document also suggests the lengths gone to in order to keep performances fresh, promising 'entirely new scenery and dress!' Even the serious performances seemed to need some levity, hence the 'MAGICAL FIGURES!' proclaimed at the bottom of the bill. Less serious evenings included pantomimes and comedies. The casting of female roles among an all-male crew was obviously an opportunity for humour, with one playbill reading: 'The only Lady in this piece, has been engaged at an Enormous Sacrifice; it being her first appearance on any Stage!!'

Walter William May adds an element of scientific interest to his 1855 illustration – mentioning, in the supplementary text, the visual effect of the weak sun and strong moon sharing the sky – but also celebrates the return of the sun to the lives of the crew. May, on his return to England, also wanted to depict some of the artefacts belonging to Franklin and his crew, having heard the news of Dr John Rae's 1854 discoveries, and published the resulting print alongside his other depictions of the *Assistance* expedition. These items, a number of which are now held at the National Maritime Museum, Greenwich, had special significance in Victorian society, as is suggested by May's use of the term 'Relics' in his title. These were some of the few remains of Franklin and his crew ever to be be found and they became important focus points for those wishing to pay respect to the crew's sacrifice.

May also used the presence of the objects to reflect on the contribution the *Assistance* had made to the search for Franklin. He pointed to the rescue of McClure and his crew and, in turn, how this had contributed to linking both known halves of the Northwest Passage together. In contrast to McClure, then, May believed the McClure and Belcher crews shared in the glory of that achievement. In 1854, Belcher ordered the abandonment of the *Assistance*, *Pioneer*, *Resolute* and *Intrepid*, in spite of protests made by members of his crew. The expedition would return home in October of that year, aboard the *North Star*, and Belcher would be acquitted at court martial. But this was not the last he, or England, would hear of HMS *Resolute*.

ABOVE

An illustration of some of the Franklin Relics
found by Dr. John Rae, published by Walter
William May in *A Series of Fourteen Sketches Made
during a Voyage up Wellington Channel* (1855).
1781.a.23

OVERLEAF

May's 'H.M.S. Assistance and Pioneer in
Winter Quarters, Returning Daylight' in
*A Series of Fourteen Sketches Made during
a Voyage up Wellington Channel* (1855).
1781.a.23

THE FATE OF FRANKLIN

The man who would eventually uncover the fate of Franklin and his crew was nothing short of a prodigy of Arctic exploration. Dr John Rae was an experienced Arctic traveller and his approach could not have been more different from that of the Navy. He was a qualified doctor hailing from the Orkney islands who – like many men from Orkney – ended up working for the Hudson's Bay Company. The island of Orkney was en route to the bay and provided a convenient place to load fresh supplies and water (indeed, Franklin himself had stopped there on his 1845 voyage), so contact was inevitable, and the pay of Arctic expeditions offered a tremendous incentive to Orkney men. For the company, the men were a boon: they were regarded as hardy, diligent and hard-working.

This was undoubtedly true of John Rae. Having survived the dreadful winter of his first expedition (1846–7), and having come to be well regarded as an explorer and man of medicine, Rae became a vital resource for the Hudson's Bay Company, in a period when opening up its inland territories was becoming of ever greater importance. In developing his skills for this task, Rae learned that the way to undertake Arctic exploration was not necessarily the way it was being done by official British expeditions. He recognised that the overland expeditions departing from Navy ships were too heavy-laden. The man-powered hauling approach left expeditions overstaffed and thus overburdened with all the material needed to survive the period of the journey. Given the numbers of men on these expeditions, living off the land was not an option, and Navy-issued clothing was rarely up to the job of travelling huge distances across the Arctic.

Rae learnt early on to develop his methods based on the approach of Arctic First Nations peoples; travelling in small teams, using tools such as snowshoes, wearing clothing based on Arctic animal skins and living off the land as much as possible. The result was that Rae charted vast areas of the Canadian Arctic and was asked on numerous occasions to look for Sir John Franklin and his crew. In 1854, on his fourth expedition in search of information about Franklin and the Northwest Passage, Rae stumbled across answers. He identified a channel that would eventually be used by the Norwegian explorer Roald Amundsen to navigate the Northwest Passage, now called Rae Strait, but, prior to this, encountered Inuit who gave him information about the fate of Franklin and his crew.

These Inuit were carrying items that had clearly originally belonged to explorers, such as a gold cap band, and Rae enquired as to where they came by these items. The Inuit had come across a large group of *kabloona* on the verge of starvation; they had been unable to help these people, who had ultimately perished. Rae was uncovering the first bits of information, which would eventually be interpreted to suggest that the crew member Francis Crozier had attempted to lead the men south to hunting grounds he imagined to be on the mainland. It was the wrong decision, as the areas passed through were devoid of animals to hunt. Rae learned that, as a result, some of the men were seen carrying grim stores of meat, which must have been parts of other members of the crew. Some of Franklin's men had turned to cannibalism and this was the story Rae carried back to Europe. In spite of four Arctic journeys, his own story was only just beginning.

A Map of the Route of Dr. John Rae (1854).

Add.MS.35308 f. 408

TOOLS OF THE TRADE

Amidst the suffering, death and failure of judgement surrounding the search for Franklin and his crew, there were also innovations which aided Arctic expeditions, and exploration more generally. One of these, despite unpromising appearances to the contrary, was Peter Halkett's 'Boat Cloak'. The boat cloak was a cloak that could be inflated to form a dinghy and, despite looking somewhat eccentric in Halkett's book of 1848 it worked. Although the boat cloak reads as one of those zany pieces of Victorian lateral thinking that have given rise to our contemporary 'steampunk' aesthetic, its utility was undeniable.

Rae, a man who went on his expeditions well prepared and carrying all the appropriate kit, took two boat-cloaks with him on his overland voyages and put them to extensive use. So pleased was he with his invention, which he used to ford rivers, ferry materials across water and, not least, keep him warm, that he termed the boat cloak one of the greatest inventions of the era. Given the products of the Victorian era, and the marks it left on the world, this might seem like a bold claim. However, Franklin had almost died years before, when his heavy canoes had become so damaged that he could not ford the Coppermine River on the return leg of his 1819–21 expedition. Cold and starving, only a short distance from what he thought was a well-stocked fort, Franklin would no doubt have considered a boat cloak a work of almost divine genius had he had one at his disposal. Viewed this way, it is no wonder that Rae held in such high esteem a boat that was not only portable but wearable and warming.

Another important point of interest as regards the boat cloak is the material used in its construction. Produced largely from India rubber, which provided a sealed chamber for the air and a waterproof covering for the cloak's wearer, the cloak reminds us that the search for the Northwest Passage was not just a story of British people heading north. Instead, it was a case of the British Empire directing all its resources and ingenuity towards filling in some of the last gaps on the map. Not just India rubber, but chocolate, rum, cotton, hemp and many other products from around the Empire were crucial to keeping ships afloat and men healthy on these long voyages. In short, the search for the Northwest Passage was not a marginal endeavour on the fringes of Empire; it was a bombastic attempt to complete the map of the world, using all the products and knowledge of a globalised world to increase chances of success.

THE PADDLER UNDER WEIGH WITH HIS UMBRELLA-SAIL &c.

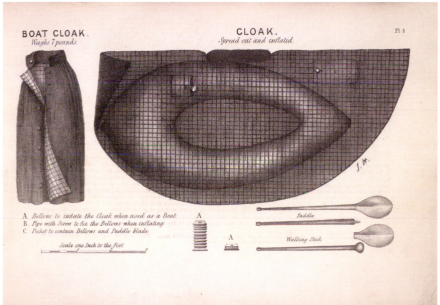

BOAT CLOAK.
Weighs 7 pounds.

CLOAK.
Spread out and inflated.

Pl. 1

A Bellows to inflate the Cloak when used as a Boat.
B Pipe with Screw to fix the Bellows when inflating.
C Pocket to contain Bellows and Paddle blade.

Scale one Inch to the Foot

A

A

Paddle

Walking Stick

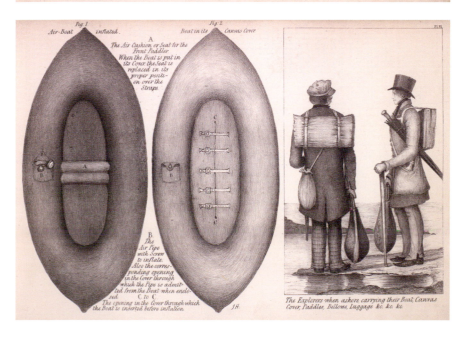

Fig 1
Air-Boat inflated.

Fig 2
Boat in its Canvas Cover.

Pl. III

A
The Air Cushion or Seat for the Front Paddler. When the Boat is put in its Cover the Seat is replaced in its proper position over the Straps.

B
The Air Pipe with Screw to inflate. Also the corresponding opening in the Cover through which the Pipe is admitted from the Boat when enclosed.

C to C
The opening in the Cover through which the Boat is inserted before inflation.

The Explorers when ashore carrying their Boat, Canvas Cover, Paddles, Bellows, Luggage &c. &c.

A series of illustrations illustrating the design and functionality of the boat-cloak from Peter Halkett's published description, *Boat-Cloak or Cloak-Boat*, (1848).

1269.d.5

Pl. IV.

The Paddler ashore cloaked.—
with Bellows, Paddle-blade &c. in his pockets.

J. H.

Since these Sketche
of his original si
light tough wood po
care should be tak
round but rather s
Paddle blade) beir
sides of the handle
fing of the thumb
dle so as to prevent

The
Umbrella
being flat, and
the stick having a
able joint or hinge
to fix at any angl
required, may be
ally as a sail, even
instead of whaleb
Umbrella from bein

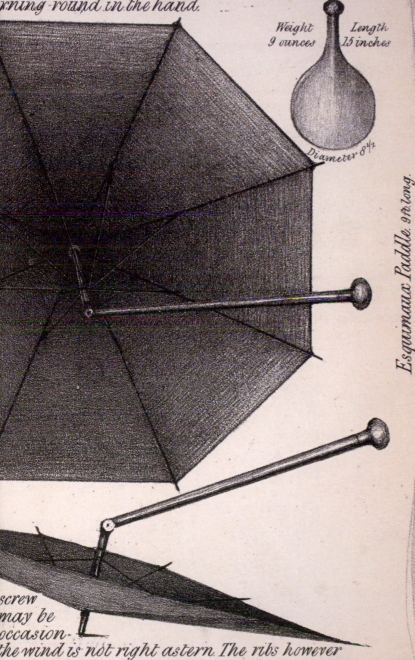

made the Inventor of the Boat Cloak instead
Paddle, generally uses now two small ones of
. These can go into the pockets of the Cloak. Great
constructing the handle which ought not to be
, the two sides (opposite the two flat sides of the
flattened and 1 ¾ inch in width. The two other
ld be rounded and ¾ of an inch wide. The cha-
s avoided and a firm hold taken of the Pad-
rning round in the hand.

Weight
9 ounces

Length
15 inches

Diameter 8½

Esquimaux Paddle. 9 ft. long.

May be conveniently used with the Boat-cloak. The Esquimaux make them of light wood,
the edge of the blade being protected by thin pieces of bone. The two rings (for preventing the water
from running down upon the hands) are made of thin strips or fibres of whalebone.

screw
may be
occasion-
the wind is not right astern. The ribs however
ould be made of stiff wood so as to prevent the
ed inside out when the wind is boisterous.

A further illustration
of the design of
the cloak. Note the
'Esquimaux Paddle' to
the right of the image.
Boat-Cloak or Cloak-Boat (1848).
1269.d.5

THE WRONG STORY

Lady Franklin was a celebrity in London society. A driving force behind her husband's success since their marriage in 1828, she was also a tremendous traveller in her own right. Franklin not only accompanied her husband to postings as far abroad as Van Diemen's Land, but also undertook journeys of her own; she was one of the very few Western women of the time to enter the Muslim holy city of Mecca. She is often remembered fondly in the places to which she travelled, a notable example being that of Hobart, where her actions led to the founding of a state college. During the search for Sir John Franklin, however, it is fair to say that there were many who did not regard her visits or letters in quite so positive a fashion.

From the time that the disappearance of her husband became a realistic possibility, Lady Franklin had lobbied London society, and the Navy Board in particular, to send expeditions to find him and his crew. Eventually occupying an apartment across the road from the offices of the Board – it was not-so-affectionately termed 'The Battery' by those facing its bombardments – Lady Franklin was, in large part, responsible for both the sending of so many ships to search for her husband's expedition and for the mythos that has grown up around Franklin and his crew. She kept the mystery about Franklin, and the events of subsequent search expeditions in the forefront of the public mind through a concerted campaign of letter-writing and meetings, which influenced important members of society, newspaper editors and, no doubt grudgingly, the Naval Board, to maintain an extensive search over a long period of time. Lady Franklin also wooed some of the most notable polar explorers of the age, including Rae, in order to get their advice and even elicit their participation in the search. She not only wrote to Rae and his employers, but also visited his home and his mother in the Orkney islands to convince

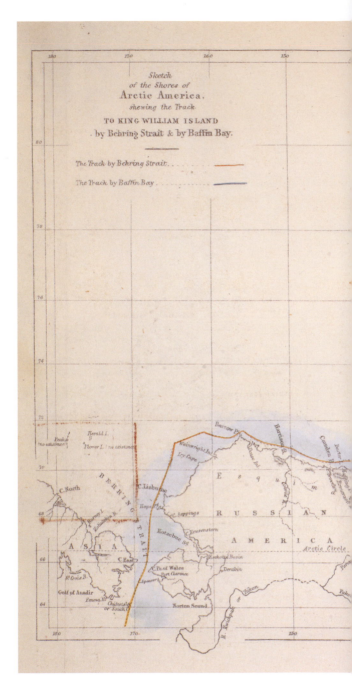

A map published in Lady Franklin's 1857 pamphlet, *A Letter to Viscount Palmerston*, showing the location she wished to be searched.
10460.e.25(5)

him to undertake the search. Lady Franklin went to vast lengths, therefore, in order to mobilise people and resources in the search for her husband; sadly, these efforts were often overshadowed by her reaction to the fate of Franklin and his crew.

Already made angry by McClure's claim to have discovered the Northwest Passage, Lady Franklin was deeply upset and outraged by the news brought home by Rae in 1854. Admittedly, Rae's news and the details about cannibalism could have been handled better by all involved, including the press, but Rae was a prodigious explorer rather than a public relations manager. He did his job well and, in the spirit of the time, reported the truth, irrespective of how unpalatable it might have been. Of course, Lady Franklin, too, could only continue to do her self-appointed job. Rae had found information and some artefacts, but nothing concrete. As far as Lady Franklin knew, some men, including Franklin himself, could still be alive, even though all rational analysis suggested this was improbable. She needed to influence public opinion in order to keep expeditions heading to the Arctic.

A WAR OF WORDS

Lady Franklin set about marshalling a new front in her campaign to keep rescue expeditions heading to the Arctic. Rae and his (accurate) account of the fate of Franklin's crew became the target of this campaign. While it is tempting to see Rae as a victim and Franklin purely as an aggressor in this situation, it is important to remember how high the stakes were. Moreover, Rae's evidence had not been witnessed directly by the rescue party, with neither the ships nor remains of officers being formally identified – both facts that left considerable questions in the public mind. The result was that these two powerful and strong-willed personalities, inevitably, locked horns.

In the renewed campaign to find Franklin, or at least salvage his reputation as an explorer and leader of men, Lady Franklin drew as many influential voices as possible into her camp. One of the most significant was the author Charles Dickens. Dickens had endless enthusiasm for the Arctic and for stories of heroic exploration in its vast, uncompromising spaces. He was an avid reader of published accounts from Arctic voyages and even took part in a production of the Wilkie Collins play, *The Frozen Deep* (1856); in an image from the *Illustrated London News*, he is shown playing the part of Richard Wardour (the despairing man with the straggly beard). A tale of adventure, love and loss, both the play and Dickens's participation in it were of interest to newspapers in England (it also marked the beginning of Dickens's affair with Ellen Ternan, whom he met while the play was being performed in Manchester).

Such enthusiasm for the Arctic, as well as an almost dogmatic belief in the superiority of British values and culture, meant that Dickens was a natural choice of ally in Lady Franklin's attempts to undermine the claims made by Rae. Using his periodical, *Household Words*, as a mouthpiece, Dickens launched a careful attack on Rae, highlighting his skill as an explorer while also attempting to paint him as naive for trusting the Inuit account he had heard. In Dickens's opinion, 'The word of a savage is not to be taken for it; firstly because he is a liar; secondly, because he is a boaster.' Statements such as this formed the backbone of his attempt to discredit the account brought back by Rae.

What Dickens displays here is not simply a distrust of the Inuit specifically, but a deep-seated racism, which affected Victorian attitudes towards people from outside the United Kingdom. The Empire bred a mindset of superiority, according to which other races were inferior and struggled with supposedly inherently British concepts such as truth, justice and heroism. It was assumed that upstanding members of British society could never stoop to cannibalism; that was something people from other cultures did. Such impressions of the relative value of Inuit culture (and that of other peoples indigenous to the Arctic) are still encountered frequently today, even though events such as the finding of HMS *Erebus*, in an area Inuit oral history has long suggested should be searched, provide ample opportunities to re-evaluate such positions.

Rae and Dickens engaged in a considerate back-and-forth in the pages of *Household Words* and Dickens's willingness to give Rae a right of reply does him some credit. However, Dickens's blinkered view of other peoples of the world suggests that a mind perceptive about issues at home was not quite as broad in a global context. The savaging Rae suffered at the hands of Dickens and other elements of the press was deeply damaging, such that his claim was discredited for a number of years and he never fully regained his reputation.

An illustration of Dickens - the prone, bedraggled man - playing the part of Richard Wardour in 'The Frozen Deep'. *Illustrated London News*, 17 January 1857.
P.P.7611

THE COPPER CYLINDER

One of the cylinders found containing
messages pertaining to the fate of the
Franklin expedition.
National Maritime Museum

Recovered on an 1857–9 expedition led by Francis Leopold McClintock, on the steam-powered vessel *Fox*, this simple copper cylinder draws one of the neater lines under the account of what happened to Franklin and his crew. South of Back Bay, on King William Island, Nunavut, a sledge party led by one Lieutenant Hobson located a cairn containing the cylinder, which enclosed a note from crewmembers of Franklin's expedition. The earliest writings on the note, dated May 1847, are positive, recording that the crew overwintered, with Franklin in charge, before signing off, 'All well'. The crew, at that point, were on the verge of navigating the Northwest Passage.

There is, however, an addition to the note, written in the margins by Captains Crozier (previously second-in-command under Franklin) and Fitzjames, from April 1848. Franklin, it reports, had died the summer previously and a further nine officers and fifteen men had died since. Something had gone terribly wrong. Even on previous expeditions that ended badly, deaths in these numbers were rare: naval commanders such as Cook had begun to stave off scurvy, for example, in the previous century. We may never know exactly what caused this disaster, though there are a number of plausible theories, including the effects of damaged tin cans on food supplies and poorly preserved anti-scorbutic items. Whatever the cause, it led to Crozier abandoning the ship, with 103 men.

Lady Franklin had lobbied for McClintock's expedition to be sent, in the hope it would show that Franklin had discovered a passage and call into question Rae's previous findings. While McClintock's evidence did allow her to argue that Franklin and his expedition were the true finders of the Passage, Crozier's decisions, as recorded on the note, lent validity to Rae's findings. Crozier wrote that he and his crew were to depart for Fish River the following day. Between them and Fish River was a vast landscape of poor hunting and, in addition, he was headed into the area where Franklin and his crew had almost starved previously. Crozier no doubt hoped that his crew would encounter an animal migration, which would provide plenty of food, before striking south to locate a Hudson's Bay Company fort or factory. This was a disastrous course of action, leading to the men's starvation and the harrowing scenes of disorientation, death and cannibalism described by the Inuit Rae encountered.

These were the best answers any Victorian was going to find. Some mavericks, like explorer Charles Francis Hall, still hoped to find survivors living among the Inuit, but only the expeditions and science of later centuries would push the narrative beyond that the Inuit and a few British explorers had found. It says much about British values at the time that a copper cylinder's contents, marked and scrawled over by various authors, was more convincing to the British than the Inuit testimony heard previously, but this was an (or at least one) end to the Franklin saga.

BELOW & OPPOSITE
Illustrations from Charles Francis Hall,
Life with the Esquimaux (1864).
10460.e.24

IG-LOOS OR SNOW VILLAGE AT OOPUNGNEWING.

Feverish interest in the search for Franklin and his crew swept Britain and its Empire, but North America had been drawn into the efforts too. North American interest in the Arctic was growing in the mid-nineteenth century, as the public became increasingly aware of adventure narratives in the media and America's economic horizons pushed into the polar north, largely following the whaling industry. As a result, many Americans became deeply enthused about the Arctic, and Charles Francis Hall was one of them. Born in Rochester, New Hampshire, before moving steadily west and ending up in Cincinnati, Ohio, Hall developed a deep interest in the Arctic through his reading and, pehaps, his work running two small newspapers: the *Cincinnati Occasional* and *Daily Press*.

Hall became determined to find survivors from the Franklin expedition, convinced that they might still be found living with local Inuit, even after Rae's news became widely known. Fired by enthusiasm, Hall searched for ways to reach the Arctic, eventually receiving free passage on the whaling bark *George Henry* through the advocacy of the merchant Henry Grinnell, a key supporter of American exploration at the time. Setting out for Frobisher Bay, Hall was determined to search for evidence of survivors in the area and spent two years working through his interpreters, Ebierbing and Tookolito (Joe and Hannah, to whalers who visited the area). His attempt to find Franklin's crew was unsuccessful, but Hall came back with exciting discoveries nonetheless.

In his published account, *Life with the Esquimaux* (1865), Hall recounts how he came across stories about previous groups of explorers who had visited the area, including some who built a boat there. On 1 April 1861, an Inuk by the name of 'Koojesse' (Hall's spelling) told Frobisher that a long time before, some 'kod-lu-nas' (Hall's spelling of *kabloonas*) had built a vessel lower down on Frobisher Bay, and, furthermore, that 'brick ("*mik-e-oo-koo-loo-oug*", small red pieces), timber, chips, &c. as having been left there'. Hall dismissed the story, because '[s]o unreasonable did the story appear of constructing a ship in such perfectly woodless country, that I thought it a waste of time and paper to make a record of it.' Days later, Hall's mistake dawns on him, as he recalls that Martin Frobisher and his men had been required

to reconstruct a ship during Frobisher's second voyage of exploration in 1577.

From this point, Hall records more details of the story, visits the relevant location, acquires relics from Frobisher's expedition and confirms that the area is indeed that where Frobisher had previously landed. While Hall is often feted for his acquisition of this information, the driver of the story is the strength of local Inuit knowledge and the capacity of oral history to store information over long periods of time. As noted previously, accounts of the arrival of the various Navy explorers survive to this day, as do some accounts that may be about Henry Hudson; these details about the presence of Frobisher in a particular location in the Arctic can be added to the list. This reminds us that not all valuable knowledge (despite Hall's methods) is written down. It also helps us to deconstruct Charles Dickens's dismissive attitude towards the use and veracity of Inuit testimony. Hall would return to an America divided by war, although this would not stop him trying to raise funds for another expedition; nor would it drive the Arctic from the public imagination.

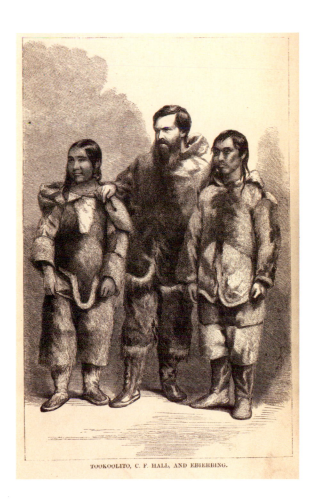

TOOKOOLITO, C. F. HALL, AND EBIERBING.

BONDS FORMED IN ICE

When HMS *Resolute* was abandoned in the Arctic in 1854, many, not least the ship's commander, thought that it was the last they would hear of the ship. However, just a few years later, the *Resolute* broke free of the ice and it was in remarkably good condition when it was encountered by James Buddington and his crew of whalers. (Buddington was in charge of the whaler *George Henry*, which, in an illustration of the close networks that governed Arctic trade and exploration, would later bear Hall north in search of the Franklin expedition.)

Buddington encountered the *Resolute* just off Baffin Island, over 1,600 kilometres away from where it had been abandoned. In many ways, the survival of the ship was a miracle; it had survived the pressures of three winters, never mind travelling so far south while unmanned. For Buddington, the vessel must have had an eerie feeling, with everything ordered and tucked away in a state of preparedness for abandonment. Buddington split his crew, to sail the *Resolute* back to the U.S., and arrived home in Connecticut on Christmas Eve 1855. The ship represented quite a prize. Henry Grinnell, along with Senator James Mason, lobbied for it to be restored to England as a 'courtesy' once it had been refurbished. This meant purchasing the *Resolute* from Buddington for the price of $40,000 – a substantial gain for his efforts – before restoring the ship and sailing it back to its original owners in England.

The reception of the *Resolute* in England was enthusiastic, to say the least. In December 1856, Queen Victoria boarded the ship when it arrived in Cowes, and toured the restored vessel. The gesture and pomp that surrounded the return were seen as marks of friendship between the United Kingdom and the U.S. – an important step for countries who had been at war only forty years previously and who still had a fractious relationship in the wake of the U.S. secession from the British Empire. Once returned, the *Resolute* saw service in home waters until she was decommissioned in 1876, but this was not the end of the story.

ENGLAND AND AMERICA
The Visit of Her Majesty Queen Victoria to the Arctic Ship Resolute, December 16th 1856

The *Resolute* had reminded all sides of the potential for friendship in trans-Atlantic relations. As a result, timbers from the decommissioned ship were used to make a number of desks, produced in the joiner's shop at Chatham Docks. One of these desks was gifted to President Rutherford B. Hayes in 1880 and, since then, it has frequently been used as the U.S. president's official desk in the Oval Office, Washington, D.C.. Prior to 1856, there was very little of the 'Special Relationship' in existence between Britain and America. The countries had been to war, wrestled over trade and vexed each other on a number of issues, but all of this began to change with the return of the *Resolute*. The ship cemented a bond of trust between the two nations and the desk made from its timbers is an everyday reminder of the fraternity that now exists. The British Prime Minister Gordon Brown showed an understanding of this when he presented President Barack Obama with a framed portrait of the *Resolute* during an official visit in 2009, and Obama is one of the many presidents who have used the desk extensively in the Oval Office. The Arctic and the search for the Northwest Passage have had an enduring impact on international politics below the Arctic Circle.

England and America. The visit of her majesty Queen Victoria to the Arctic ship Resolute - December 16th, 1856... (1859) engraved by G. Zobel after a painting by W. Simpson. An illustration capturing the patriotism and spirit of friendship embodied in the return of HMS Resolute.
Library of Congress

SANTA CLAUS'S ROUTE.

RELOCATING SANTA

In many ways, North American interest in the Arctic, the finding of Franklin and the recovery of British artefacts can all be seen in the context of the growing cultural and colonial horizons of an expanding nation. American whalers were an increasing feature of life in the Arctic in the nineteenth century, much to the later dismay of Canadians, and the North Pole was increasingly seen as a site for the performance of American derring-do, an expression of cultural and technical achievement similar to the attempt to chart the Northwest Passage. Further to this, less than fifteen years after Rae's claim that he had discovered the fate of Franklin, the U.S. undertook one of its last great land expansions. The Alaska Purchase, completed in March 1867, added the huge North American landmass (which had previously belonged to Russia) as a new state, the only American land north of the Arctic Circle. As well as whalers and explorers, many other American citizens could now find an Arctic home, including not just fishermen and trappers but prospectors, bar owners, bankers and administrators.

All of this was having a dramatic cultural impact in the U.S. The idea of a 'Manifest Destiny', America's ultimate status as a continental nation stretching from the east coast to the west, had acquired a northern dimension; Alaska and the Arctic were the final frontier for North American continental dominance and mastery of all the landscapes the New World had to offer. The cultural expression of this dominance was felt through a wide range of media, including newspapers, music and maps, and involved a wide cast of characters, the most surprising of which, perhaps, was Santa Claus.

Thomas Nast was a cartoonist who spent much of his career drawing for *Harper's Weekly*, and Santa was a favourite figure of his, often used politically. During the American Civil War (1861–5), Nast began to illustrate Santa at Christmas. Nast depicted Santa as a figure of benevolence and support for the Northern states, bringing gifts to men serving on the front lines at Christmas. As an expression of good – and, in his original role as a saint, a representative of godliness – the use of Santa in this context underscored the belief that the men of the North fought on the side of right. What is also interesting about Nast's depictions of Santa is that they relocate him. Boxes brought to soldiers are marked 'North Pole', while Santa's workshop is also shown near this location.

An illustration from an 1890 compendium of Nast's work, shows that this construction of Santa continued throughout Nast's career. Indeed, Santa continued to be a favourite festive figure for Nast, and his characterisation of the man – portly, jolly and clad in red (as opposed to the more traditional depiction: jovial, hale and clad in green) – became the archetypal image of Santa Claus. The decision to relocate Santa to the North Pole was part of a broader re-articulation of cultural boundaries, moving him from his traditional home in northern Europe to one increasingly understood by Americans to be within their sphere of influence. By doing so, Nast inadvertently began a great push-and-pull between Canada and the U.S for Santa's identity. As late as 2013, a Canadian minister asserted that Santa must be Canadian since, not only did he live in the Arctic, but he wore a very Canadian shade of red.

The fascination with the Arctic shared by consumers in Europe and North America had developed as a result of nineteenth-century Arctic exploration, the search for the Northwest Passage and, in particular, the search for Franklin and his crew, and it enabled the Massachussetts-born Romantic painter William Bradford to turn a passion into a profitable enterprise. In this regard he was part of a massive industry of writers, printers, sketch artists and painters who catered to this market, but Bradford was one of the few artists, and the only painter of large-scale scenes, who had actually visited the Arctic: he had visited Labrador and Greenland in 1861 and the landscape had become his passionate focus as an artist. As a result, Bradford produced some of the most striking depictions of ships trapped in ice, forging through the pack or sitting under the stunning colours of an Arctic sky. These are the work of someone on whom the landscape has made a lasting and intimate impression.

Painting was not Bradford's only medium, as he produced beautiful photographs for publication and sale, as well as for reference in his painting. In 1869, Bradford undertook an expedition to photograph the Arctic land and seascapes around Greenland on the sealing ship *Panther*. Funded by the New York art collector and banker LeGrand Lockwood, Bradford also took two Boston-based photographers, George Critcherson and John Dunmore. The expedition itself was not a long one, leaving Newfoundland on 3 July and forced by dangerous pack ice to turn back in mid-August, but there was still time to linger at sites of visual and anthropological appeal. The resulting photographs were published in London during Bradford's two-year sojourn in the city, which seemed to make its mark on the artist as he donated an oil painting of the *Panther* to Queen Victoria.

The book resulting from these journeys, *The Arctic Regions, etc.* (1873), is a unique publication in terms of its ambition. A large volume with tipped-in photographic plates, the book is an early example of photograph and text existing in dialogue with each other in the same publication. Bradford used the text to accentuate features and highlights of the views and people photographed on the journey. In particular, the text is used to heighten the romanticism of a view and the anthropological reflections on local Inuit made by the expedition's camera-workers.

The Arctic Regions is a milestone in printing and in the imaginative depiction of the Arctic, representing the first printed photographic book on sale to a market that was already hungry for depictions of the north. The contents of the book are similar to those produced today in visual accounts of the Arctic: sublime views emphasising the grandeur of the landscape, frail and tiny human bodies dwarfed by it, an anthropological fascination with northern peoples and a keen interest in local flora and fauna, although the focus was on collecting zoological samples rather than conserving them. One particular photo, showing members of the crew standing outside the ship with polar bear carcasses in front of them (overleaf), suggests just how much the Arctic has changed today. Here, the polar bears, paraded as trophies, are shown as mere animals, sacrificed to more predatory instincts. Today, the polar bear is an emblem of the conservation movement and, in particular, the perils of climate change; the visual register and way we see the Arctic has shifted but Bradford put in place some of the first principles for photographing the Arctic.

THE

ARCTIC REGIONS

ILLUSTRATED WITH PHOTOGRAPHS TAKEN

ON AN ART EXPEDITION TO

GREENLAND.

BY

WILLIAM BRADFORD.

WITH DESCRIPTIVE NARRATIVE

BY THE ARTIST.

LONDON:

SAMPSON LOW, MARSTON, LOW, AND SEARLE,

CROWN BUILDINGS, FLEET STREET.

1873.

RECORDING AN ARCTIC EXPEDITION

Photographs from Mitchell and White's
*A Catalogue of Photographs Taken during
the Arctic Expedition of 1875-76* (1877).
Maps 20.c.12-13

The Arctic expedition led by Nares is an often forgotten piece of Britain's history of polar exploration. Nares himself had been part of this history for much of his career, serving as a mate on HMS *Resolute* in 1852, and leading HMS *Challenger* on a scientific research expedition to the Antarctic from 1872 to 1874, during which this ship became the first steamer to enter the Antarctic Circle from the Indian Ocean. Nares's Arctic expedition was tasked with using two ships, HMS *Discovery* and *Alert*, to try to reach the North Pole, while also exploring the coast of Greenland and adjacent islands. As a result, it forms part of the broader British narrative in the Arctic, its main geographical locations and trade routes. The expedition also included Albert Markham, a lieutenant at the time, who would rise to become a council member for the Royal Geographical Society and a firm supporter of British polar exploration. Markham also set a new 'furthest north' record on this expedition, reaching over 83°N by hauling his sledge from the ship.

Latitude records were not the only significant thing about Nares's expedition, however. Nares had insisted that the expedition be equipped with cameras, and photographers accompanied both ships. George White, Assistant Engineer for the *Alert*, and Thomas Mitchell, Paymaster for the *Discovery*, were trained to operate the camera equipment and become not just the expedition's photographers but the first British camera-workers to accompany an official naval expedition. Mitchell and White were not the first photographers to take equipment to the Arctic but the context in which they carried out their work is noteworthy.

Despite their training, both photographers were essentially amateurs, tasked with grappling with the unwieldy equipment of the time in a hostile environment. Nonetheless, they compiled an extensive photographic record, which now forms two large photographic volumes in the British Library's map collections. Mitchell and White documented various aspects of the expedition: illustrating the ships in their Arctic environment; men as they undertook their surveying and hauling work; Inuit who visited the crews; and hunts, possibly for the purpose of specimen collection. Through these photographs, their composition, selection of subjects and production, Mitchell and White established a framework for expedition photography that went on to influence the heroic age of exploration. Marking a shift from the modes of representation used by earlier explorers, those of the heroic age depended heavily on photography for recording, communication and self-promotion. Along with William Bradford's *The Arctic Regions*, the documentation of George Nares's polar expedition of 1875–6 began to establish a template for the way in which the Arctic was viewed and understood from remote, metropolitan heartlands.

11

London Stereoscopic and Photographic Company,
110 AND 108, REGENT STREET, AND 54, CHEAPSIDE.

8

London Stereoscopic and Photographic Company,
110 AND 108, REGENT STREET, AND 54, CHEAPSIDE.

35.

London Stereoscopic and Photographic Company,
110 AND 108, REGENT STREET, AND 54, CHEAPSIDE.

26.

London Stereoscopic and Photographic Company,
110 AND 108, REGENT STREET, AND 54, CHEAPSIDE.

Mitchell and White
photographed various
subjects during the
expedition. While
the ship was often
the focus of images,
the crew, visiting
Inuit and the results
of a hunt were also
depicted. *A Catalogue
of Photographs Taken
during the Arctic
Expedition of 1875-76*
(1877).

DISCOVERING A LEGACY OF POLLUTION

Despite the enthusiasm for exploration of the Northwest Passage generated by British imperial dominance and endeavour, the Northeast Passage, sought by Englishmen such as Joseph Billings in the eighteenth century, as well as a host of other European navigators, was in fact navigated first, in 1878–9, by the Swede Adolf Erik Nordenskiöld. Relatively unknown in the British history of Arctic exploration, Nordenskiöld undertook various voyages to Spitsbergen, Novaya Zemlya and Greenland, as well as achieving a navigation increasingly thought to be impossible. As the nineteenth century drew to an end, the navigation of the Northeast Passage can be seen as the closing of an era, the realisation of dreams from a previous generation. Men like Nordenskiöld also drew attention to future subjects of interest in the Arctic.

Nordenskiöld's expeditions to Greenland yielded not just geographical discoveries but also, so Nordenskiöld thought, completely new minerals. On his journeys to Greenland in 1867 and 1883, Nordenskiöld repeatedly came across hollows of meltwater made in the ice. Although these holes providing drinking water for the expedition, they were treacherous, as men could easily fall into them. They also contained an unusual powder. In the 1879 English translation of an earlier work, *The Arctic Voyages of Adolf Erik Nordenskiöld*, the author notes that the material might contain feldspar and augite, as well as some black grains that were attracted to a magnet. Nordenskiöld called the substance 'Kryokonite', before noting that further work on it was needed. After his 1883 expedition to Greenland's interior, Nordenskiöld had even more information and published a series of papers full of conjecture about the powder.

At this point the nature of the material was not known, but Nordenskiöld and his collaborators noted that, as it was not clay-based, it could not originate from known parts of Greenland: either it

A map of Nordenskiöld's 1883 expedition to the interior of Greenland, *Karta öfver 1883 ars Svensiva Expedition på Grönlands Inlandsis under befäl af A. E; Nordenskiöld. Af Expeditions topograf* (1884). Maps 35250.(3.)

came from somewhere not yet explored, or hailed from outside the island. This is the crucial bit of evidence: the material in question was not, in fact, a new mineral but coal residue. Later chemical analyses identified that coal dust, originating from the burning of fuel in North America and Europe, was falling back to the ground in Greenland and then absorbing extra heat, leading to the melting of surrounding ice.

Nordenskiöld had, therefore, discovered some of the earliest evidence of the global circulation of pollutants, and shown how fossil fuels burnt in the sub-Arctic could affect ecosystems in the Arctic itself. The developing knowledge of these currents would underpin future scientific discoveries made at the poles. The mechanisms uncovered as a result of Nordenskiöld's find are the same as those now known to convey Chlorofluorocarbons (CFCs) to the poles, especially the Antarctic, resulting in the depletion of the ozone layer. This is another example of scientific research with global implications being conducted at the poles.

Nordenskiöld's relationship with climate change is more complex than this suggests, however, as coal dust deposits themselves are not an acknowledged mechanism of large-scale climate change. However, their discovery does illustrate the dramatic effect of fossil fuels on polar ecosystems and the globalised nature of climate; an important component in our understanding of the potentially catastrophic consequences climate change could have for both poles.

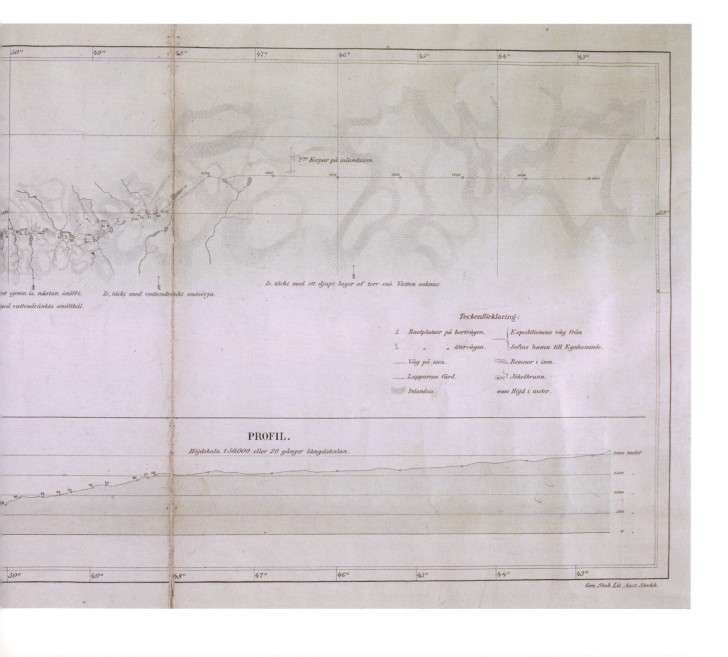

ZOOLOGY AND CONSERVATION

The role of zoology in the history of exploration can be traced in a number of parts of this book, not least its intersection with commercialised hunting, as in William Scoresby's *An account of the Arctic Regions* (see pp. 102–5). Scoresby's account reminds us that, incongruous as it may seem, being a whaler and a professional naturalist went hand-in-hand in the early days of the science. For commercial hunters, and whalers in particular, the areas of the Arctic opened up by explorers represented a bonanza of profitable, albeit risky, opportunities to be exploited. Arguments have been made that, in the early years, this human presence, while invasive and destructive, was not on a large enough, or indeed successful enough, commercial scale to catastrophically affect Arctic ecosystems. Whether or not this is true is open to debate, but what is beyond doubt is that the increasing industrialisation of hunting practices that occurred in the nineteenth and twentieth centuries had a catastrophic impact on many Arctic and, later, Antarctic species.

Alexander Mikhailovich Nikolsky was a Russian-Ukrainian zoologist, whose career extended from 1877 to the end of his life in 1942. An expert in reptiles and amphibians, he would become director of herpetology at the zoological museum of the Russian Academy of Sciences, St Petersburg, in 1895 (when he was thirty-seven years old), a position from which he would publish his 1900 work, *Лѣтнія поѣздки натуралиста* (Summer travels of a Naturalist). *Лѣтнія поѣздки натуралиста* focuses on a number of the different landscapes covered by the vast borders of contemporary Russia and a significant amount of the book is dedicated to the shores of the Russian Arctic.

Nikolsky was attracted to these locations by the opportunities provided by the expanding sphere of colonial influence, as was the case for naturalists from other nations, including Charles Darwin. The urge to understand what lay within the geography or influence of the state exerted a powerful pull on naturalists who wished to observe, classify and understand the flora and fauna of new areas. This resulted in publications documenting the wide range of birds, mammals, reptiles, crustaceans and fish to be found in the Arctic, as well as the people and cultures who depended on harvesting them. To a present-day reader, *Лѣтнія поѣздки натуралиста* is also a catalogue of creatures put in danger by these expanding horizons, as fauna such as the common eider duck, various species of whale and even fish have eventually been threatened or made extinct by the opening up of such frontiers.

Books such as *Лѣтнія поѣздки натуралиста* are important cornerstones of international conservation movements. The pressures placed on wildlife populations such as those described were the first warnings that polar environments and ecosystems were not as unyielding to the impact of human commerce and culture as might, at first, be assumed. As a result, these books record what has been lost or placed under threat and act as an impetus to conserve and protect what remains.

95. Птичьи горы.—Тревога.

NAVIGATING THE NORTHWEST PASSAGE

In the end, the Northwest Passage would not be navigated fully by a member of the British Navy or even a Canadian overland explorer, but by the Norwegian Roald Amundsen. From an early age, Amundsen had set himself the goal of becoming the pre-eminent polar explorer of his generation, a goal from which he would not be dissuaded despite disastrous early endeavours and continual financial problems; such as the debts that almost saw his ship, the *Gjøa*, seized before his Northwest Passage expedition left port. Amundsen learnt quickly how to approach polar exploration, not least by listening to the advice of his mentor, Fridtjof Nansen, who was chief scientist on the first expedition to the North Pole (see below)

Amundsen's approach could not have been more different from that of the naval explorers who had sought the passage before him. He was instead inspired by men like John Rae, and his use of Inuit and First Nations people's approaches to travelling over snow and ice. Early on, Amundsen realised that travelling light, with a small team and, crucially, in a small craft was the best way to approach the Passage. An early twentieth-century illustration of Amundsen's *Gjøa* shows that the ship did not have the same proportions as HMS *Erebus* or *Terror* or the many other Arctic exploration ships before it – It was small, with limited space for provisions and a shallow draught. The crew had to be resourceful and live off the land, as setting off with all the supplies they could possibly need was not an option.

After leaving Oslo in summer 1903, having only narrowly evaded Amundsen's creditors, by September the expedition had reached a location now known as Gjøa Haven, in Nunavut. Here, Amundsen spent the winter in close contact with local Netsilik Inuit, who came to trade. Learning how to live by hunting on the sea ice and acquiring the equipment, most notably apparel, he would need for later exploration, Amundsen was in awe of how well adapted to their Arctic environment the Inuit were. In a later publication, Amundsen wrote '[The Inuit] could travel easier than we, could find delights where we experienced only suffering … could regale in abundant food where we should starve …The adaptation is perfect.'

Once freed from the ice at Gjøa Haven, Amundsen and his crew managed to negotiate the Northwest Passage, but early contact with another ship, the *Charles Hansson*, meant that he quickly had to forge a path overland to the nearest telegraph station in order to break the news first. Having made the journey, in the end Amundsen broke the news second, which cost him a significant amount in publisher exclusivity rights. However, he had achieved what many before him had not: he had navigated the Passage by ship. A small team, a nimble vessel, the right equipment and an ability to think creatively had proven to be the key requirements, and it would not be the last time the British way of going about polar exploration would lose out to Amundsen. Perhaps more importantly, Amundsen had internationalised the story of Arctic exploration again. Having been, for years, a sphere of British imperial action and North American commerce, the Arctic was opening up to a new generation of explorers, traders and, sadly, fighters, who would engage with the high north in very different ways.

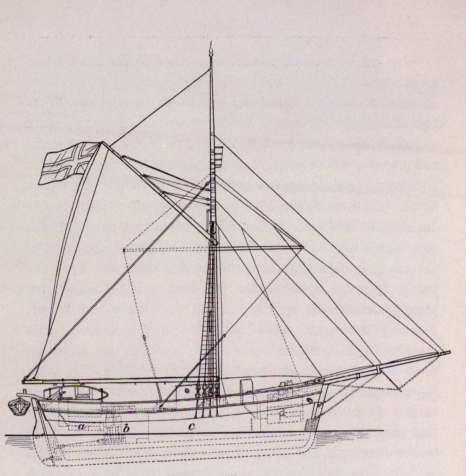

GJØA — 47 R.-TONS.

a. AGTERKAHYT.   c. STORRUM.

b. MOTORRUM.   d. FORKAHYT.

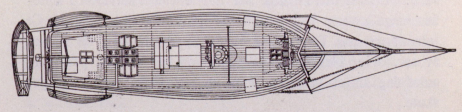

GJØAS DÆK.

A depiction of the vessel *Gjøa* from Roald Amundsen's account, *Nordvest-Passagen. Beretning om Gjøa-ekspeditionen, 1903-1907* (1907).

10460.v.6

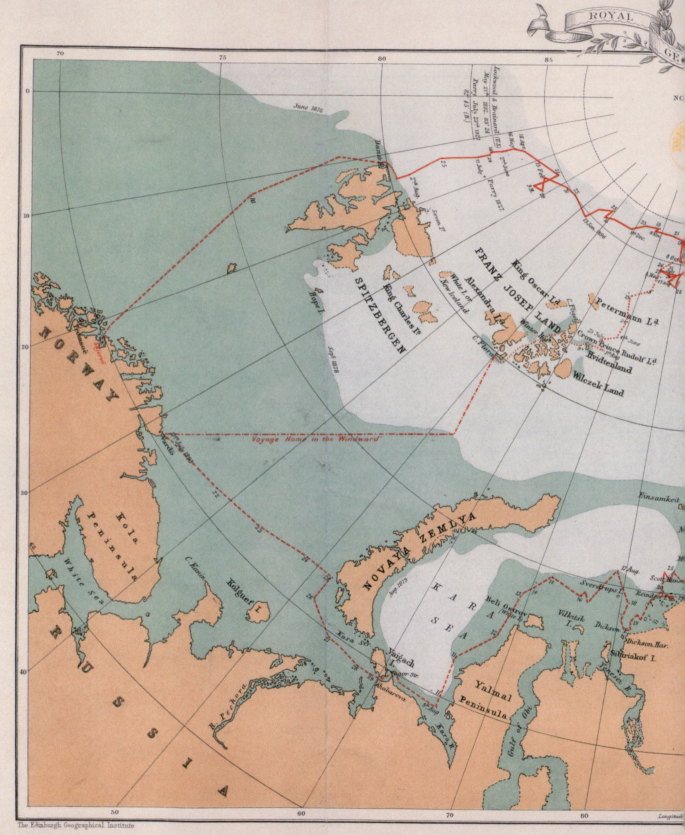

June 1876

Lockwood & Brainard (U.S.)
May 13th 1882, 83° 24'
Parry, July 23rd 1827
83° 45' (B.)

18 Apr.
25 May
16 Apr.
14 Oct. 29
7th Sept.
12 Feb. 24
Parry, 1827
7th Aug.

Duke's B.

FRANZ JOSEF LAND

King Oscar Ld.

Petermann Ld.

C. Fligely
23 July 4 June
Crown Prince Rudolf Ld.
Winter Hut
C. Flora
Hvidtenland
Wilczek Land

SPITZBERGEN

King Charles Is.

White I.
New Iceland
Alexandra Ld.

Hope I.

Sept 1878

NORWAY

Obdorsk

Voyage Home in the "Windward"

Einsamkeit

Kola Peninsula

White Sea

C. Kanin

Kolguev I.

NOVAYA ZEMLYA

Aug 1879

KARA SEA

Sverdrups I.
Scott Han
Reind.
Vilkitski I.
Dickson
Dickson Har.
Beli Ostrov
(White I.)
Sibriakof I.

RUSSIA

R. Pechora

Kara Str.

Vaigach I.
Yugor Str.
Khabarova
Kara R.

Yalmal Peninsula

Gulf of Obi

5 Aug.

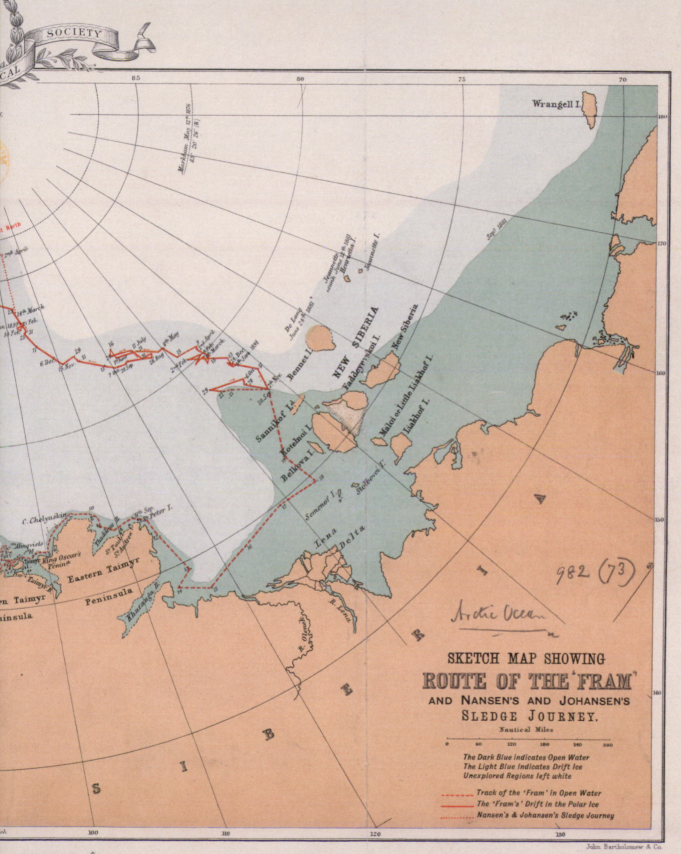

SKETCH MAP SHOWING
ROUTE OF THE 'FRAM'
AND NANSEN'S AND JOHANSEN'S
SLEDGE JOURNEY.

Nautical Miles

The Dark Blue indicates Open Water
The Light Blue indicates Drift Ice
Unexplored Regions left white

Track of the 'Fram' in Open Water
The 'Fram's' Drift in the Polar Ice
Nansen's & Johansen's Sledge Journey

982 (73)

Arctic Ocean

FEBRUARY 1897

John Bartholomew & Co.

The first expedition made by the *Fram* (Forward) to the North Pole had been conducted between 1893 and 1896. Otto Sverdrup was captain of the ship and Fridtjof Nansen chief scientist of the expedition. The expedition was set to take a different route from that attempted by previous teams that had attempted to reach the pole by foot: Nansen and Sverdrup's intention was that the ship should drift to the most northerly part of the world. Nansen was confident that the ice covering the Arctic flowed, driven by currents in the water underneath, and that such movements would eventually carry a ship to the North Pole. The *Fram* had been specially designed to survive becoming wedged in the open ice. Its wide and shallow hull was constructed to float on the deep ice, effectively raising it out of the range of the otherwise huge tensions and pressures below the surface.

A map (shown on pp. 180–81) was produced for Nansen's lecture at the Royal Albert Hall, London, on his return in 1897 and is an illustration of just how popular the adventures of explorers were at the end of the nineteenth century. It shows the route eventually taken by the ship, which, steered by the ocean currents, missed its main goal but proved the theory of Arctic drifting to be sound. Nansen had eventually attempted to reach the pole by sledge but failed in this endeavour too. Heading back, he was picked up by the British explorer Frederick Jackson. The expedition may not have been a complete success but Nansen had developed a technical approach to polar exploration and his work was to be hugely influential on other explorers in the early twentieth century. Most notable among these was Amundsen, who would use the *Fram* during his successful attempt to beat Robert Falcon Scott and his team to the South Pole in 1911. As a result, the *Fram* would reach the furthest north and south of probably any wooden ship.

While the *Fram* linked Nansen and Amundsen's expeditions to the poles, Amundsen would eventually undertake expeditions that would diminish the role of the ship in polar exploration. Despite carrying men on the historic attempt to reach the South Pole, Amundsen did not think ships were the future of polar exploration. By the 1920s, he was convinced that the air was the next frontier of polar exploration, providing a new way of looking at the earth and a new sphere of technical development. For Amundsen and others, who might prove that an airship, whether aeroplane or zeppelin, was capable of flying to and over the North Pole, it was not just fame that awaited but potentially lucrative market opportunities.

If the aim of reaching and flying over the pole could be achieved, a new route of transit could be opened up. Mail, messages and, one day, items for trade, could be flown over the Arctic, the shortest distance between Eurasia and North America, providing some semblance of the trade route sought since the days of the Cabot family, Francis Drake and Martin Frobisher. The Arctic would then fulfil its promise, albeit by air as opposed to sea. In the end, Amundsen proved this was possible, taking the airship *Norge* from Europe to Alaska and, in spite of a bumpy landing, marking a transition from the age of the ship to that of transport through the air.

THREE

THE
ARCTIC
AND
THE
MODERN
WORLD

After centuries of attempts, the Arctic was finally beginning to yield viable trade routes, albeit by air rather than the Northwest Passage. This did not mean the era of exploration was over, however. Nationalist ambitions remained to be realised, personal glory still tempted, Arctic sea routes retained a perilous allure and the charting of air routes still required significant and dangerous work before those routes could be made viable. The air may have opened up and Northwest Passage been navigated but the story was still evolving.

In fact, the twentieth and twenty-first centuries would see the pressures that drove those from southerly latitudes north continuing to increase. Arctic resources, not least oil, would become increasingly tempting, climate change reopened the door to Arctic sea travel and global political pressure continued to grow in the age of Cold War and Intercontinental Ballistic Missiles (ICBMs). The Arctic also held an enduring allure for artists, not least those wielding photographic equipment, and inspired writers on myriad subjects, catering to audiences still eager to consume news, ideas and fantasies about the Arctic.

Despite centuries of contact with indigenous peoples, many continued to think of the Arctic as a blank space. However, centuries of interaction had in fact changed the world for Arctic indigenous communities, tying them into a system of global economic and cultural exchange, not to mention the circulation of virulent diseases. In short, our contemporary interaction with the Northwest Passage and the Arctic at large is still informed by desires and activities that have their roots in the days of the silk roads.

Photographs from
William Bradford's
The Arctic Regions (1873).
1785.d.7

NEW ROUTES

The development of aerial travel, and the 'air mindedness' that gripped Europe and the U.S. in the early twentieth century, meant the Arctic would, eventually, be looked to as a source of new, quick air routes over the northern hemisphere. Roald Amundsen had actively participated in the early stages of this fascinating advance and provided proof that the route could be navigated with his reasonably successful flight of the airship *Norge* from Europe to Alaska, via the Arctic, in 1926.

By the 1930s, the aeroplane was becoming an increasingly prevalent means of travel, and aircraft manufacturers and aviators began to seriously consider crossing the northern hemisphere via the Arctic. Any travellers who tune into their 'moving map' on a long-haul flight will know that, on account of the curvature of the earth, the quickest way from point A to point B in intercontinental transit is not necessarily a 'straight line'. For example, the quickest way from London to Vancouver is not to fly, as a map might suggest, across the Atlantic – over Toronto, Winnipeg and so on until you reach British Columbia – but instead to fly up to the Arctic Circle, over Greenland and down via Canada's northern territories.

However, in the early twentieth century, no one knew how the journey would affect aviation technology; there was a lack of information about, for example, temperature minima and maxima and wind speed. Knowledge of Arctic areas, in particular Greenland, was also insufficient to allow accurate charts to be drawn up in order for pilots to orientate themselves. As a result, the British Arctic Air Route Expedition of 1930–31 was proposed in order to chart a possible route over Greenland and suggest the feasibility of such an aerial feat. A small team, sponsored by the Royal Geographical Society (RGS), would attempt to catalogue data about Greenland's coast and plateau, map it using aerial photography, and collect supplementary data regarding ornithology and geology from three camps, including that of Ice Cap Station, at the highest point of the route.

The account of the expedition, published in 1932, is heavily influenced by the style and tone of those accompanying previous British polar explorations, especially those sponsored by the RGS, such as Robert Falcon Scott's Antarctic expeditions of the 1910s. Organisation is stringently detailed and the writing conveys a strong sense of the expedition's 'stiff upper lip'. In late 1930, one Augustine Courtauld was trapped, alone, at Ice Cap Station with diminishing supplies – evidence of the most serious danger facing the expedition. Courtauld was, after some errors, eventually relieved, apparently as his food and fuel were about to run out, but the author recounts that the rescue team paused to 'record the site of the camp' in photographs before rescuing him. This suggests that any sense of danger and drama had, by this point, long left the minds of Courtauld's colleagues. These camp photographs and others from Courtauld's rescue are included alongside text in the 1932 publication.

Through the work of the British Arctic Air Route Expedition, the Arctic was opened up to different types to travel and, latterly, exploitation, as advancing technology made new routes and forms of communication possible. The result was that the Arctic was placed under greater threat but also became more visible to an increasingly wide and informed public.

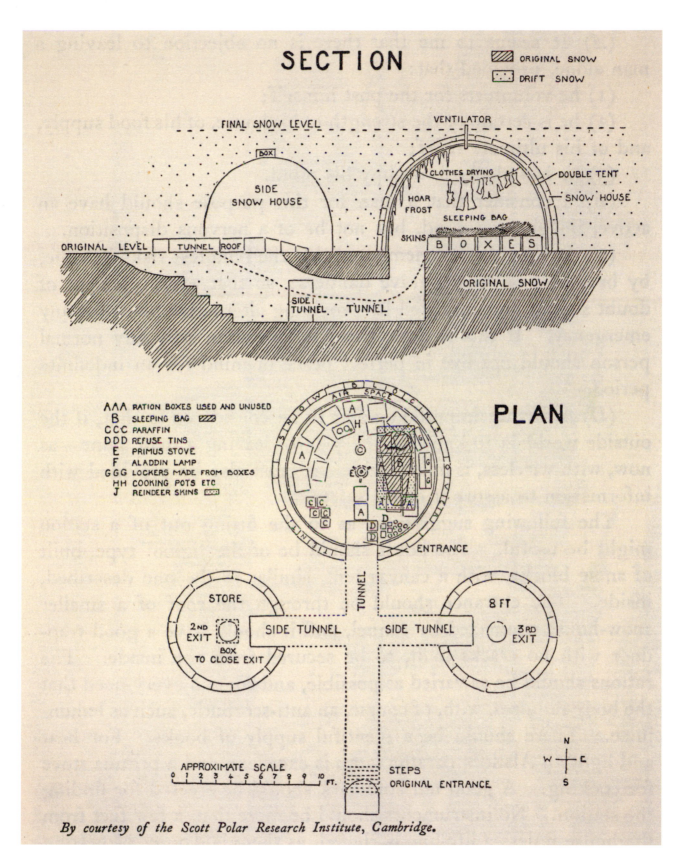

SECTION

ORIGINAL SNOW
DRIFT SNOW

FINAL SNOW LEVEL

VENTILATOR

BOX

SIDE
SNOW HOUSE

CLOTHES DRYING

HOAR
FROST

SLEEPING BAG

DOUBLE TENT

SNOW HOUSE

ORIGINAL LEVEL

TUNNEL ROOF

SKINS

B O X E S

SIDE
TUNNEL   TUNNEL

ORIGINAL SNOW

PLAN

AAA RATION BOXES USED AND UNUSED
B   SLEEPING BAG
CCC PARAFFIN
DDD REFUSE TINS
E   PRIMUS STOVE
F   ALADDIN LAMP
GGG LOCKERS MADE FROM BOXES
HH COOKING POTS ETC
J   REINDEER SKINS

SNOW BLOCK AIR SPACE

ENTRANCE

STORE

2ND
EXIT

BOX
TO CLOSE EXIT

SIDE TUNNEL

TUNNEL

SIDE TUNNEL

8 FT

3RD
EXIT

APPROXIMATE SCALE
0 1 2 3 4 5 6 7 8 9 10 FT.

STEPS
ORIGINAL ENTRANCE

N
W   E
S

By courtesy of the Scott Polar Research Institute, Cambridge.

An illustration of the quarters from which
Courtauld was rescued. Included in Chapman's
account of the expedition, *Northern Lights:
the Official Account of the British Arctic
Air-Route Expedition 1930-1931* (1932).
10460.h.26

PLATE XLIV

WATKINS SPEAKING TO COURTAULD THROUGH THE VENTILATOR

PLATE XLV

WATKINS CUTTING THROUGH THE TENT TO REACH COURTAULD

PLATE XLIII

COURTAULD IMMEDIATELY ON HIS RETURN TO THE BASE

PLATE XLVI

COURTAULD EMERGING FROM THE TENT

ROUTES, SCIENCE, COOPERATION

Ships also underwent significant technological changes during the early decades of the twentieth century. The steam revolution championed by the early nineteenth-century British polar explorer John Ross (see p. 127), among others, bore fruit later in the nineteenth century, as the technology's capacities caught up with its promise. By the early twentieth century, Russia, Canada and the U.S. were able to construct massive, ocean-going icebreakers. These ships had a displacement of around 8,000 tonnes and used their modern steam engines and reinforced hulls to break ice and forge new paths.

The establishing of the Soviet regime in Russia saw a renewed enthusiasm for exploring, claiming and exploiting the Arctic environment, now inflected with a communist ideology. The possibility of conquering the Arctic seas and taming the ice represented, as it had for the British Navy's expeditions in the nineteenth century, an expression of power in the region and on the world stage. In this vein, the performance of Soviet technological and scientific expertise in the Arctic Ocean was an opportunity to display the abilities of a young state that had only just extricated itself from civil war and conflict with various international neighbours.

It was in this context that the icebreaker *Georgiy Sedov* set out on a scientific expedition around Russia's Arctic waters. It was 1937 and the *Sedov*'s second major Arctic expedition, after a 1929 journey to Franz Josef Land, north of Russia; the ship attempted to chart a northern sea route across Russia, as many had done before, but became locked fast in the ice. Drifting like Fridtjof Nansen's *Fram* (pp. 180–83), the ship became the first floating Arctic science station, and the crew and scientists on board were themselves tested. For over 800 days, the ship was trapped in ice – sometimes accompanied by other ships, such as the icebreaker *Malygin* – taking astrological, meteorological and geomagnetic readings over a long period of time. The ship was freed in 1940 by the largest Soviet icebreaker of the time, *I. Stalin*.

The published account of the expedition is very much a statement about Soviet achievement and makes liberal use of the iconography of the state, including the colour red and an imposing portrait of Stalin. Like the mission itself, the book is a performance of power, illustrating the Soviet Union's achievements and prowess in the Arctic – a theme that would continue through the twentieth and twenty-first centuries. Despite this and the other achievements of the *Sedov* and *Malygin* and their crews – including the first Arctic meeting with a dirigible aircraft, the *Graf Zeppelin* – the explorers returned to a state soon to be at war and which became increasingly paranoid. Many of the scientists celebrated as heroes in this book would later be sent to the Arctic gulags as victims of Joseph Stalin's purges.

ДВАДЦАТЬ СЕМЬ
МЕСЯЦЕВ
НА ДРЕЙФУЮЩЕМ
КОРАБЛЕ
«Георгий Седов»

Издательство Главсевморпути
Москва — Ленинград
1940

«Седов» во льдах (март 1938 г.)

Title page and photograph of
the Sedov locked in the ice,
from *Dvadtsat' sem' mesiatsev
na dreifuiushchem korable
'Georgii Sedov'* (Twenty seven
months on the drifting ship
'Georgii Sedov', 1940)
010460.L.13

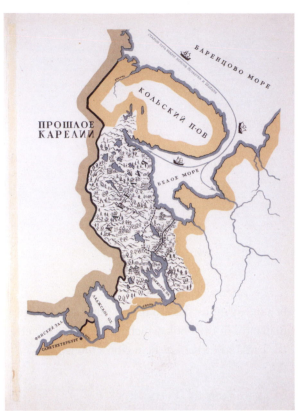

LEFT & BELOW

The White Sea-Baltic Canal area illustrated before and after the canal's construction though the use of a transparent overlay. Not only do factories appear after the construction of the canal but the ships transition from sail to steam. *Belomorsko-Baltiiskii kanal imeni Stalina : istoriia stroitel'stva* (The White sea canal named after Stalin: an account of the construction, 1934)

20087.b.27

OVERLEAF

The suggested effect of the White Sea Canal. *Belomorsko-Baltiiskii kanal imeni Stalina : istoriia stroitel'stva* (1934).

20087.b.27

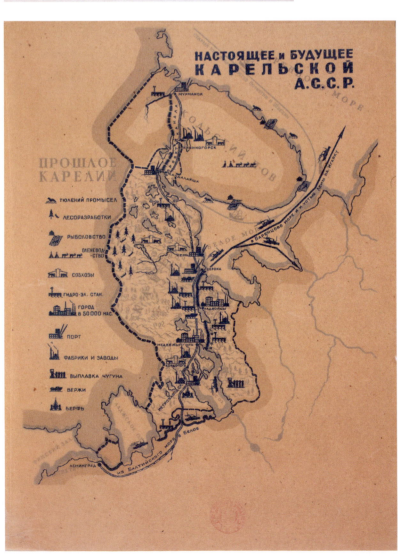

REMOULDING THE LANDSCAPE

Constructed in less than two years and opened in 1933, the White Sea–Baltic Canal in the northwestern corner of Russia was a monumental feat of Soviet engineering and state cruelty. It attempted to connect Russia's northwestern Arctic regions, and the rest of its Arctic hinterland, to the state's industrial hubs via Leningrad (now St Petersburg). The canal is another example of Soviet attempts to illustrate strength and industrial might by modifying the Arctic landscape and shows a continuation of the desire to bend Arctic trade routes to the will of a state – even where that meant the use of brute force, prison labour and a huge volume of explosives.

The construction of the canal relied on the forced labour of prisoners who dug through the granite strata and canalised rivers and three lakes separating the White Sea from the Baltic Sea to create a waterway some 230 kilometres in length. The work of these labourers (and even the canal designers, who were imprisoned while working on the canal) was used to serve a narrative of 'redemption through labour', whereby the Stalinist regime intended to illustrate that character could be reformed through manual work and physical endurance, building individuals fit to live in and contribute to the Soviet Union.

Maxim Gorky was tasked with the creation of a collaborative publication detailing the achievements of the project. Resulting from a tour for over 100 artists and writers, who travelled down the canal as it neared completion, the book is a lavish production complete with photographs and maps, mostly in an avant-garde and dramatic Soviet style. A map shown early in the book sets out the role of the canal in uniting the Soviet Union with its Arctic regions, so that Arctic shipping would no longer have to be directed around enemy capitalist states to gain access to Leningrad. The canal formed the core of an interconnected Arctic network and the heart of a newly industrialised region (illustrated by a map later in the book, which imagines the effect the canal will have on the region's industrial potential).

Arctic imagery and rhetoric ran through all levels of the project. Not only was the public-facing side of the endeavour focused on Arctic connections, but the prison labourers involved in construction were embedded in a narrative whereby the cold symbolised their incarceration. This is best summed up by a piece of worker propaganda associated with the project that reads 'Canal Army Soldier! The heat of your work will melt your prison term.' This rhetoric reinforces the idea that coldness was synonymous with incarceration in pre-revolution Russia and the Soviet Union continued this association. The Arctic had long been used as a space of imprisonment and exile and Stalin's regime embraced this use of the Arctic to terrible effect.

The idealised map of the function of the White Sea–Baltic Canal illustrates that this huge undertaking was just one in a series of attempts to turn the Arctic and a possible Northeast Passage to Russia's advantage. Yet the failure of ships such as the *Sedov* to chart this route reminds us, once again, of the folly of attempting to tame the Arctic through human endeavour and technology. While the canal stood as testament to Russian engineering achievement and was of use in connecting the industrial heartlands to Russia's northwestern Arctic regions, it never reached its full potential. The dream of a productive Arctic coast and shipping route was still some way off.

КАРТА

ИЗ ЛЕНИНГРАДА ЕДУТ В ОБХОД СКАНДИНАВИИ.
НАША СТРАНА ТЕРЯЕТ МНОГО ВРЕМЕНИ И ДЕНЕГ.

ЛЕНИНГРАД

ПОВЕНЕЦ   АРХАНГЕЛЬСК

ПУТЬ К УСТЬЯМ ОБИ И ЕНИСЕЯ ОСВОЕН.

ПАРОХОД С ГРУЗОМ ДОШЕЛ
ДО ПОВЕНЦА. ДАЛЬШЕ НЕПРО-
ХОДИМЫЙ ЛЕС.

КАРАВАНЫ ИНОСТРАННЫХ СУДОВ
ЗА ЛЕСОМ. ВЗАМЕН ПРИВОЗЯТ МА...

В МОСКВЕ: ЦК ПО ДОКЛАДУ ТОВ
КАГАНОВИЧА ВЫНЕС РЕШЕНИЕ:
"РАЗРЕШИТЬ ЗАДАЧУ ОБВОДНЕНИЯ
МОСКВА — РЕКИ ПУТЕМ СОЕДИНЕНИЯ
С ВЕРХОВЬЯМИ ВОЛГИ"

ТЕ ТРАКТОРЫ, О КОТОРЫХ ГОВОРИЛ ЛЕНИН
ПРИШЛИ НА ПОЛЯ. КУЛАК ЛЕДЕРКИН В ЯРОСТИ
ПОДЖИГАЕТ ЗДАНИЕ КЛУБА.

ЖЕЛЕЗО

МАГНИТОСТРОЙ   ЖЕЛЕЗН. РУДА

СТАЛИНГРАДСКИЙ
ТРАКТОРНЫЙ ЗАВОД
ОКОНЧЕН.

УГОЛЬ

КУЗБАСС

БАТУМ

НЕФТЬ

ИЗ БАКУ В БАТУМ ПРОВЕДЕНЫ ТРУБЫ.
ПО НИМ ПЕРЕКАЧИВАЕТСЯ НЕФТЬ.

БАКУ

ПУСТЫНИ ОРОШАЮТСЯ. ВСЮДУ ПРО-
РОЮТ КАНАЛЫ. В КНИГЕ ВЫ ПРО-
ЧТЕТЕ О ВРЕДИТЕЛЬСКОМ ДЕЛЕ
ИРРИГАТОРОВ, РАСКРЫТОМ ЗДЕСЬ.

СИБИРЬ И ТУРКЕСТАН СОЕДИНЕНЫ.
ТЕПЕРЬ НУЖНО СВЯЗАТЬ ОТДЕЛЬНЫЕ
ПРОМЫШЛЕННЫЕ РАЙОНЫ.

ДЕХКАНЕ СЕЮТ ХЛОПОК.
ИДЕТ ВСПАШКА НОВЫХ
ЗЕМЕЛЬ.

ДОКОЛЫ ДЕЛАЮТ ЭТО МОРЕ СУДОХОДНЫМ.

ЗДЕСЬ УСТРОЕНЫ
ОЛЕНЕВОДЧЕСКИЕ КОЛХОЗЫ.

А ЗДЕСЬ В ХРЕБТАХ ЕСТЬ УГОЛЬ, ЗОЛОТО И МЕДЬ.

ОКАЗЫВАЕТСЯ
ЗДЕСЬ МОЖЕТ РАСТИ ПШЕНИЦА.

СССР В 1931 г.

САХАЛИН

ЭТОТ РЕЙД С МОРЯ
ПОХОЖ НА БАКУ.
НА САХАЛИН В ЭТОМ
ГОДУ ПРИЕХАЛИ
21000 РАБОЧИХ.

ОНА НЕ ПОХОЖА НА СТАРЫЕ КАРТЫ.
ПЯТИЛЕТКА В ДЕЙСТВИИ.
БЕЗРАБОТИЦА УНИЧТОЖЕНА. ВСЕМ
НАШЛОСЬ СТОЛЬКО РАБОТЫ, ЧТО
160 МИЛЛИОНОВ ЛЮДЕЙ НЕХВАТАЕТ.
ЗДЕСЬ НЕ ОТМЕЧЕНЫ СОТНИ ГРОМАД-
НЫХ СТРОИТЕЛЬСТВ — НА КАРТЕ ДЛЯ
ВСЕХ СТРОЕК НЕХВАТИЛО БЫ МЕСТА.

THE GROWING STATE

Expansion into the Arctic was nothing new in the twentieth century: Russia had expanded massively into the European and North American Arctic up until the mid-nineteenth century. The Alaska Purchase of 1867, however, marked this land's formal arrival as a new Arctic state under the control of the U.S. Britain, meanwhile, had more of an informal northern presence in the North American territories. This was through the activities of the Hudson's Bay and North West Companies, but the period following Canada's confederation (also in 1867), and especially the early twentieth century, saw a determined expansion of the new Canadian state into what would become the Canadian Arctic. Previous to this, Canada had been a dependent territory administered locally but with a government structure still beholden to the Palace of Westminster in London. It was in July 1867 that the region was organised into a semi-autonomous state known as the Dominion of Canada, originally comprising New Brunswick, Nova Scotia, Ontario and Quebec but gradually expanding to form the nation we recognise today. Once the process of confederating the lower parts of Canada was complete, the work of affirming Canada's Arctic sovereignty began.

The contemporary reasons for this were multiple, but prevailing concerns were the U.S. Arctic expansion, the unrestricted operation of whalers and a desire to further understand Canada's Arctic territory. Indeed, some of these were compound issues: the independence of American whalers, who ran some areas of the Arctic nominally claimed by Canada and the British Empire as their own independent centres of trade, could conceivably be used to develop an American claim to this territory. The Canadian government therefore wanted to exert control over this space.

To do this, Canada sent an expedition to Fullerton Bay and Churchill in 1903, led by the North West Mounted Police (NWMP). The mission had multiple aims: to 'show the flag' to local Inuit and whalers, to document social and medical conditions around various whaling stations and Inuit camps, to establish NWMP barracks and, perhaps most importantly, to document the process through photography. By doing so, the Canadian government hoped to extend the control mechanisms of the state northwards, and document them in tangible ways that could be used as evidence against possible territorial claims by other states. Such activities, as well as cairns built by previous British Arctic expeditions, still form a core part of Canada's Arctic sovereignty claims to this day.

Group of Esquimaux Women and Children
Fullerton 1906.

Of particular note among the characters employed in this expedition is Captain J. D. Moodie, whose wife, Geraldine, was a photographer well known for her portraits of First Nations culture in Canada's southern provinces. She visited her husband during his tenure as leader of the Canadian government's Arctic mission, becoming one of the few white women of this period to see the Canadian Arctic first hand. Most importantly, Geraldine Moodie took her camera.

Moodie's camera, like that of her husband and his fellow expedition member, A. P. Low, concentrated on the work of the mission and the people with whom it came into contact. Significantly, however, Moodie's work – made from a personal photographic studio constructed to give her a private space away from the men of the mission – provides a different perspective on the people encountered. Whereas the photographs of J. D. Moodie and Low depict people as subjects of the state's gaze, photographed for classification or the diagnosis of medical ailments, Geraldine Moodie produced portraits. Individuals and their unique stance and garb are shown, emphasising that these are people from a distinct culture and not simply anonymous subjects of the state's attention.

One of the few Arctic photographs taken by Moodie outside of a studio, 'Group of Esquimaux Women, Fullerton, 1906'.
HS85/10/18546

RELIGION AND
PRINT CULTURE

Missionary activity has had a huge role to play in the development of North America and its impact was also felt in the Arctic, as connections were made between colonial settlers and indigenous peoples. Soon after the sixteenth-century French explorer Jacques Cartier, and his later equivalent Samuel de Champlain, initiated French efforts to colonise and capitalise the area now known as Quebec, they were followed by missionaries, predominantly Jesuits, who sought to convert the local First Nations groups to Christianity. The British, Dutch and Spanish were also involved in missionary activity throughout the Americas.

Much late-twentieth-century writing about missionary activity in the Americas has focused on the negative impact of western religion on First Nations culture. The erosion or forced destruction of indigenous culture and religious practices, the role of religion in building western colonial hegemony in North America, and the involvement of religious orders in the abusive practices of institutions such as residential schools are all important elements of this history that need to be understood in the twenty-first century. There were, however, other roles undertaken by religious orders or individuals that need our attention and complicate any understanding of the action of Christian religion in the Americas as being uniformly negative.

The role of missionaries in the Arctic is no exception in either regard. The relationship between missionary culture, religious practice and the state in the Arctic is no less problematic than it was in the rest of the Americas, especially as regards residential schools and the removal of Inuit children from their families and cultural groups, but there are also positive consequences, not least in the area of print culture. In Europe, the relationship between Christianity (especially Protestantism) and print is long established, and this culture of printing and reading was often exported to the colonised world. The challenge

missionaries faced, from the time of de Champlain up until the twentieth century, was how to convey religious teaching in textual form to cultures with no standardised form of written communication, especially if that form of communication had been lost due to the homogenising effect of contact with colonial settlers and governments.

Missionary societies, then, dedicated time to the development of syllabic languages, which could be printed and distributed on a large scale to communities speaking the language, aiding missionaries in their work to communicate with and convert peoples spread across vast geographical distances. This work was carried out in colonial centres such as London and led to the creation of many instructional and devotional texts in the form of small, portable, syllabic books. The British Library in London has the largest collection of North American syllabic religious works in the world.

Whatever your stance on these matters – the attempts at conversion and the effect these sometimes (certainly not universally) had on indigenous Inuit culture – it is clear that such investment in written language has had important consequences for contemporary Inuit society. As discussed in this book's first chapter, in relation to *Kaládlit Okalluktualliait* (Greenland Legends, 1859–63, see pp. 14–19), the consequences of missionary teaching for Inuit artists, writers and communicators should not be underestimated. *Kaládlit Okalluktualliait* and other similar projects sowed the seeds for today's burgeoning art-print industry. Contemporary Nunavut is a dual-language society with all official and political notices being communicated in written, syllabic Inuktitut and other regional languages, and the base for this written language is the syllabic structure developed for missionary use. In short, missionary work, while it hindered Inuit culture, also supplied the tools for it to develop and thrive in the twentieth century.

Syllabarium.

	ā	e	o	u
	▽	△	▷	◁
p	∨	∧	>	<
t	∪	∩		
k				
g				
m				
n				
s				
l				
y				
v				
r				

A Magnificent Trophy

THE NEW NORTH

*Being Some Account of a Woman's
Journey through Canada
to the Arctic*

BY

AGNES DEANS CAMERON

*WITH MANY ILLUSTRATIONS FROM PHOTOGRAPHS
BY THE AUTHOR*

NEW YORK AND LONDON
D. APPLETON AND COMPANY
1910

Title page and photographs, including the
playing of 'Farthest North Football' from
Agnes Cameron's, *The New North* (1905).
010470.ee.18

Farthest North Football

We Tell the Tale of a Whale

The First Type-writer on Great Slave Lake

The end of the nineteenth and beginning of the twentieth centuries saw a notable increase in the number of people who chose to travel around the globe for little more than amusement and intellectual stimulation. Arctic tourists predate this trend – indeed, artists such as the American painter William Bradford (see pp. 166–9) were often seen as this kind of traveller – but, from the late nineteenth century onwards, the globalisation of a world of empires and the increased capacities of transport, and aerial transport in particular, opened up ever more opportunities to travel to the Arctic out of curiosity. This, in turn, changed the kinds of people who could visit the Arctic, allowing it to become, not solely the preserve of male explorers and agents of the state but increasingly accessible to female travellers. Some, such as Geraldine Moodie, came to the Arctic because of family connections whereas others, such as Agnes Deans Cameron, journeyed there out of a more general impulse to travel.

Although there were many earlier travellers, the timing of Cameron's arrival is particularly important. Setting out in the early 1900s, she wished to see and report on a key area of North America, where a wilderness, as she imagined it, was coming into increasing contact with the industrialised society that administered it. As Cameron argued, this contact was central to many of the landscapes that defined the emerging Canadian and North American nations. Travelling north from Chicago to the mouth of the Mackenzie River in Canada, Cameron encountered industrial metropolises, the emergent grain belt and the former lands of the Hudson's Bay Company before arriving at the coast once charted by Franklin and other members of British naval expeditions. Sponsored by the Western Canadian Immigration Association, Cameron was the first woman to undertake a large-scale round trip to the Arctic Ocean.

All of this marks the beginning of an age in which the Arctic, still remote from the urban centres of London, New York and even Ottawa, is increasingly accessible to a wide range of travellers, explorers and prospectors. It also evidences the technological advances of the age: travellers were able to take new, functional products to aid them on their journeys, which in turn became a greater part of the stories being told about the Arctic in published accounts and lectures, 'back home'. Cameron's inventory included comfortable travelling clothes and a portable Kodak camera, which would produce a record of how metropolitan travellers perceived a space increasingly open to personal travel.

What is more, Cameron brought back an account of the Arctic at a very significant point of change. Her 1909 publication is a story of the Canadian state's northerly expansion, in which whalers still work the shores and Inuit groups are enmeshed in the economies and cultures of whaling and sealing. Cameron's photographs capture this hybridisation, as portrayed by her images of Inuit children playing 'farthest north football' in the Arctic summer.

AN ANTIDOTE TO MODERN LIFE

Another enthusiastic traveller, though working some years later, was Rockwell Kent. He led a diverse professional life – at different times an architect, dairy farmer, left-wing political activist and writer – but is perhaps best known for his work as an illustrator. He produced a best-selling illustrated edition of Herman Melville's *Moby-Dick* (1930), as well as notable versions of Casanova's memoirs (1908) and Geoffrey Chaucer's *Canterbury Tales* (1930). He also proved to have a taste for the Arctic, its landscape and the peoples living there. This resulted in two of Kent's written works, the more notable of which is an account of his 1931–2 winter trip to Greenland called *Salamina* (1935), which he also illustrated.

Salamina – Kent's *kifak* (housekeeper) during his time in a small hut on the island of Illorsuit, off the west coast of Greenland – is the central character of this book, which is effectively a series of vignettes depicting Kent's experiences and encounters there. The account covers not just Kent's experiences but the habits, culture, life and loves of the Inuit and Danish inhabitants of the area, all framed by the text and, later, illustrations the author composed. Kent's illustrations are unique: they bear the abstraction of Inuit woodblock- and screen-printing while also, perhaps, reflecting some of the aesthetic of socialist movements seen in the Soviet Union and industrial areas of Europe and North America.

Of all these illustrations, however, the map at the front of Kent's book deserves the most attention. It pokes fun at previous explorers' habit of inscribing the names of expedition sponsors onto the landscape: '[I]est the backers of the expedition be disappointed with its results it must be explained that some-one, unfortunately, had already given names – and what names! – to the larger bodies of land and water.' A short blurb then proposes that, in a following expedition, 'it would be advancing the glory of America to write [the sponsors'] names upon the map – even if we have to scratch out the old ones.' Across the map the viewer can then see some incongruous names, such as 'Pan-American Airways Corp. Ice Cap' and 'General Electric Co. Ice Cap'.

In this map, Kent is satirising the previous history – British, Russian, French, Dutch and North American – of writing Inuit and other Arctic cultures off the landscape only to re-inscribe it with the dull, useless nomenclature of Western backers and businesses. This humorous ploy, which perhaps possesses a biting edge, was no doubt driven by Kent's feelings about Greenland, the Arctic more generally, and their relationship to capitalist society. Written in the mid-1930s during America's recovery from the Great Depression, Kent's introduction reflects on his feeling, in relation to Greenland at least, that a move back to a de-industrialised nation more in touch with its environment would be welcome.

Put another way, Kent sees Greenland and the Arctic as a soothing antithesis to North American – and, more generally, Western – industrial and consumer culture. Most importantly, he feels that these landscapes, and their peoples and culture, should be protected from the rapacious desires of the West in order that some of their pre-industrial 'innocence' (although Kent does not use the word) should be preserved, perhaps showing the error of Western ways. Kent's is a lone voice in the context of the looming global conflicts that would shortly arrive – the Second World War and the Cold War – during which the Arctic and its peoples would increasingly be used in the posturing of the world's great powers. He also provides a narrative framework and evocative set of terms for the works of future travellers to the Arctic and other remote spaces – one that is still in use and popular today.

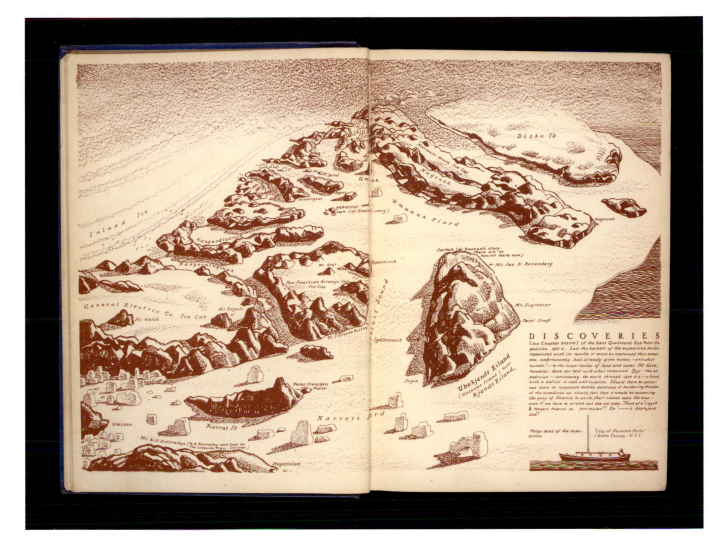

A map of 'discoveries' and their new names,
such as 'General Electric Motors Ice Cap',
from Rockwell Kent's *Salamina* (1935).

This is Salamina — apparently hanging out nothing but a clothes pin. If I had given her wash it would have covered up her hands. She always tried to cover them, for they were working hands. This book permits of no concealment.

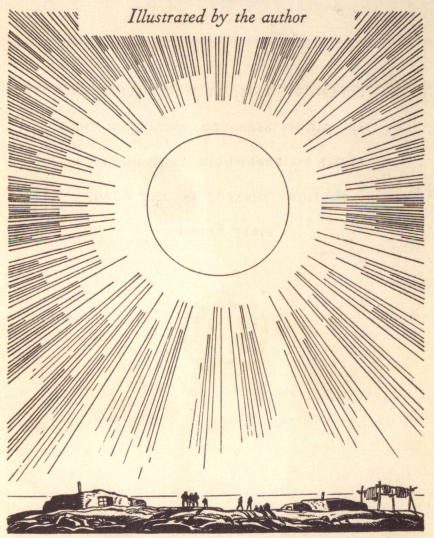

SALAMINA

BY ROCKWELL KENT

Illustrated by the author

HARCOURT, BRACE AND COMPANY
New York, 1935

THE NORTHWEST PASSAGE
IN A GLOBAL WAR

Photographs from Larsen's official
account, *The North-West Passage,
1940-42 and 1944* (1952).
C.S.E. 63/12

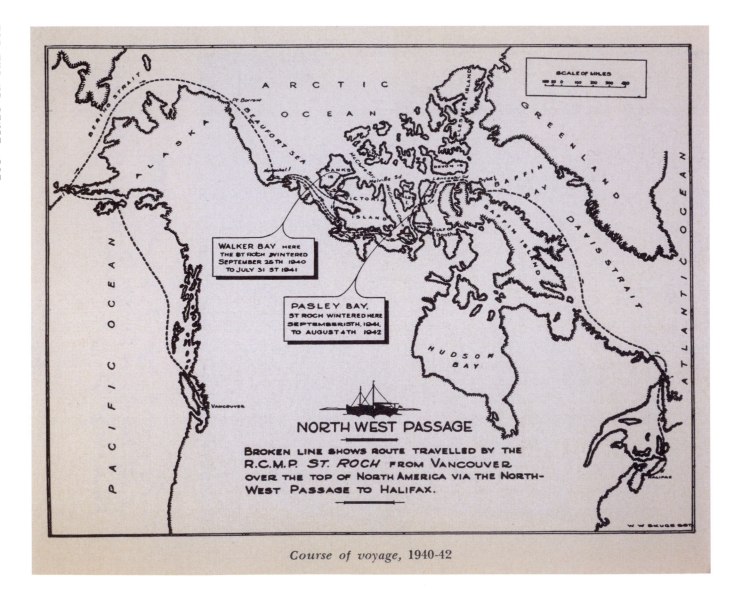

Course of voyage, 1940-42

Taking on fresh water from pools on the ice.

Progress stopped, September, 1944. In McClure Strait.

Arctic trade routes thus far had proved to be a failure even as an expression of British naval power, with lost ships, men and supplies littering the territory by the end of the nineteenth century. Despite this, Arctic trade routes did have a role to play in the Second World War. Of most note were the Arctic convoys that ran from North America, Iceland and Britain to the Soviet Union, predominantly to the ports of Arkhangelsk and Murmansk, between August 1941 and May 1945, carrying supplies, arms and even tanks. These convoys risked the ice, freezing temperatures and appalling weather, and also ran the gauntlet of formidable Nazi forces operating out of occupied Norway. The route itself was not on the scale of the great passages dreamt of by earlier explorers, but it did resemble those established by the Muscovy Company in the sixteenth century (see pp. 30–31) and thus shows the way in which European and North American uses of Arctic routes continued to evolve in the face of financial, political and military requirements.

This was not the only Arctic route in use at this time. Perhaps surprisingly, there were attempts to reinvigorate the Northwest Passage as a communication link in the theatre of war. Amundsen's voyage at the beginning of the century (see p. 178) had proven that navigation of the passage was possible and, when German U-boats threatened Atlantic shipping and, after the invasion and annexation of Denmark, there seemed a potential risk of Germany occupying Greenland, options were explored to see if a counter-occupation of this strategic location would be feasible. The British Arctic Air Route Expedition had already shown that Greenland was invaluable in terms of controlling air transit and, therefore, Atlantic sea passages. As a result, any possible control that could be gained there, even using the capricious Northwest Passage, had to be attempted. Furthermore, Greenland's coast contained a number of harbours potentially useful to submarines, as well as an operable mine for cryolite (a mineral used in the production of aluminium).

It was in this context that the fortified schooner St Roch, captained by Royal Canadian Mounted Police (formerly the NWMP) Sergeant Henry A. Larsen, was the first ship to sail the Northwest Passage from west to east, taking over two years to trace, in reverse, a route similar to that taken by Amundsen and his crew in the Gjøa. After the war, Larsen insisted that his journey, which also saw him return through the passage, was about enforcing sovereignty in the Arctic, but in reality he had been sent to scout a route with a view to establishing an occupation of Greenland. Once again, the plan was scotched by uncooperative ice in the Passage, and also by the actions of the U.S., which objected to any Canadian occupation in the area. Both the Arctic convoys and the St. Roch expedition illustrate that, even in the twentieth century, Arctic transit routes were desirable, unreliable and an important part of politics – and wars – originating further south.

Canada
Department of Mines and Resources
SURVEYS AND ENGINEERING BRANCH
HYDROGRAPHIC AND MAP SERVICE

NORTHWEST TERRITORIES
AND
YUKON

Scale 80 miles to 1 inch or 1:5,068,800

50   0   50   100   150   200   250

Datum is mean sea level.

1939

Reference

Railway	Wireless Station
Road	Seaplane Anchorage
Trading Post	Hospital
Post Office	School
Height in feet	Industrial Home
R.C.M.P. Post	Boundary of Arctic Islands Preserve - revised 1945

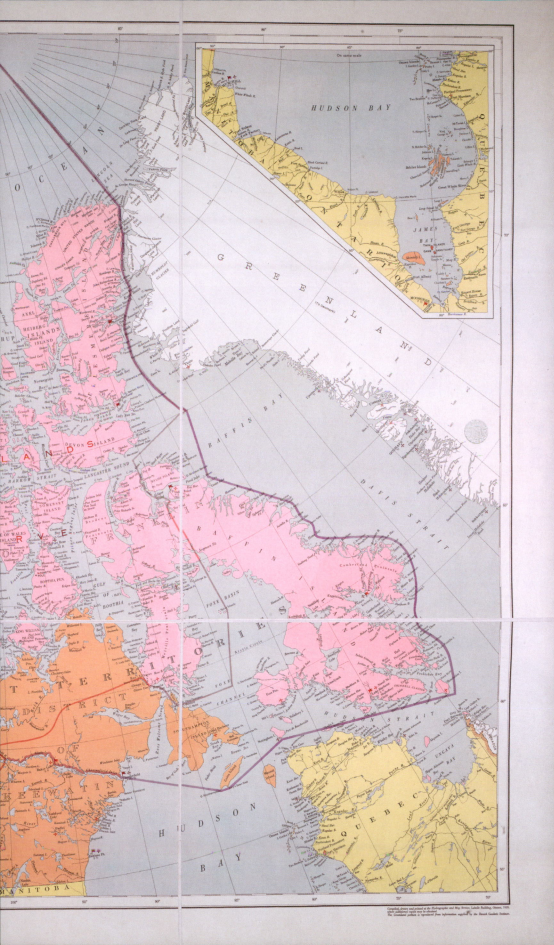

The Canadian use of the Sector Theory displayed in an official chart, *Northwest Territories and Yukon. Scale, 80 m to 1 inch* (1948). Maps 70420 (38),

THE GEOMETRY
OF STATECRAFT

Contemporary Canada's efforts at enforcing its presence in the Arctic are remarkably similar to those undertaken by J. D. Moodie: touring the land, 'showing the flag' and undertaking research. However, in the sphere of international politics – even in the case of Russia's dramatic twenty-first-century activities in the Arctic Ocean – occupation and flag-planting will only get you so far. Sovereignty is also subject to the parameters of the international community.

The international Law of the Sea, various Arctic conventions and ideas such as Sector theory are important elements in this international system of conventions. Sector theory is the principle of territorial demarcation based on the earth's parallels and meridians and it became most closely aligned, in the early twentieth century, with the Canadian government's attempts to articulate its complex northern coastline for administration and mineral-extraction purposes. The theory and its application provide a more scientific and rational perspective on territorial demarcation in the Arctic, where lines of influence are often permeable.

While Sector theory may provide a rational end result, however, it is still based on the previous work of explorers. The start and end points of the sector lines are claimed as Canadian territory because of information that is contained in British exploratory accounts, embodied in the cairns left behind and evidenced by other points of notice constructed by expeditions passing through the Arctic archipelago. In short, the continuing influence of historical explorers on contemporary land claims is never far away.

Combined with the rewriting of the landscape by explorers, who named places after backers, monarchs, politicians and moods, and often overwrote the names and meanings of indigenous cultures, this is a challenging issue when one considers the growth of indigenous agency in the Arctic.

NEW ROUTES,
NEW POLITICS

After the conclusion of the Second World War, former allies renewed their centuries-long geopolitical competition in the Arctic, with the technologies pushed forward during the war years forming the backbone of a new era of competition. The potential for air travel to open up the Arctic as a thoroughfare for communication was realised once war-time innovations were implemented in military and commercial spheres. Longer flight ranges and developing jet technologies meant that flying over the Arctic to reach other parts of the polar world, and indeed the globe, became a technical possibility. This, in turn, renewed the possibility of the Arctic becoming a sphere of conflict between European and North American powers.

The USSR Polar Location map shown overleaf was formerly classified as 'secret' and was in the possession of the British Ministry of Defence. It uses a polar stereographic projection to show flight paths as straight lines, while also noting the location of towns and their proximity to each other in miles. Tellingly, it also includes settlements in 'areas under Soviet influence'. The technical character of the map is worth dwelling on in light of the other maps discussed in this book. In previous chapters we have seen the Arctic landscape projected onto various media and in ways that support particular modes of use. Inuit mapping details landmarks and areas of use (see pp. 20–21) while the various maritime maps of the sixteenth century onwards aggrandise European exploration and attempts to tame the Arctic. In short, humans manipulate their representation of the Arctic to correspond to their modes of engaging with it. The polar stereographic projection seen here operates in the same vein, displaying the Arctic in such a way that aviators can navigate their journeys with ease.

As well as providing a new perspective on the Arctic, the map also articulates the geopolitical games being played out across it. Russian and British interests in the Arctic have already been discussed in this book, with informal cooperation and formal competition marking the two nations' interactions in various areas of the European and North American Arctic. This map provides an insight into the role the Arctic played in British, Soviet and North American relationships in the decades following the Second World War, as the Soviet Union grew and Cold War suspicion replaced previous wartime alliances. Secret maps such as this one functioned very differently from those made by the Navy during the nineteenth century. They are a confidential articulation of preparedness and perspective on the developing spheres of the Cold War. Such preparedness would become even more important in later years, as the Arctic shifted from a space of conflict to one of transit for weapons of unparalleled destructive capacities.

OVERLEAF
A formerly classified USSR Polar Location Map from the Ministry of Defence (1951).
Maps MOD GSGS Misc 1524

Geographical Section, General Staff, (Misc.) 1524.
Published by the War Office, 1951.
First Edition, 1951.

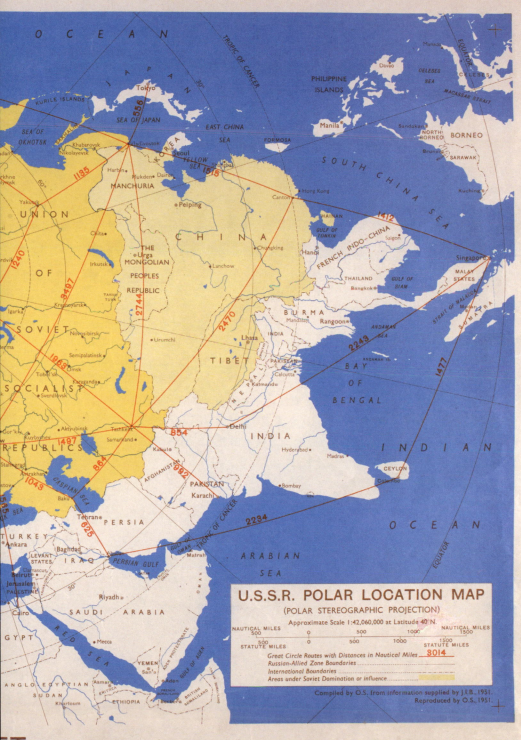

O C E A N

TROPIC OF CANCER

PHILIPPINE
ISLANDS

Manado

Davao

CELEBES
SEA

CELEBES

EQUATOR

MACASSAR STRAIT

J A P A N

Tokyo

KURILE ISLANDS

SEA OF JAPAN

EAST CHINA
SEA

FORMOSA

Manila

Sandakan

NORTH
BORNEO

BORNEO

Brunei

SARAWAK

Kuching

556

SEA OF
OKHOTSK

Khabarovsk
Nikolayevsk

Vladivostok

KOREA

Seoul

YELLOW
SEA

Shanghai

1518

S O U T H   C H I N A   S E A

rkhne

1195

Harbin

Mukden

Dairen

MANCHURIA

Peiping

Canton

Hong Kong

1412

Yakutsk

U N I O N

Chita

C H I N A

HAINAN

GULF OF
TONKIN

Hanoi

FRENCH INDO-CHINA

Saigon

Singapore

MALAY
STATES

rdvk

1240

THE
Urga
MONGOLIAN

PEOPLES

Irkutsk

3497

Chungking

Lanchow

2744

REPUBLIC

TANNU
TUVA

Krasnoyarsk

2470

THAILAND

Bangkok

GULF OF
SIAM

Medan

STRAIT OF MALACCA

SUMATRA

O F

Urumchi

Lhasa

BURMA

Mandalay

Rangoon

ANDAMAN
SEA

S O V I E T

Novosibirsk

Semipalatinsk

1969

Omsk

T I B E T

INDIA

ANDAMAN IS.

B A Y

2243

erma

Tobol'sk

Karaganda

PAKISTAN

Calcutta

O F

1477

S O C I A L I S T

Sverdlovsk

NEPAL

Katmandu

B E N G A L

Gor'k

Kuybyshev

Aktyubinsk

Tashkent

854

Delhi

I N D O N E S I A

1497

Samarkand

I N D I A

Hyderabad

Madras

R E P U B L I C S

864

Kabul

AFGHANISTAN

8982

PAKISTAN

Karachi

CEYLON

Colombo

1043

CASPIAN SEA

Baku

Bombay

Tehran

625

P E R S I A

TROPIC OF CANCER

2234

O C E A N

I N D I A N

TURKEY

Ankara

Baghdad

LEVANT
STATES

I R A Q

PERSIAN GULF

Matrah

GULF OF OMAN

OMAN

Damascus

Beirut

Jerusalem

PALESTINE

A R A B I A N

S E A

EQUATOR

Cairo

Riyadh

SAUDI   A R A B I A

RED SEA

Mecca

U.S.S.R. POLAR LOCATION MAP
(POLAR STEREOGRAPHIC PROJECTION)

Approximate Scale 1:42,060,000 at Latitude 40°N.

NAUTICAL MILES				NAUTICAL MILES
500	0	500	1000	1500

STATUTE MILES				STATUTE MILES
500	0	500	1000	1500

Great Circle Routes with Distances in Nautical Miles 3014
Russian-Allied Zone Boundaries
International Boundaries
Areas under Soviet Domination or Influence

Compiled by O.S. from information supplied by J.I.B., 1951.
Reproduced by O.S., 1951.

EGYPT

YEMEN

San'a

GULF OF ADEN

Aden

ANGLO-EGYPTIAN
SUDAN

Asmara

ERITREA

FRENCH
SOMALILAND

BRITISH
SOMALILAND

Berbera

Khartoum

ETHIOPIA

THE ARCTIC AND
THE APOCALYPSE

Both Europeans and North Americans quickly realised the potential for rapid travel and undetected strike action that the desolate Arctic air routes would open up. Unlike the icy and capricious seas, which made naval travel unpredictable as late as the 1940s and the *St Roch* expedition, the air provided relatively few challenges that could not be surmounted by experimentation and research. It is cold at altitude regardless of latitude and indeed, threatening high-altitude weather was not restricted to the Arctic, so these routes lacked the unique physical barriers provided by similar shipping routes. This would become increasingly relevant as the Iron Curtain descended and the Cold War became focused on the frozen north of the world.

Until the Cuban Missile Crisis of 1962, Arctic routes were the shortest possible way a Russian ICBM might travel from the Eurasian landmass to the cities of North America. The severity of the potential threat this posed and the average citizen's ability to do anything about it (other than building a very secure, well-stocked bunker next to their house) are matters up for debate, but the North American response at the time was the construction of the Distant Early Warning (DEW) Line: a system of radar stations in the far north. While the militarisation of the Arctic and its peoples by European and North American states can be traced all the way back to the time of the Reformation and the armies of the Swedish ruler Gustav II Adolf, the post-Second World War era saw this occurring on an unprecedented scale.

There are two features in particular that jump out from the U.S. Air Force map of the DEW Line opposite. First, the presence of Thule airbase in northwest Greenland. For centuries a fictional location, forgotten by Europeans (see pp. 22–3), Thule had been resurrected from the ice, like a modern Atlantis, by the U.S. during the Second World War. Used as a base for establishing aerial superiority over Greenland and polar Europe, as well as a location from which to launch anti-submarine operations, Thule represented the militarisation of the Arctic landscape and of European mythology. After the war, the base became an important northern hub of the DEW Line. Second, the thirty radar sites representing the system's line of first warning, which do an uncanny job of tracing much of the Northwest Passage.

This reforming of the Arctic landscape, whereby the quest for oceanic superiority is relinquished in order to establish aerial defences, also had a significant impact on the people of the Arctic. Inuit groups were inevitably drawn to the radar stations for trade, food and company which establish a whole series of interactions as complex as those between Inuit and explorers and whalers in the centuries before. By the time the Cold War wound down, the western Arctic, irrespective of national political boundaries, had been imprinted with the U.S.-Soviet Union geopolitical tussle, with effects for the Arctic, its landscape and politics that endure to this day.

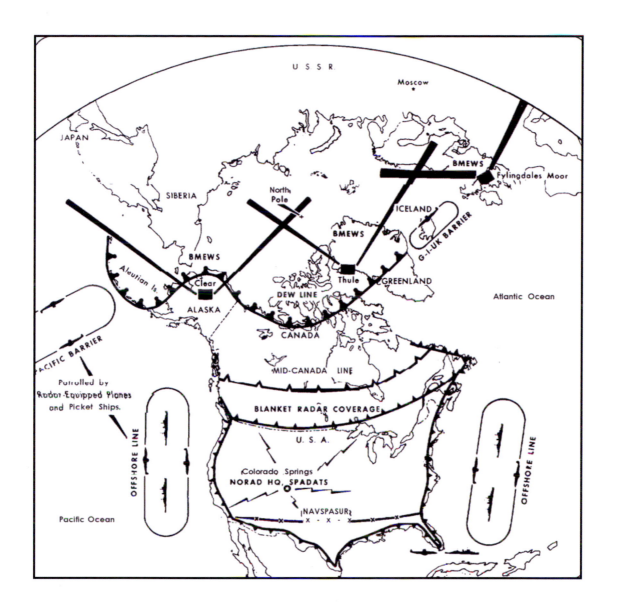

ABOVE
A map showing the continental
air defence system and DEW line.
Note the reappearance of Thule
on the map.
USAF Museum

LEFT
A photograph of the American Stars
and Stripes and the Canadian red
ensign flying at the DEW Line radar
site near Cambridge Bay in the
Canadian Arctic.
Canadian Forces Photographic Unit

THE SCIENCE
OF STATECRAFT

The continuing importance of mapping in the claims of Arctic states is clearly illustrated by Russia's *Atlas Arktiki* (Atlas of the Arctic), an official publication produced in 1985. This state-sponsored atlas covers a wide range of Arctic subjects, mapping multiple expeditions to the North Pole that took place between 1897 and 1973 (with an emphasis on Russian activities), providing an early chart of the historical geographical movements of Arctic peoples, and also showing how the cartographic understanding of the Arctic had changed in preceding centuries. Illustrating this last history are various European maps attached to past expeditions, as well as some examples of early 'theoretical' Arctic cartography and its uses, highlighted at the start by way of an introduction to Arctic cartography. This acts as an invitation to consider how far mapping of the Arctic has come, not least in the context of this particular Russian atlas.

While the atlas is broad in scope, the overall perspective emphasises a scientific approach to understanding the Arctic and its morphology. As we can see from the history of the Antarctic, in the decades since the Antarctic Treaty of 1959, twentieth- and twenty-first-century scientific research has become increasingly aligned with principles of international cooperation and environmentalism, but this has not precluded the use of scientific principles and practices for the justification of territorial claims. The *Atlas Arktiki* can be viewed as laying the groundwork for some such claims, especially in the context of the all-encompassing geological perspectives cast upon the region. Using a projection that centres on the North Pole, many of the maps included here provide a god-like perspective on the Arctic and give the viewer access to information usually hidden under its icy surfaces and seas.

In the 1980s, the technology required to undertake this work was still relatively rudimentary compared to the tools for fieldwork and visualisation – not to mention the possibilities opened up by satellite imagery – that are available today. In spite of this there are still clues to important geological features, which would become increasingly significant as technology developed further and the claims and counter-claims of Arctic geopolitics heated up again over the coming decades. Just below the middle of one map, connecting northern Russia to northern Greenland, runs a jagged pink-and-blue line, which represents one of the region's tectonic plate boundaries. This particular line of geological instability is the Lomonosov Ridge, an area of elevated underwater terrain that made the news worldwide when an advanced submersible vehicle planted a Russian flag on it in 2007.

Planting a flag in the depths of the Arctic Ocean is in some ways an equivalent to America's planting a flag on the moon. Both illustrate nationalistic pride and technical prowess, and both also make a geopolitical claim to ownership; in Russia's case, one that has caused a great deal of consternation among the other Arctic powers. This act does not exist in isolation, however, as the Russian claims it dramatically represents are based on the more comprehensive scientific view presented in works such as *Atlas Arktiki*. The use of scientific data to make geopolitical claims is based on a subjective analysis of raw facts and how they apply to real-world discussions of politics and law. Nonetheless, it represents a strong counter-example to the cairns, flags and occupancy touted by other nations elsewhere in the Arctic.

THE ARCTIC IN A RESOURCE-HUNGRY CENTURY

In the early post-war years, another challenge arose for the newly emerging world order, when fears over the population explosion that occurred after 1945 generated a worldwide search for fresh resources. A massive demographic shift was taking place in the Western world, as rising standards of living, improved modern medicine and healthcare institutions such as the British National Health Service began to drive population numbers rapidly upwards. To accommodate this growth, states and businesses began to investigate previously untapped sites in what were regarded as the less hospitable parts of the world.

As part of this general movement to expand the resource horizons of the world, a map published by Barclays Group of Banks *c.* 1958 identifies the Arctic and Antarctic as areas with potential for exploitation. It has been drawn according to the Atlantis stereographic projection, which accentuates the poles and thus makes the Arctic and Antarctic the focuses of the upper and lower sections of the map respectively. At the same time, an illustration to the right alludes to barren deserts and 'frozen wastes', and depicts benign indigenous peoples who, it suggests, would be welcoming of the economic development that would accompany the extraction of resources from these areas. In this regard, the polar regions are represented as not quite *terra nullius*, but spaces in which resource extraction is rendered simple by developing technology and proceeds unhampered by borders and resource rights.

By 1958, the potential of science and technology to unlock the world's subterranean energy reserves was enabling the exploitation of the world's oil resources to previously unattainable levels. These years were also, supposedly, infused with a spirit of international cooperation: multinational research parties joined together in the Antarctic, and the first charter flight from Britain to Moscow flew in 1958. However, in reality, the Cold War and extreme technical difficulties would be an impediment to the development of resource extraction in the Arctic.

Geopolitical competition and international scientific cooperation would combine to stem corporate desires to exploit the Antarctic as a site of resource extraction too. The Antarctic Treaty of 1959 was informed by lessons learnt when technological progress and uninhibited commercial imperatives combined to put severe pressure on species vulnerable to predation: the result was the devastation of whale and seal populations in the southern seas. In subsequent years, one of the many outcomes of this treaty was to demarcate the Antarctic continent as being off-limits to all human exploitation beyond the pursuit of scientific knowledge. The spirit of cooperation this map posits for the Arctic finds form in the Antarctic Treaty but in the interests of closing down areas for exploitation rather than opening them up.

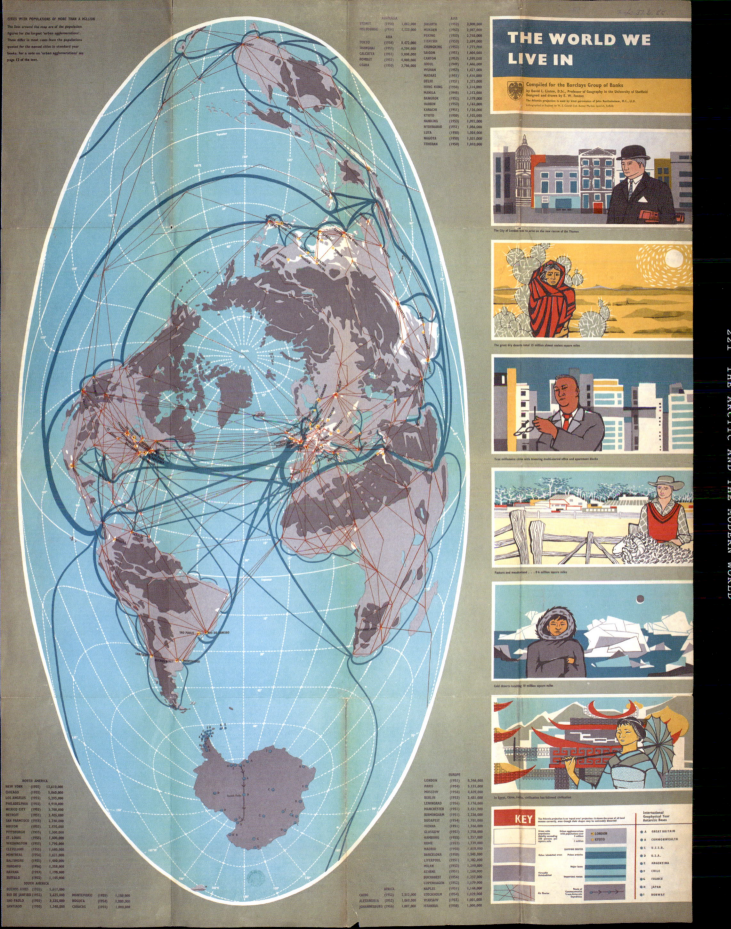

THE WORLD WE LIVE IN

Compiled for the Barclays Group of Banks

by David L. Linton, B.Sc., Professor of Geography in the University of Sheffield
Designed and drawn by E. W. Fenton

The Atlantis projection is used by kind permission of John Bartholomew, M.C., LL.D.

Lithographed in England by W. S. Cowell Ltd, Butter Market, Ipswich, Suffolk

KEY

The Atlantis projection is an 'equal area' projection: it shows the areas of all land
masses correctly, even though their shapes may be seriously distorted

Areas with populations thinly exceeding 200 persons per square mile	Urban agglomerations with populations over 1 million
	● LONDON
	● KYOTO
Areas inhabited but sparsely	Prime arteries
Virtually uninhabited	Major lanes
	Important routes
Air Routes	

International Geophysical Year Antarctic Bases

◆ A	GREAT BRITAIN
◆ B	COMMONWEALTH
◆ C	U.S.S.R.
◆ D	U.S.A.
◆ E	ARGENTINA
◆ F	CHILE
◆ G	FRANCE
◆ H	JAPAN
◆ I	NORWAY

A HISTORY OF NAMING THE POLES

The operation of British scientific bases on the Antarctic continent has meant that, throughout the twentieth century, postage stamps and a postal infrastructure have been required in order to allow researchers (and now tourists) to communicate with friends and family back home. In the UK, we are used to seeing the head of Queen Elizabeth II on our stamps, her profile portrait changing over the years as a steady reminder of the passage of time, and the head of the Queen (or a historical reigning monarch) has also adorned the postal stamps of various colonial territories, including Canada, Australia and New Zealand. The stamp displayed here, in which a young Queen Elizabeth II's portrait hovers over the British Antarctic Territory and an expedition ship, is, perhaps, more unusual.

From the point of view of the state, stamps have a long history as part of mechanisms of control, organisation and meaning. Their significance is evident wherever European states have developed their empires, the most notable example being the role of tax stamps in sparking the American War of Independence. In the Antarctic, and the Arctic, the production and use of unique area stamps have been, not just an important means of communicating, but also one of the many ways of illustrating Briain's presence in and control of an area (the same is also true for other colonising powers). As a result, various British scientific missions and expeditions to the Antarctic have had their own polar stamps produced.

It is as part of this history that we must view the stamp shown here, intended for use in the British Antarctic Territory (BAT) between 1963 and 1969. The latter part of the twentieth century saw the Antarctic become a space of international cooperation, but also one in which the British government had to work ever harder to justify and maintain its claims, as states such as Chile, Argentina and Australia all began to develop their own notions of Antarctic statecraft. The British Crown is an important point of continuity for British claims in these situations, providing a public sense of continuity and legal frameworks which underpin colonial and imperial claims across the various successions of monarchs and royal families.

y

This is the main reason why the names and titles of British monarchs are written on maps of the Arctic and Antarctic, in locations such as Canada's Victoria Island, named by Peter Warren Dease and Thomas Simpson in 1839, or Prince Regent's Inlet, which confounded William Edward Parry in the nineteenth century, having been inscribed there by the actions of the explorers discussed earlier in this book. This tradition continues today: the coronation of Elizabeth II saw the Queen Elizabeth Islands in Canada so named in her honour, while 2012 saw part of Antarctica renamed Queen Elizabeth Land as part of the Diamond Jubilee celebrations.

Both of these acts of renaming coincided with heightened geopolitical interest in these areas – the Cold War's effect on Canada, and increasing Argentinian claims in the Antarctic in the twenty-first century respectively – while the commissioning of the 1963 BAT stamp coincided with the increasing internationalisation of Antarctica in the wake of the Antarctic Treaty. These acts of naming and the formation of imaginative geographies through the use of maps, photographs and stamps are part of the same system of national claim, geopolitical pressure and resource requirements explicated in this book. The systems of claiming and naming employed on the Northwest Passage and in the Arctic inevitably ended up being applied to the southern pole as well.

Artwork for the British Antarctic Territory: 1963-69 3d deep blue stamp. Crown Agents Philatelic and Security Printing Archive, British Library

THE POWER OF NAMING

There have been various points in history at which, to a Western observer, Inuit and other indigenous peoples' agency and sense of ownership in the Arctic has been clear, be it through the woodblock prints of *Kalâdlit Okalluktualliait*, maps carved from driftwood (see pp. 20–21), the resistance offered up to explorers like Martin Frobisher (see pp. 40–41), or the importance of their advice in the nineteenth-century search for Franklin and his crew. In spite of this, as this book has sought to show, history also relates the changing nature of this agency. Each voyage of exploration and every industrial project increases the number of ways in which the Arctic is bound into the systems and exchanges of the metropolitan, Western world, exposing Arctic peoples to new technologies, invasive religious cultures and virulent Western diseases.

The map has played a key role in this process: maps of the Arctic created by Europeans and North Americans have, over the last 500 years, charted the lands, coasts and seas of the Arctic for all to see, but they have also inscribed this landscape with a Western nomenclature, as discussed above. These names are sometimes important nodes in a geopolitical network, as is the case for the Queen Elizabeth Islands, or commemorative of expedition sponsors or, as is often the case in the northern Arctic, expressions of profound disappointment at the end of a gruelling trek, such as Franklin's 'Point Turnagain'.

Each of these names, irrespective of why they were given, overwrites a landscape rich in the language and knowledge of another, indigenous culture. Long before explorers contemplated visiting the Arctic, its landscapes were richly named, with words suggesting what could be found in a place, its spiritual significance or perhaps that it was simply of no use to humans at all. These names are freighted with deep cultural significance and their removal from the landscape has a significant and negative impact on the cultures that placed them there; if they are forgotten, then important parts of that culture are lost, too, and it begins to fragment.

The resurgence of Inuit political agency in the late twentieth century and the beginnings of increasing political autonomy necessitated a promotion of Inuit culture and heritage, creating a pressing need to re-inscribe the landscape with Inuit meaning. A map of Nunavik, Canada, from 1990–1 (overleaf) represents one of a number of attempts to undertake such a project, placing Inuit language, names and meaning back onto a printed map of the region (which is in northern Quebec). Using Inuit syllabic characters (developed, in part, through the activities of Western missionaries and preachers, as discussed above), the map overlays modern, Western cartography and naming with an extra layer of Inuit meaning. This layer is an intervention, an arrest, of the previous history of fragmentation, and part of an effort to codify Inuit knowledge of space so that it may endure.

Creating this map in a style analogous to that employed in Western cartographic practices also represents a statement of intent and ability. It makes Inuit knowledge directly comparable to Western naming and asserts this culture's right to endure and have political agency in its own lands. The map, then, attempts to appropriate Western systems of cartography in order to control space and wrest the land back into the indigenous sphere. A long battle has ensued, as many in the West – not just resource extractors, but politicians, celebrities and conservation groups too – continue to ignore the Inuit place in the world.

BAIE D'HUDSON

HUDSON BAY

TASIUJARJUAQ ᖅᐱᕐᑕᐃᔪᒃ QIKIRTAIJUK

ADMINISTRATION

RÉGIONALE

KATIVIK

Editor / Research, Concept, Cartographic Design): Ludger Müller-Wille

Associates / Associés : Helen Ohosetaaluluk, Johnny Palliser,
Linna Weber Müller-Wille

Contributors / Collaborateurs: Inuit Elders of Nunavik
Anciens(nes) inuit du Nunavik

Cartographer / Cartographe: Richard Bachand

Elevation in metres above mean sea level
Contour interval ....10 metres

Altitude en mètres au-dessus du niveau moyen de la mer
Équidistance des courbes ....10 mètres

Scale 1 : 50 000 **Échelle**

Metres 1000   0   1   2   3   4 Kilomètres
Mètres   Kilomètres

1   0   1   2 Miles
                                                         Milles

A chart from the publication,
Nunavik: Inuit Place name map series (1990).
Maps X.1559

ᐊᕕᑕᖅ ᐱᐅᓯᑐᖃᓕᕆᕕᒃ INSTITUT CULTUREL **AVATAQ** CULTURAL INSTITUTE

ᐃᓄᐃᑦ ᐊᑎᖏᑦ ᓄᓇᕕᒻᒥ: ᓇᕐᓵᓗᒃ
Inuit Place Names in Nunavik: Narsaaluk — **Toponymes inuit au Nunavik: Narsaaluk**

ᐊᑎᖏᑦ	Name / Nom	Entity / Entité		Name / Nom	Entity / Entité
1	Qikirtaaluup Kuunga	river/rivière	43	Kakiatmalnk	lake/lac
2	Upingivik	point/pointe	44	Tasikailak	lake/lac
3	Qikirtaaluup Kangiranga	point/pointe	45	Tasikallaup Inuarlunga	lake/lac
4	Qikirtaluk	island/île	46	Amaamaalunp Tasinga	lake/lac
5	Mippivik	point/pointe	47	Amaamaak	hill/colline
6	Quurngnaq	narrow/détroit	48	Iqaluppilik	lake/lac
7	Siutainnaq	island/île	49	Qavvasitinq	lake/lac
8	Qikirtaaluup Kangirsualuangata Qaangaa	bay/baie	50	Narsaaluk	creek/ruisseau
9	Isurtaaraq	lake/lac	51	Kangirsualuk	bay/baie
10	Aichmaaq	creek/ruisseau	52	Kangirsualuup Qikirtanga	island/île
11	kpaluqartauunaq	lake/lac	53	Tikirnapik	point/pointe
12	Tasiquivirnrik	lake/lac	54	Tikiraalok	point/pointe
13	Ikuriaq	creek/ruisseau	55	Kangirtuxaaluk	isthmus/isthme
14	Nunak	hillside/flanc de coteau	56	Ivigartaaq	point/pointe
15	Kangirsukstaaq	bay/baie	57	Tikiraaluup Qikirtanga	island/îles
16	Aanaakkisiurvik	creek/ruisseau	58	Kangikitnaq	point/pointe
17	Kuugaruittusiurvik	creek/ruisseau	59	Tikirammark	point/pointe
18	Kuugajuaraaluk	creek/ruisseau	60	Quirteinaq	rock/rocher
19	Iqaluppilik	lake/lac	61	Tungalaittuq	point/pointe
20	Saaninguinq	lake/lac	62	Itilliruap Nuvanga	point/pointe
21	Narsaaluk	creek/ruisseau	63	Isilliruat Kangirunga	bay/baie
22	Tasialuup Kangitsualunga	bay/baie	64	Itilliruaq	isthmus/isthme
23	Tasixluup Quumgunga	narrow/détroit/file	65	Sunganujarnaap Tikirakailaalunga	point/pointe
24	Nuluarniavik	lake/lac	66	Sunganjarnaq	point/pointe
25	Salbilik	lake/lac	67	Qikirtakutaaq	island/île
26	Tasialuup Tikiranga	point/pointe	68	Kangikitnaq	point/pointe
27	Kuuk Tariutiarvik	creek/ruisseau	69	Qattaujartalik	point/pointe
28	Tasikutaagaltuk Qikirtalik	lake/lac	70	Qikirtakallak Naujaaluik	island/île
29	Kivviagartalik	lake/lac	71	Aanaakkisiurvik	creek/ruisseau
30	Kuukallak	river/rivière	72	Tikirakutaaq	point/pointe
31	Isunrsiovik	confluence	73	Kangirnulakaat	bay/baie
32	Qinngilrivik	island/île	74	Qikirtaijuk	foreshore flat/batture
33	Aariarusluk	lakes/lacs			
34	Quurnguuluk	narrow/détroit/file	75	Narsaaluk	valley/vallée
35	Kuukallak	narrow/détroit/file	76	Quiarpuluk	lake/lac
36	Tasikutaaq	lake/lac	77	Tasikutaaraapik	lake/lac
37	Ikaartariaq	ford/gué	78	Qarqaq Majuralk	hill/colline
38	Innaaluup Tasinga	lake/lac	79	Kivviagartalik	bay/baie
39	Innaaluk	mountain/montagne	80	Narsaaluk	valley/vallée
40	Innaaruluapik	lake/lac	81	Kapisillisiuvik	bay/baie
41	Ikaartariaq	lake/lac	82	Sanganjarnaq	bay/baie
42	Innaalulik	lake/lac	83	Kangirsualuk	bay/baie
			84	Innaaruluapik	cliff/falaise
			85	Snkkakallak	hill/colline

ᓄᓇᐃᑦ ᐊᑎᖏᑦ ᓄᓇ ᓴᓂᐊᓂᒃ ᑐᑭᓯᒋᐊᕐᓂᖅ ᐱᔭᐅᔪᑦ
Place Names from Adjoining Maps — **Toponymes provenant de cartes adjacentes**

Sheet/Feuillet			Name/Nom	Entity/Entité
34F/14	25		Anurituuq	inlet/anse
34K/4	40		Qullinaap Kuunga	river/rivière
34K/4	46		Ikuriaq	creek/ruisseau
34L/8	67		Tasiqarjuaq	bay/baie

This list is taken from / Cette liste est tirée de:

Müller-Wille, Ludger. Inuttitut Nunait Atingitta Katinsutuuninglit Nunavimmi (Kupaimmi, Kanatami). Inukjuak: Avataq Piusitugalirivik 1987: 174-176.

Gazetteer of Inuit Place Names in Nunavik (Quebec, Canada). Inukjuak: Avataq Cultural Institute 1987: 174-176.

Répertoire toponymique inuit du Nunavik (Québec, Canada). Inukjuak: Institut culturel Avataq 1987: 174-176.

ᓴᖅᑭᔭᐅᑎᑦ **LEGEND LÉGENDE**

ᓄᓇᐅᑉ ᖃᓄᐃᑦᑐᖓ / Topographic feature / Caractéristique topographique

ᐃᒪᖅ ᖃᓄᐃᑦᑐᖓ / Hydrographic feature / Caractéristique hydrographique

ᐃᓄᖃᖅ ᐊᑐᖅᑕᖓ / Human feature / Caractéristique humaine

ᓄᓇᕕᒃ **Région Nunavik Region**

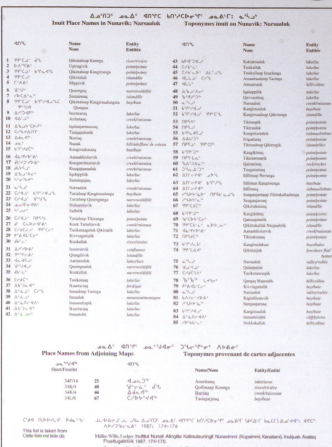

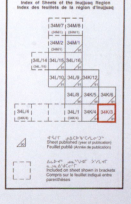
Index of Sheets of the Inujjuaq Region
Index des feuillets de la région d'Inujjuaq

The grid on the map is the Universal Transverse Mercator grid (U.T.M.); the sides of each square equal 1000 metres.

Le quadrillage représenté sur la carte est le quadrillage U.T.M. (Universel transverse de Mercator); chaque carré a 1000 mètres de côté.

Designed and prepared by Indigenous Names Surveys (Department of Geography, McGill University). Published by Avataq Cultural Institute, Inukjuak (Nunavik). Printed by Les Presses Solidaires.

Conçu et préparé par Relevés des noms indigènes (Département de géographie, Université McGill). Publié par l'Institut culturel Avataq, Inukjuak (Nunavik). Imprimé par Les Presses Solidaires.

© Ludger Müller-Wille & Institut culturel AVATAQ Cultural Institute/1991
ISSN 1180-5773

Dépôt légal - 3ᵉ trimestre 1991. Bibliothèque nationale du Québec.
Dépôt légal - 3ᵉ trimestre 1991. Bibliothèque nationale du Canada.

Copies may be purchased from / Ces cartes sont en vente au:

Avataq Cultural Institute / Institut culturel Avataq, Inukjuak, Nunavik (Québec) J0M 1M0

Avataq Cultural Institute / Institut culturel Avataq, 294, carré Saint-Louis #1, Montréal (Québec) H2X 1A4

NARSAALUK
SHEET / FEUILLET
34 K/3

DIGITALLY REIMAGINING THE LANDSCAPE

The re-mapping of the Arctic to reflect the histories, naming, practices and politics of indigenous peoples has continued into the twenty-first century. Indeed, it has accelerated through the possibilities opened up by digital mapping and geographical information systems (GIS). In many ways, Canada's vast northern landscapes played a part in inspiring the development of these technologies. During the 1960s, the Canadian government was successfully lobbied to form the first computerised mapping department, in order to successfully map this huge area for settlement and possible resource extraction. Since then, the capabilities of digital mapping technology have grown massively as companies such as Esri, Google, and now a whole slew of start-up online mapping producers, have expanded the reach of the technology and the tools available to manipulate geographical information.

It is in this context that the possibilities of digitally mapping the Arctic, and projects such as the Pan-Inuit Trails Map specifically, have grown. An outcome of the broader research project 'Northwest Passage and the Construction of Inuit pan-Arctic Identities', led by the academics Claudio Aporta, Michael Bravo and Fraser Taylor, this map has been constructed from published accounts, letters, maps and other illustrations that make mention of Inuit activities around the area of the Northwest Passage, and from which geographical coordinates of some description can be gleaned. The result is a map that illustrates Inuit agency in the Arctic landscape and its

historical depth. Also, and more importantly, this is a living map, as many of these trails are still used by Inuit groups and hunters to this day.

This opens up an important point highlighted by the research leaders in their introduction to the map, that '[u]nderstanding Inuit routes is essential in order to appreciate the Inuit history and occupancy of the Arctic'. Inuit naming practices are also key here, as they preserve information about the landscape's features: the possibilities for hunting, camp locations and the utility of any given valley or track as a route within this broader network of trails across the Arctic landscape and its seas. This information is crucial for Inuit survival in the landscape and now supports a broader quest for cultural cohesion and political agency in a landscape generations of Inuit have called home.

These digital maps and their ability to layer up-to-date, satellite-based geography and historical information regarding Inuit occupation are an evolutionary step forward from the maps of the 1990s, which reclaimed the Arctic landscape for Inuit nomenclature. This practice represented a reappraisal of the landscape, and its digital iterations allow for the scale and resolution of the mapping to be improved while multiple layers of historical information are added. Furthermore, the variable scale and interactivity of the map allow the viewer to move around the virtual space, following their own interests, and clearly perceiving the deeply entrenched Inuit use and inhabitation of the Arctic environment.

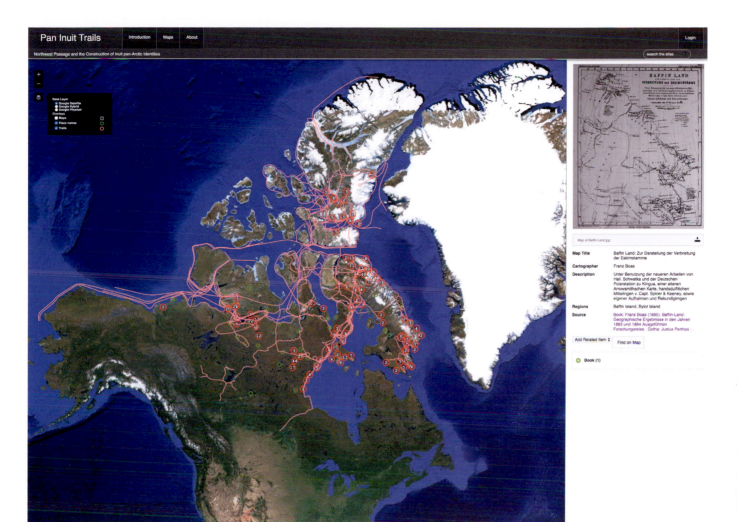

The Pan-Inuit Trails Map (2014)

Dalhousie University, University of Cambridge
and Carleton University

POLITICS, RESOURCES AND MAPPING CLIMATE CHANGE

The climatic extremes have always meant that the Arctic is a challenging and constantly changing environment: sea ice shifts, icebergs crack and cliffs erode with a speed that is frightening to those from gentler climates. But a more significant, fundamental shift in the Arctic's landscapes, seascapes and natural rhythms is also occurring. Climate change has a huge impact across the globe but the effects are felt particularly keenly in the fragile ecosystems of the Arctic. Not long ago, the polar regions were viewed as areas supremely resistant to human influence; but, as pollution has become global and scientific horizons have broadened, it has become increasingly clear that this superficial perspective masks the underlying fragility of the region. There have been attempts to comprehend the scale of change through the use of modern satellite and digital mapping techniques.

Humanity's parallel explorations into space have provided the first true views of our globe, and the satellite and imaging technology that has been developed as a result of space exploration has allowed us to understand its workings in ever more intricate ways. The data sourced, combined with meteorological and geographical information collected on the ground, has allowed agencies such as NASA to create complex models of our shifting climate. On a smaller scale, this data has also been used to illustrate changes such as those occurring in the sea ice levels during the Arctic winter. The NASA website includes a page devoted to showing the expansion and contraction of the ice over the latter decades of the twentieth century.

While the picture produced is complex (as described previously in this book, ice is capricious and behaves in unexpected ways), the noticeable decrease in winter maxima and lack of enduring summer ice in many parts of the Arctic illustrate a dramatic change, which most other sources of evidence suggest is linked to anthropogenic climate change. This adds extra significance and complexity to the projects of renaming engaged in by indigenous communities. A changing landscape makes this work simultaneously both harder to complete and more important. If the landscape shifts beyond all recognition then efforts need to be made to preserve existing knowledge about it.

In the meantime, visualisations such as those produced by NASA show the continued evolution of ways of seeing the Arctic. Indeed, courtesy of the voluminous logbooks kept on past voyages of exploration to the polar regions, these new ways of seeing can also be extended into the past, potentially improving and contextualising our understanding of present changes and providing new, more creative, ways of engaging with both the past and present.

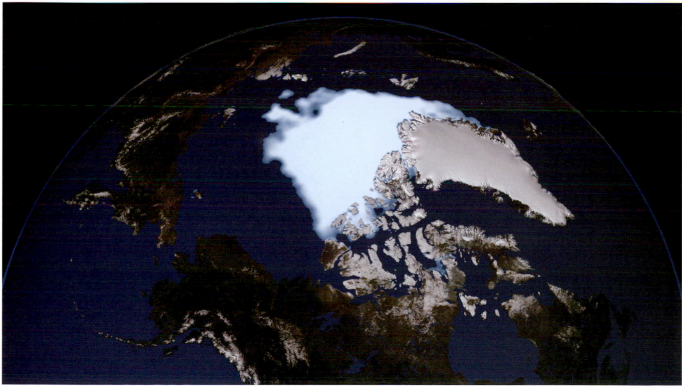

Two stills from NASA's dynamic
visualisation of changing ice levels
over the period 1979-2012 (2012).
NASA

THE CONTINUING SEARCH FOR FRANKLIN

In 1993, a new expedition set out to try to find evidence relating to the fate of Sir John Franklin and his crew. Barry Ranford, Mike Yaraskavich and John Harrington undertook a summer expedition to King William Island in Nunavut, Canada, where, the summer before and under direction from local Inuit, Ranford had located what he thought was an old Franklin crew campsite. The Northwest Territories government supported the expedition, which returned with important evidence: 300 bones from Franklin's crew, of which 90, when analysed by specialists, were revealed to bear scoring marks that suggested a knife had been used to remove meat from the bone. Here was scientific evidence, over 100 years since John Rae and Charles Dickens had indulged in their lengthy print arguments (see pp. 156–7), that the doctor's testimony and the narrative provided to him by his Inuit contacts was correct. Franklin's crew had, under incredibly strenuous circumstances, resorted to cannibalism. These results are recorded in a format unusual for this sort of expedition, as Harrington was both an artist and diarist, who compiled his sketches and writing into a notebook for small-run publication. The images

Artist's depictions of expedition camp and bones found during a Franklin search expedition in 1993, from John Harrington, *The Franklin Recovery Expedition* (1994). New British Library acquisition, awaiting shelfmark.

shown below portray the working camp of the team, and the grisly evidence collected, through the lens of the artist's impression.

Ranford, Yaraskavich and Harrington are not the only people to have set off looking for Franklin and his crew in the long years since the search was officially called off in the nineteenth century. Indeed, many have followed in the footsteps of Rae, James Ross and others who attempted to locate the crew and discover their fate. In 2014, this persistence paid off and, after years of trying, HMS *Erebus* was located by the crew of a Parks Canada expedition. Further expeditions are now planned to the site each summer season, in an attempt to examine the ship and see if more information about the fate of Franklin's crew can be found.

Just as Franklin and the expeditions searching for him were bound up in a nineteenth-century network of geopolitical factors, so the twentieth-century searches have followed the same pattern. In the wake of the Cold War, searches for the remains of British expeditions in the Canadian Arctic have remained an important way of exercising sovereignty in the Arctic, and the 2014 find

was no exception, undertaken in the light of increasingly bold claims from Russia as to its own Arctic influence and North American bids to use the Northwest Passage as an international waterway. The continuing importance of the Inuit knowledge so maligned by Dickens in 1854 is also reaffirmed by this find. Ranford and team relied on Inuit guides but, more significantly, the *Erebus* is in a location where Inuit oral history had long asserted a boat would be found should anyone go to look.

Continuing searches for Franklin are a reminder that a number of the issues dealt with in this book are not only still relevant but have recurred continually throughout the long period discussed. Geopolitical pressures, claims of ownership, the marginalisation of significant (and correct) Inuit voices (and the possibilities opened up when these are listened to) are just some of the themes we see returning with Harrington's book. The recovery expedition and the location of HMS *Erebus* illustrate the complex and hybrid cultural and political space the Arctic has come to be, in which insiders and outsiders, past and present, continually rub against and abrade each other.

THIS SITE APPEARS TO BE AN INUIT CAMPFIRE OR IS IT FROM FRANKLIN'S MEN? JIM'S TENT (AND LAUNDRY) 50 METERS AWAY IS ON THE LEFT, MINE IS IN THE MIDDLE AND BARRY'S IS ON THE RIGHT. PEOPLE CAN BE SEEN WORKING ON THE SITE IN THE BACKGROUND. EREBUS BAY IS ON THE LEFT HORIZON CAN YOU FIND THE SEAL BONE & PIECE OF WOOD NEAR THE FIREPLACE?

37

I THINK I CAN MAKE DEREK OUT FAR TO THE WEST OF ME. AS I GET CLOSER I CAN TELL THAT IT IS DEREK AND HE IS STANDING BESIDE WHAT IS CLEARLY A GRAVE SITE! AS I APPROACH HIM HE TELLS ME THIS ISN'T THE HALF OF IT! HE HAS ALSO FOUND A WOODEN BUILDING STILL INTACT AND BONES AND RUSTY CANS EVERYWHERE! THERE ARE TWO GRAVES CLOSE TO EACH OTHER. ONE IS ADULT SIZE AND IT READS: "JANE KLENGENBERG - BORN AN 14, 1926 DIED MAY 17, 1944" THE OTHER ONE IS CHILD SIZE AND IT READS: "N.P. KLENGENBERG PAST AWAY AUGUST 4 1943" THE BUILDING PROVES TO BE MOST INTERESTING AS WE APPROACH IT. IT IS IN PRETTY GOOD SHAPE HAVING SAT

THE TWO GRAVES ARE ON TOP OF A HILL APPROX 20 FT APART

PATCHES OF DARK MOSS HAVE BEEN PLACED ON THE SURFACE. PROBABLY TO ENCOURAGE FLOWER GROWTH

N.P. PASSED AWAY FIRST (AUG /43), JANE WAS ONLY 18 YRS OLD AND DIED THE NEXT SPRING (MAY 44). I SENSE A LOT OF PAIN & HEARTACHE IS REPRESENTED HERE!

78

LOOKING AT HISTORY
THROUGH DIGITAL MAPS

A recent British Library exhibition, *Lines in the Ice: Seeking the Northwest Passage* (1 November 2014 – 29 March 2015), was composed from historic and contemporary artefacts in the Library's collections, but objects were created specifically for the display too. An online Google Map, created by Digital Writer-in-Residence Rob Sherman, reflects upon the history of exploration, the author's own journeys and a fictitious character's attempt to save Franklin. The result is a myriad of points and lines, mostly focused around the Northwest Passage, which blend history, experience and imagination into multiple layers of a single map and cast a new light on engagement with the frozen north.

'On My Wife's Back' (2014–15), the project from which the map arose, is the story of Isaak Scinbank, a fictitious captain enrolled by Lady Franklin in the search for her husband. Scinbank may be a sailor but he also enjoys his home comforts, such that the Lincolnshire countryside is often on his mind and his ship's log is a repurposed fishing journal, complete with a notch cut in the top in which to rest a fishing rod. This journal was constructed by the British Library's conservation team and used as a medium for Scinbank's story. 'On My Wife's Back' is a digital project, but it has one foot firmly planted in the material world: the ship's log is handwritten in the first instance, while the author also made various physical items, such as a ship's biscuit, and arranged found items, including a fake scrimshawed whale's tooth, to further develop the narrative.

The real locations that inspired parts of Scinbank's story and Scinbank's character are located on the Google Map, creating pseudo-real points that exist alongside the history of explorers such as John Ross and Franklin, blurring the line between fact and fiction in the developing narrative. Such an approach is not new in Arctic exploration; sailors often invented stories to explain away events or decisions from which punishment may otherwise have followed. In works of Arctic literature such as Mary Shelley's *Frankenstein* (see pp. 100–101), the construction of the story in a world grounded in the contemporary adds to the sense of dislocation, danger and drama.

Sherman himself notes that such creative engagements perhaps represent their own form of cultural imperialism, writing the author or character's story onto a landscape already richly covered by different cultures and histories. However, they also serve as a comment on this tradition of writing stories onto foreign landscapes. The approach taken here, where various stories exist simultaneously and the 'fiction' acts as a lens through which 'fact' can be questioned and reinterpreted, encourages the viewer to reconsider their understanding of the history of Arctic exploration and all that it has changed in the north. A map is an ideal way in which to achieve this because of the way viewers are drawn into its layers of information and meaning, layers that are only becoming deeper as the variable levels of focus found in vector mapping open up new cartographic perspectives. In the case of 'On My Wife's Back', the map also prepares the viewer to play an online game, in which the player engages with Scinbank's fictitious search for Franklin.

Rob Sherman's digital maps blend historical and fictional sites to create an immersive experience of the Arctic.
Property of Rob Sherman

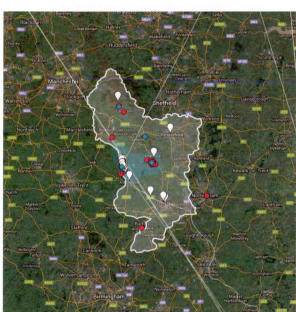

INUIT PRINT CULTURE

Franklin, Rae, Frobisher and others like them are not the only ones who have set the tone of Arctic representations. Through maps like the Ammassalik depictions of the Greenland coast, and the illustrations of Sami culture found in Charles II's 1680 atlas (see pp. 64–5), among other materials, Inuit, Sami and other Arctic cultures have also made their mark on European and North American cultures, as explorers have drawn these two worlds together. This interchange continues in the twentieth century, as the art and cultural practices of indigenous peoples across the Arctic have become bound up in globalised networks of art and literary publishing, not to mention a diverse world music scene.

The early seeds of what is now a global Inuit art industry can be understood as developing from when Hinrich Johannes Rink taught Aron Kangek (a local Kalaallisut hunter) the techniques required to undertake woodblock printing and illustrate a book on Greenland's legends and history (the *Kalâdlit Okalluktualliait*). Global enthusiasm for Arctic art more generally can be understood as having grown from interest in the artefacts brought home by explorers and, later, some of the first European and North American tourists to the north, such as Agnes Deans Cameron. From the mid-twentieth century onwards, Inuit printing, on various substrates, has grown into a substantial part of the global art industry, underpinned by the accompanying growth in demand for Inuit sculpture and carved art. As a major branch of this industry, Inuit prints produced by artists in the Canadian Arctic are regarded as being a distinct creative entity.

A number of Canadian artists and filmmakers have become nationally and internationally renowned, and have seized opportunities to work across different media forms, including books. Germaine Arnaktauyok, who illustrated *Stories from Pangnirtung* (1976), is one such well-known artist. Hailing from the Igloolik hamlet in Nunavut, she has produced artwork in the latter part of the twentieth century and the twenty-first century. Arnaktauyok's work focuses primarily on Inuit heritage, folklore and tradition, and is executed as lithographs, etchings and screen-prints. Her style is bold and distinctive, with figures usually conveying a strong sense of movement. The book *Stories from Pangnirtung* gathers tales from the settlement named in the title, in the Qikiqtaaluk region of Nunavut. The book illustrates the richness of Inuit oral culture for non-Arctic eyes, and Arnatauyok's distinctive style and flair for capturing the essence of a story adds further depth. By showing the Arctic as a lived-in and culturally rich area – not just a space of exploration, transit and resource extraction – these creative works challenge the perception of the Arctic as a blank and empty space, just as the Inuit prints produced by Aron Kangek in the nineteenth century did.

Two Germaine Arnaktauyok illustrations from *Stories from Pangnirtung* (1976).
X.808/33335

Arnaktauyok's illustrations bring the recollections and histories told by Pangnirtung elders vividly to life on the page. *Stories from Pangnirtung* (1976).

X.808/33335.

HUMAN MARKS

The dominant Arctic stories of explorers, resource extraction, inhospitable environments and extreme temperatures can serve to mask the simple but important fact that the Arctic is an inhabited space. As previous chapters have shown, this is reflected not just in the culture and history of indigenous Arctic peoples, but also in land and seascapes marked by settlements, infrastructure and year-round human activities. Indigenous communities and, today, more heterogeneous communities composed of people from all over the world cover a great deal of the Arctic Circle, especially on the coasts of Eurasia, North America and Greenland.

This is nothing new. As we saw in the first chapter of this book, legends and histories still survive of the medieval Inuit and Viking communities that existed, and to some extent co-existed, on the southern shores of Greenland. While these sites were lost, possibly because of changes in global climate, today Greenland, the Canadian Arctic, Alaska and the Arctic states of Europe are host to a number of permanent indigenous and immigrant towns and cities. Some are historic sites of seasonal indigenous settlement, strongly embedded by history, culture and meaning; others are politically important, like Nunavut, the main hub of contemporary Arctic politics in Canada; some have been shaped by conflict, as was the case for the U.S. base Thule on the DEW Line; and many others have grown up around the resource extraction industries in which both Inuit and Western communities work.

While politics, conflict, commerce and culture leave their own distinct marks on these sites, there are also smaller, more intimate human marks, which make their impression on the ice. Nancy Campbell, a writer and artist who has spent many years studying and interpreting the Arctic, has focused on these intimate human marks in her work, which includes a recent artist's book called *Itoqqippoq* ('washing line' in Greenlandic, 2014). The book is structured around a series of photographs of a frozen washing line hung in Ilulissat, west Greenland, where, according to the author, 'laundry is left out to freeze-dry all winter long, but these sheets were dancing in the wind – a sign of spring'.

The *itoqqippoq*, both a human mark and a line over the ice, speaks to the small-scale, individuated impact of human life in the Arctic; it also conveys the dynamic relationship between humans, and the polar regions and their annual cycles. In the Arctic, therefore, the small habits that people form, and the way in which these habits change with the seasons, are reminders that humans are part of an annual cycle and can live in harmony with it, for all the attempts at control, exploitation and domination discussed in this book.

Three parts of Nancy
Campbell's work
Itoqqippoq (2014).
RF.2014.a.12

RELICS, POLITICS AND
INDIGENOUS KNOWLEDGE

The slightly eerie image of HMS
Erebus lying on the sea floor. It
was created from a side-scan sonar
and was the first image released to
publicise the finding of the ship.
Parks Canada

The search for the ships of Sir John Franklin's lost expedition has captured the European and North American imagination for generations. The vigorous publicity campaign run by Lady Jane Franklin and the well-established allure of the Arctic and its exploration ensured that the missing ships and the fate of their crew have continued to inspire the imagination since the mid-nineteenth century. So strong is this pull that the Canadian government, as we have seen, has continued to intermittently sponsor expeditions to the Arctic with the sole aim of locating the ships *Erebus* and *Terror* and other information that may shed further light on the fate of Franklin and his crew.

Summer 2014 was a milestone in this venture. At first what seeped back from the north were rumours, a whisper that something of significance had been found by the Parks Canada expedition dispatched that summer. Excitement built among Arctic enthusiasts and newspapers eager for stories but hopes were muted: small relics, a new site where Franklin's men had camped or perhaps a significant clue as to the location of the *Erebus* or *Terror* were expected by most. When the news broke that a ship had been found, accompanied by the image opposite of *Erebus* lying on the sea bed, largely intact and in relatively shallow water, it was a revelation few had expected.

Presenting his findings at the British Library in November 2014, the Parks Canada archaeologist Ryan Harris detailed the finding of the ship and what it contained while simultaneously reminding listeners as to the allure of Arctic artefacts to non-Arctic, metropolitan audiences. Harris's lecture, like the accounts of many of the explorers detailed in this book, was a tale of diligent exploration and scientific research that pushed back another frontier in a place that still captures our modern imagination. As a result, the publications and objects that arise from Park Canada's continuing work on the *Erebus* site will be enmeshed in the long story told by this book.

Like the ventures detailed earlier in this book, the work of Parks Canada is not a purely apolitical undertaking. When confirmation was received that *Erebus* had been found and a toast raised on board HMCS *Kingston*, then moored off Baffin Island, Canada's then Prime Minister, Stephen Harper, was on board to celebrate. The locating of *Erebus* was one exceptional achievement of the Harper administration's Arctic strategy, which sought to assert Canada's sovereignty at a time when other nations, whether they possessed Arctic territory or not, were looking to take advantage of the political, trade and mineral opportunities of a changing Arctic.

Finding *Erebus* was not an explicitly political venture. It was undertaken by explorers and researchers with an interest in the Arctic and the history of its exploration who sought to answer some of the remaining questions left from the period of nineteenth-century exploration. However, like those same expeditions carried out by whalers, adventurers and Navy men detailed earlier in this book, these activities were never conducted in isolation from the intensely political world surrounding them.

The locating of *Erebus* speaks to one final argument this book has sought to draw out, namely the significance of the agency and knowledge of indigenous Arctic peoples. Inuit oral history has long attested that one of Franklin's ships may have been located where *Erebus* was found and, in turn, been dismissed by many non-indigenous experts. This book has shown numerous times the strength and importance of indigenous knowledge and how it has aided explorers and traders who sought to profit from the Arctic, only for it often to be erased by the historical record. Here too, as we celebrate the locating of *Erebus* by Parks Canada, it is important to remember that for many years Inuit oral testimony has provided a map to a significant part of Arctic history.

FINAL LINES: CONCLUSIONS

Keen-eyed readers will notice that the majority of artefacts in this book have been drawn from the collections of the British Library, London. There are materials from elsewhere, items such as the Ammassalik map (National Museum of Greenland), or the copper cylinder, in which notes on the Franklin expedition were found (National Maritime Museum, Greenwich, London), as these help to pull the narrative along and add some context from areas of material culture not represented in the British Library collection. Wood, after all, has never been a core part of the Library's collecting policy. That so much material has come from the collections of the national Library, an institution not often regarded as holding significant collections on polar exploration, may surprise many, but this very fact illustrates an aspect of this book's argument. As is set out in the introduction to the text, *Lines in the Ice* seeks to draw out one point above many others, that polar exploration and trade has drawn European interest for centuries and had a distinct influence on all those cultures effected – indigenous, Eurasian and North American.

There are few places which illustrate this influence better than the collections of the British Library, precisely because it is not a polar collection – instead, it aims to provide a world-leading library for scholarly research through collections which reflect British and global cultures in their broadest sense. As a Legal Deposit Library, it also provides unique insight into the subjects of interest to British (not to mention global) authors, scholars and publishers over a historical period lasting centuries. That the Arctic, and the polar world in general, should feature so prominently in these collections is a testament to the enduring allure of these regions – an allure which has existed since Greek geographers

articulated their ideas of the far-off Thule. The significance of the high north to British research, exploration, trade and politics can be seen in materials which originate from those known as the 'Founder Collectors', historical figures such as George III, Joseph Banks and Thomas Grenville.

These are only three of the individuals whose collections formed the bedrock of the early British Museum Library (a cornerstone of today's British Library) but, for each of them, the polar world was of profound significance. Grenville seems to have collected many of the major British narratives of exploration available in his day, while George III, 'The Map King', acquired polar maps from around the world. Banks, perhaps best known for his voyage on the HMS *Endeavour* with then-lieutenant James Cook between 1768 and 1771, had a fascination with the high latitudes of the world that predated his journey to the southern hemisphere. He journeyed to Newfoundland and Labrador in his twenties and then travelled to Iceland when his attempt to join Cook's second expedition failed to bear fruit. The knowledge accumulated on these voyages was stored in his Soho Square library and, as we have seen in this book, influenced numerous subsequent Arctic scholars and explorers.

All of this speaks to how pervasive the draw of polar exploration was as well as how knowledge about it, accumulated over centuries of expeditions, circulated among those who had an interest in northerly latitudes. The scale of this circulation, I hope, is illustrated by *Lines in the Ice*. This book does not represent all of the Arctic material held at the British Library, which, in turn, does not represent all of the books, maps, sheet music, photography and other materials ever created about the polar regions. Instead, these are highlights, selected to show the scale and variety of production, as well as to give a sense of the voracious consumer appetite that drove their production.

Lines in the Ice has also sought to illustrate how this interest has changed the Arctic. Indigenous voices have not been silent here; indeed, indigenous people's ways of engaging with the Arctic, as well as their experience of contact with Europeans and North Americans, shows, profoundly, that the blank spaces in the European imagination were far from desolate wastes before 'discover'. Instead, they were diverse environments inhabited by rich cultures with distinct relationships to the ecologies, landscapes, seascapes and icescapes around them. This makes the use of the Arctic as a geopolitical playground both problematic and tragic. The key argument of this book has been that the interest in the Arctic displayed by today's European governments, American companies and global consumers – the seeking of open-water trade routes, new sites of resource extraction and geopolitical advantage, in an area under the influence of dramatic climate change – is not new or unique. Instead, the same desires drew Martin Frobisher, Henry Hudson and many others north. The framework of global political competition has shifted, historically; from the British competing against the Spanish, to the Canadians cautious of the Russians – mariners now search for oil, 'black gold', rather than a new El Dorado. But what we see are similar dynamics playing out over a long historical arc.

One constant in this history is that we still do not know how to predict precisely how ice will act in the short or long term. The overall ice cover in the Arctic is diminishing, but it will still surge in some years, while, in the Antarctica, the behaviour of the ice sheet confounds many experts. The ice reminds us that, while understanding its changes is an important aim drawing many scientists north, we are still far from understanding, let alone being able to fully control or mollify, the extreme environments of the polar regions. This does not call into question the reality of global climate change or its effects on the polar regions, instead it makes a mockery of those who would seek to benefit from any change they predict may happen. The desire of many in this book, such as nineteenth-century Secretary to the Admiralty Sir John Barrow, that ice should behave in the way they predicted and was beneficial to their endeavours, and the human consequences of their actions, should act as a warning to all seeking to profit from this era of ecological change.

In short, this history shows us that we must be cautious in our engagement with the polar regions. The Arctic is full of indigenous cultures whose use of the high north deserves respect from non-polar societies, and those same cultures, politicians and businesses must look to their own past to understand that what look to be certainties and glistening opportunities can often turn out to be fool's gold – worthless treasure which draws adventurers to reach far beyond their grasp.

Nonetheless, the high north will continue to inspire people to travel there and their marks are not just those of greed or ambition. Throughout the history of exploration detailed above, the Arctic has inspired the creation of beautiful works of art, cartography and literature. It reminds us that not all engagement with this polar world, indeed our world in general, is destructive; instead, the feeling of beauty, awe and humility that inspires such work shows the best in us and how we can positively relate to the Arctic in a rapidly changing world.

INDEX

Page numbers in *italic* refer to the illustrations

Picture Credits

All images © The British Library Board except:
p.21 © Greenland National Museum and Archives; p.101 © Estate of Lynd Ward; p.158 © National Maritime Museum, Greenwich, London; p.182 National Library of Norway; pp.205–7 © Rockwell Kent/College Foundation/SUNY-Plattsburght; p.216 above © USAF, below Canadian Forces Photographic Unit; p.237 GCRC at Carleton University; p.231 NASA; pp.232–3 © John Harrington; p.235 © Rob Sherman; pp.237–9 © Germaine Arnaktauyok; p.241 © Nancy Campbell; p.242 Parks Canada.

Select Bibliography of Secondary Works

1.   Althoff, W. F., *Drift Stations: Arctic Outposts of Superpower Science* (Lincoln, 2006)
2.   Axelsson, R., *Last Days of the Arctic, Cornwall: Polarworld* (2010)
3.   Balzer, M. M. (ed.), *Shamanic Worlds: Rituals and Lore of Siberia and Central Asia,* (London, 1997)
4.   Berton, P., *The Arctic Grail: the quest for the Northwest Passage and the North Pole, 1818–1909* (Toronto, 2001)
5.   Bockstoce, J. R., *Whales, Ice and Men: The History of Whaling in the Western Arctic* (Seattle, 1995)
6.   Brandt, A., *The Man Who Ate His Boots* (London, 2010)
7.   Bravo, M. and Sörlin, C., *Narrating the Arctic: a cultural history of Nordic scientific practices* (Canton, 2002)
8.   Brown, S., *The Last Viking: The Life of Roald Amundsen, Conqueror of the South Pole* (London, 2012)
9.   Bryars, T. and Harper, T., *A History of the 20th Century in 100 Maps,* (London, 2014)
10. Cosgrove, D. and della Dora, V., *High Places: Cultural Geographies of Mountains, Ice and Science* (London, 2008)
11. David, A., *The Charts and Coastal Views of Captain Cook's Voyages, Vol. 1* (London, 1988)
12. Davidson, D., *The Idea of North* (London, 2004)
13. Day, A., *Historical Dictionary of the Discovery and Exploration of the Northwest Passage* (Lanham, 2006)
14. Dodds, K., *The Antarctic: A Very Short Introduction* (Oxford, 2012)
15. Dodds, K. and Powell, R. (eds.), *Polar Geopolitics? Knowledge, Land Regimes and Resources* (Cheltenham, 2014)
16. Doel, R., Wrakberg, U. and Zeller, S. (guest eds.), *Science, Environment and the New Arctic, special issue of the Journal of Historical Geography* (2014)
17. Driver, F., *Geography Militant: Cultures of Exploration and Empire* (London, 2001)
18. Driver, F., 'Intermediaries and the Archive of Exploration' in Konishi, S., Nugent, M. and Shellam, T. (eds.), *Indigenous Intermediaries: New Perspectives on Exploration Archives* (Canberra, 2015)
19. Eber, D., *When the Whalers were up North: Inuit Memories from the Eastern Arctic* (Montreal, 1989)
20. Eber, D., *Encounters on the Passage* (Toronto, 2009)
21. Emmerson, C., *The Future History of the Arctic* (London, 2010)
22. Evans, J., *Merchant Adventurers: The Voyage of Discovery that Transformed Tudor England* (London, 2014)
23. Frankopan, P., *The Silk Roads: A New History of the World* (London, 2015)
24. Harris, P. R., *A History of the British Museum Library, 1753–1973* (London, 1998)
25. Hatfield, P. J., 'The Material History of the Endeavour: the collections of Joseph Banks at the British Library' in Chambers (ed.), *Endeavouring Banks: Exploring collections from the 'Endeavour' voyage, 1768–1771* (London, 2016)
26. Hayes, D., *Historical Atlas of the Arctic* (Seattle, 2003)
27. Herbert, K., *Heart of a Hero: The Remarkable Women Who Inspired the Great Polar Explorers* (Edinburgh, 2013)
28. Keighren, I. M., Withers, C. W. J. and Bell, B., *Travels Into Print: exploration, writing and publishing with John Murray, 1773–1859* (Chicago, 2015)
29. King, J. C. H. and Lidchi, H. (eds), *Imaging the Arctic* (London, 1998)
30. Lambert, A., *Franklin: Tragic Hero of Polar Navigation* (London, 2010)
31. Levere, T. H., *Science and the Canadian Arctic: A century of exploration 1818–1918* (Cambridge, 1993)
32. Lewis-Jones, H. and Herbert, K., *In Search of the South Pole* (London, 2011)
33. Lopez, B., *Arctic Dreams* (London, 2001)
34. Madelbrote, G. and Taylor, B. (eds.), *Libraries within the Library: the origins of the British Library's Printed Collections* (London, 2009)
35. McCannon, J., *A History of the Arctic: Nature, Exploration and Exploitation* (London, 2012)
36. McGhee, R., *The Last Imaginary Place: A Human History of the Arctic* (Chicago, 2005)
37. McGhee, R., *Canadian Arctic Prehistory* (New York, 1978)
38. McGoogan, K., *Fatal Passage: The True Story of John Rae, the Arctic Hero Time Forgot* (New York, 2002)
39. Mills, W. J., *Exploring Polar Frontiers: A Historical Encyclopedia (2 vols.)* (Santa Barbara, 2003)
40. Piper, L. (guest ed.), 'Comparative Issues in the history of Circumpolar Science and Technology', special issue of *Scientia Canadensis* (2010)
41. Potter, R. A., *Arctic Spectacles: The Frozen North in Visual Culture, 1818–1875* (Seattle, 2007)
42. Slezkine, S., *Arctic Mirrors: Russia and the Small Peoples of the Arctic* (New York, 1996)
43. Sörlin, S., *Science, Geopolitics and Culture in the Polar Region* (London, 2013)
44. Spufford, F., *I May be Some Time: Ice and the English Imagination* (London, 2003)
45. Stern, P. R., *The A to Z of the Inuit* (New York, 2009)
46. Wenzel, G. W., *Animal Rights, Human Rights: Ecology, Economy and Ideology in the Canadian Arctic* (Toronto, 1991)
47. Wheeler, S., *Magnetic North: Notes from the Arctic Circle* (London, 2010)
48. Williams, G., *Arctic Labyrinth: the quest for a Northwest Passage* (Berkeley, 2011)
49. Woodman, D. C., *Unravelling the Franklin Mystery: Inuit Testimony* (Kingston, 1991)
50. Woodward, F. J., *Portrait of Jane: A Life of Lady Franklin* (London, 1951)

Acknowledgements

A book like this, despite what it says on the front, is never the work of just one person. Family, friends, colleagues, peers, interested individuals and complete strangers have all been generous with their time and opinions in the formation of this book. First and foremost I must thank the British Library's Eccles Centre for American Studies, specifically Phil Davies, Jean Petrovic and Cara Rodway, for their complete and enthusiastic support throughout the various phases of this project. The British Library would be a poorer place without them and the Centre. The book would also be much poorer if it weren't for the contributions of Tom Harper and Rosanna White, who helped locate some of the material found in this book. I must also thank the Delmas Foundation who, through their sponsorship of work on some items found in this book provided me with time to do further and more thorough research. A line is also due to Tom Harper and Rosanna White who, as contributors, have given a huge amount to this project.

Curators are often invisible presences in books such as this, unless their name is on the front, and yet they shape the content and ideas they contain through their expertise and generosity for sharing knowledge. The European and Americas Collections at the British Library gave much to this project, with Peter Hellyer, Barbara Hawes, Carole Holden, Marja Kingma, Katya Rogatchevskaia, Matthew Shaw and Teresa Vernon providing particular support. Colleagues from Maps, Manuscripts and Printed Historical collections have also lent support and ears along the way. Particular mention has to go to Adrian Edwards, who tolerated innumerable questions and a request to visit the King's Library Tower. I should also thank Neil Chambers, of Nottingham Trent University, who encouraged an interest in the collections of Sir Joseph Banks which underpin many areas of this book.

I am also indebted to those who read this book, provided comments and insight as to how it could improve. It has been an absolute joy to work with British Library Publishing and the team are doing great things with the imprint. Klaus Dodds and Felix Driver, who both read an early draft and have championed this project throughout, have made a huge impression on this book and improved it no-end. They also represent the enduring impact of Royal Holloway (my alma mater) and its Geography Department on my writing and my career; it is a university with an ethic of care and support that endures long beyond the time a student dons a cap and gown.

While this work particularly focusses on the collections of the British Library it does cast eyes elsewhere and there are numerous thanks to be given for help and inspiration. The National Maritime Museum (especially Clare Warrior), Natural History Museum, Scott Polar Research Institute, British Museum, Library and Archives Canada, Library of Congress and the Canadian High Commission have all left marks on this book in one way or another. Mention is also due to Kari Herbert and Huw Lewis-Jones, of Polar World, whose work, ideas and support to someone nudging into this fascinating field have been invaluable.

My family has endured hard times while this book has been taken root. My parents, and their determination to thrive in the face of hardship when others would fail, have been an inspiration. Likewise, Madeleine Hatfield, my wonderful wife, has given ears, eyes and time to this book irrespective of what else was going on. It would not be half of what it is without you. I would not be half of who I am without you. The final mention goes to our son, Joshua, only three months old at the time of writing. I hope you some day enjoy this book and become an enthusiastic little Arctic monkey.

June 2016

First published in 2016 by
The British Library
96 Euston Road
London NW1 2DB

Published simultaneously in North America by McGill-Queen's University Press

Text copyright © Philip J. Hatfield 2016
Images © the British Library Board and other named copyright holders 2016
Designed and typeset by Daniel Streat, Visual Fields
Picture research by Sally Nicholls

Cataloguing in Publication Data
A catalogue record for this publication is available from The British Library

Printed and bound in China by C&C Offset Printing Co., Ltd

Library and Archives Canada Cataloguing in Publication
Hatfield, Philip J., 1984–, author
Lines in the ice : exploring the roof of the world / Philip J. Hatfield.
Includes bibliographical references and index.
Issued in print and electronic formats.
Co-published by The British Library.

ISBN 978-0-7735-4820-6 (cloth)   ISBN 978-0-7735-9987-1 (ePDF)

1. Arctic regions–Discovery and exploration–History.
2. Arctic regions–Discovery and exploration–History--Pictorial works.
3. Northwest Passage–Discovery and exploration–History.
4. Northwest Passage–Discovery and exploration–History–Pictorial works.
    I. British Library, issuing body II. Title.

G620.H38 2016   910.9163'27   C2016-904080-1   C2016-904081-X

PAGES 4, 6-7, 12-13, 90-91, 184-5, and 248-9
Photographs from William Bradford,
The Arctic Regions (1873).
1785.d.7

PAGES 244-5
'Noon in Mid-Winter', from William
Henry James Browne, *Ten Coloured Views
taken during the Arctic Expedition
of Her Majesty's Ships 'Enterprise'
and 'Investigator', under the command
of Captain Sir James C. Ross... With
a summary of the various arctic
expeditions in search of Captain Sir John
Franklin... and his companions in
H.M. ships 'Erebus' and 'Terror'* (1850).
1259.d.11